Filled with Laughter

OTHER BOOKS BY RUFUS LEARSI

OUTLINE OF JEWISH KNOWLEDGE: A History of the Jewish People and an Anthology of Jewish Literature. Three Volumes. With the collaboration of Samson Benderly.
ISRAEL: A History of the Jewish People
FULFILLMENT: The Epic Story of Zionism
THE JEWS IN AMERICA: A History
KASRIEL THE WATCHMAN AND OTHER STORIES
SHIMMELE
SHIMMELE AND HIS FRIENDS
PLAYS FOR GREAT OCCASIONS
THE WEDDING SONG: A Book of Chassidic Ballads
THE BOOK OF JEWISH HUMOR

Filled with Laughter

A Fiesta of Jewish Folk Humor

by

Rufus Learsi

Then was our mouth filled with laughter, and our tongue with singing (Psalms 126:2).

New York · THOMAS YOSELOFF · London

Library of Congress Catalog Card Number: 61-6926

Thomas Yoseloff, Publisher

11 East 36th Street

New York 16, New York

Thomas Yoseloff Ltd.

123 New Bond Street

London W.1., England

Printed in the United States of America

To Kalman Whiteman

Philosopher, Colleague, Friend:

In Memoriam

Acknowledgments

THE TALES that make up this assemblage have been drawn from various sources. Most of them have been frequently told and retold. For the present retelling, in which the author did not hesitate to take what he considered permissible liberties, he alone, of course, is responsible. Out of the many sources he singles out for special acknowledgment the works of Ausubel, Davidson, Druyanov, Herzberg, Moszkowski, Olsvanger, Sadan and Steiner. He is grateful for the help he has had from Sundel Doniger, Daniel Persky, Mrs. Wilbur Barker and the most faithful of all his helpers—his wife.

Contents

THE QUIPS AND PRANKS OF HERSHELE OSTROPOLYER

PAGEANT OF THE HUMAN COMEDY

GALLANT AND GAY: Humor of Reborn Israel

Preface

What, in the economy of nature, is the function of laughter? What gives rise to it? A variety of answers have come to these questions from the philosophers. Thomas Hobbes found the origin of laughter in the elation we feel when we become aware that we are superior to others—to the stupid, the inept, the gullible. What we then experience he characterizes by the rapturous term "sudden glory." This theory, of course, ascribes to laughter a function that is personal or individual.

Henri Bergson, on the other hand, considers the function of laughter to be primarily social. It is an important social corrective, not so drastic as fines and jails, but often more potent. Laughter, he says in effect, is the penalty we lay on the artificial when it pretends to be natural. We laugh when puppets jerk their limbs and wag their heads. We laugh when the upstart apes the manners of the aristocrat. We impose the same penalty on the nonconformist, or freak, as we are pleased to call him, who defies the conventions which the group considers normal and natural. The slavish imitator and the flaunting rebel—both receive their punishment in ridicule and laughter.

There were other renowned thinkers who offered explanations. Spencer and Freud were not far apart in theirs, the first finding the cause of laughter in the release of pent-up energy, the second in liberation from inhibitions. Kant and Schopenhauer seem to be in accord: both saw laughter springing from the sudden perception of incongruity. But is there a single explanation that is all-embracing? If there is, it is yet to be discovered.

The "sudden glory" of Hobbes may explain the happy laughter of superiority, but laughter may also be harsh and bitter. One may even laugh at oneself, and experience what is perhaps the most salutary kind of laughter. Ridicule certainly plays an important role as censor and corrector, but Bergson's punitive theory, as it may be called, fails to explain why the normal individual has a craving for laughter. Why do little girls go off into the giggles for no apparent reason whatever? Why do we join someone caught in an uncontrolled fit of laughter, without knowing what it's all about? Don't we pay to see clowns and comedians in the expectation that they will provide us with what appears to be a basic vitamin for the health of the spirit?

It should be no surprise, therefore, that a people which for so many centuries has found itself between the upper and nether millstones of history should have taken this vitamin in large doses. Of course, the Jew has not been gay or flippant about life—its meaning, its trials, its duties. Imbued with the conviction that life has a sublime purpose, his laughter could not be like the pagan's, lighthearted and boisterous. But he was able to find in ironic laughter a release from his inner tensions as well as from those which his hard lot inflicted upon him.

Laughter brought him relief from the tension which his stern and lofty conception of life's meaning, his religion, imposed upon him, the tension of the infinite. He developed a relation with his Deity that was peculiarly intimate and quaint. "Father in Heaven," he prays, "why don't you help me? You are helping Pavel and Nikita and Ivan, who are strangers to you, and me, Jacob Isaac ben Abraham, you don't help?" Nor does the "prayer" impugn his awe of his Creator any more than his laughter at the speculations of a certain wag impugns his faith in the Hereafter. "It is clear," says the wag, "that this world belongs to them, the *goyim*. But the World-to-come, ah! that belongs to us." And he pauses and adds: "Would I laugh if the World-to-come also belonged to them!" Quips like these, which some may find touched with cynicism, are in reality a refuge from the inner tension imposed by ineffable religious concepts and rigorous commands.

More important than its role as spiritual cathartic was the relief which his humor afforded the Jew from the sorrows of his bitter struggle against penury and persecution. It brought him balm in laughter for what would otherwise seek relief in tears; and doesn't that explain why so much of Jewish humor hovers on the brink of tears?

In the teeming communities of Eastern Europe, where Jewish folk humor attained its richest efflorescence, it was the only weapon with which he could avenge himself against his enemies. For this purpose, his humor took the form of a caustic and often bitter irony, that found its principal *point d'appui* in the intellectual inferiority of his adversary. It was a victory of a sort to expose the thickheadedness of his persecutor, it brought him, if not an access of "sudden glory," then a measure of vindication. The banker, who the previous day had stood at the baptismal font, makes up a financial report full of errors. "Look," says his Jewish colleague, "you've been a *goy* only twenty-four hours and you are already an ass."

In its role as avenger his irony is, of course, aimed at the *goy*; as a source of relief from the tensions of his struggle against penury, he himself is its target. The "jolly pauper" is one of its stock characters. "Rejoice, *kabtsn,* dirt is cheap!" is his motto and battle-cry. The aplomb of the professional beggar is an inexhaustible source of merriment, as well as the shifts and devices of the matchmaker, the shoestring trader, the perspired little broker and other cane-twirlers. The purse-proud moneybag and heartless miser are lampooned and pilloried without mercy.

This life full of zest and color, alert and creative in spite of poverty and persecution, and aglow with an immemorial idealism, is no more, mown down by the scythe of a bestial destroyer. To the American Jew, nurtured in a far different environment, some of the characters in the human comedy presented in these pages may be unfamiliar—the befuddled *melamed,* the indomitable *shadchn,* the proud beggar, and others. They are not, however, too unfamiliar as human types for their adventures and misadventures to be understood and relished.

Nevertheless, it should be noted that the rapid march of recent history has relegated at least one stock theme of Jewish humor to the limbo of the unregretted past. This theme of self-derision lurks in the story of the lion-hearted tailor who jumps into a free-for-all, is treated to a fiery slap in the face and runs away. It stands out more baldly in the following jibe at "Jewish heroes:" In the Song of Songs we are told that King Solomon's litter was guarded by "threescore heroes of Israel." "Why so many heroes?" asks the quipster. And he answers: "They were heroes of Israel, *nebach*."

The heroes of reborn Israel have made the jibe almost unintelligible, and that alone should be sufficient justification for including the gay and trenchant humor of the restored Jewish state in this compilation.

The Valiant Rooster

and Other Tales—Wry, Droll, and Merry

Foreword

We all love stories; we love to make them up; to tell them, to hear them. That is why the folk tale is the principal component in the folklore of all nations. For the Jews, it was the Bible which, from the earliest times, provided the means to satisfy this universal passion—from the earliest time to our own days, when the same source serves as an inspiration to story-tellers of other nations also.

The majestic narratives with which the Book abounds were an eternal fountain of delight, but they served also as a stimulus to the story-making urge. How lovingly and endlessly those narratives were expanded and embroidered! The numerous legends that came into being are folktales in the full sense of the term, forming a major part of the Midrash as well as the Agada, the non-juridical portion of the Talmud. It was only in the Middle Ages that Jews began to be attracted by other sources, but even then, as the *Maaseh Buch* (Story Book) and other compilations attest, the pristine source was still without peer. Often in these tales the prophet Elijah appears as the *deus ex machina* and plays his traditional role: he consoles, he rescues and, when necessary, he punishes.

Very few of those legends and parables answer to the description "wry, droll, and merry." Their purpose was not to amuse, but to instruct and edify. But in the later centuries a number of rollicking stories began to circulate among the Jews of eastern Europe that did deserve those adjectives, among which were some that managed to combine moralistic purpose with genuine drollery. For not even the spirit of drollery could suppress the passion of the Jew for justice and the vindication of the righteous against the wicked.

In the tales that follow the present compiler must confess that he has often played the role of author rather than editor. He has combined, extended, altered, embellished and even invented. But he has striven to preserve the spirit of the folktale, and of the particular folk which these tales represent. For the rest, the stories themselves must be his justification.

The Valiant Rooster

In the reign of King Solomon there lived a farmer in the Land of Israel named Joash, who once had the good fortune to save the life of the king's youthful son and heir.

The lad was a keen horseman and was riding one day on a path near a field which Joash was plowing. Suddenly a huge serpent reared up on the path in front of the horse and rider, and the animal plunged in wild panic towards the edge of a cliff that dropped straight down to a dizzy depth. Joash was just in time to seize the bridle with his powerful hands, and at the risk of his own life, he brought the animal to a halt.

The following day a herald of King Solomon stopped at the farmer's door. "The king," he cried, "commands you to appear before him in his palace in Jerusalem without delay!"

Joash, who was a modest man, meek and subdued, was smitten with terror. But his wife Mara was of tougher texture. Mara, in fact, ruled him with an iron hand, so much so that the neighbors jeered at him and nicknamed him "the Apron." Neighbors are sometimes kind, sometimes cruel. "That woman," they said, "is always wiping her hands on him."

"Why do you stand there like a wooden post?" she snapped at him. "The king wants to reward you for saving his son's life. What else could he intend? So go with the herald and see that you bring back everything the king gives you. And don't step into any of the taverns on the way."

The fact was that the farmer did have a habit of stepping into a tavern now and then. Who will blame a man for seeking a little relief from such a vixen of a wife?

Nevertheless she was right. The woman was right.

"My good man," said King Solomon to the farmer, "How can I help being grateful to you all my life? Name your reward and I will grant it."

The farmer felt a hot perspiration break out all over him. What should he ask for? Anything he might bring home—gold, silver, jewels—would at once be appropriated by his wife. He would become even more ridiculous in the eyes of his neighbors. Nevertheless he must ask for something. He must, or the king would be offended. He might even punish him for spurning his gifts.

In his anguish a good angel came and whispered in his ear. At once he knew what to ask for.

"Great king!" said Joash, "who does not know how vast is your knowledge, how deep your wisdom? Nothing on earth is hidden from you. You even understand the language of the beasts and the birds. My humble request, therefore, is that you teach me that I too may understand what the beasts and the birds say to each other."

King Solomon knit his brows. What a strange request for a simple farmer to make! Strange and bold. But the king had promised, and a king's word is not lightly given. Especially to someone to whom he owed so much.

"Joash," said the king at length, "your request shall be granted. Stay with me for three days and nights and I will teach you to understand the language of the birds and beasts. But you must know that I do so on one condition. You must not reveal to anyone that you have acquired this secret knowledge. If you do, I will at once become aware of it—don't ask me by what means—and you will forfeit your life."

Was there ever a farmer named Joash placed in such a dire dilemma? But our Joash did not ponder the matter too long.

"I accept the condition," said he to the king. So at the end of three days and three nights, the farmer, by the marvelous methods employed by Solomon, learned to understand the language of the animals and birds he knew.

And was it really so strange that Joash should be eager to acquire this knowledge? Not at all! Whenever his wife's railing and ranting became more than he could endure, it was his habit to retire to his barnyard and stable in search of peace. There he sat and watched his hens and rooster, his dogs and sheep, his horse and cattle. And more than once, as he gazed at the creatures, he was sure they were holding converse with each other, and he felt it would be just thrilling to understand what they were saying. What queer thoughts will not come to a man whose brain has been relieved, if only for a short while, from the pounding of a woman's tongue?

Joash returned to his home and his sorrows, and Mara began her operations immediately. Why had he stayed away so long? What escapades had he been up to? She heard there were loose women in the capital, so how about that, hey? But be that as it might, let him produce the gold and silver he obtained from the king. What? No gold, no silver? Did he think she would believe that? Well, what about the precious stones and jewels? No precious stones? No jewels? He must be out of his mind to think he could palm off such lies on her! Was he out to drive her to desperation? So the king gave him nothing, he gave him nothing for saving his son's life! He did give him something? He did? So why didn't he produce it? Let him produce it at once! At once!

Poor Joash! What could he say? How could he tell her? Life was bitter enough, but death would be still more bitter. He ran out of the house and hid in the stable. And suddenly he felt a thrill that smothered all the bitterness in his soul. His ox and his horse were holding a colloquy, and he understood! He understood everything they were saying!

But Mara knew no mercy. She must know, she must know what King Solomon had bestowed on her husband! Day and night she hounded him and pounded him. Could he make his stable or his hennery his permanent home? Gradually his resistance wore thinner and thinner. Life, he decided, was not worth living. If he held out against her, he would suffer a lingering and torturous death. If he told her, death would at least be swift and merciful. He decided to tell her and then leave at once for the capital and give himself up to the king. It was better that way, more dignified. Why should he wait for the king's officers to come and drag him away?

He trimmed his beard, put on his Sabbath garments, and told Mara he was going out and in an hour would be back and tell her what she was so avid to know. He is behaving strangely, said she to herself, but the prospect of at last knowing his secret drove every other thought from her head. She would be there, she told him, waiting for him.

Joash stepped out of the house into the barnyard. It was a lovely morning, bright and sunny. He sat down on a log for a final hour of contemplation before embarking on his somber ordeal. At the door of the kennel his faithful old dog lay sprawled, his gray chin tucked in between his paws. Not far away his old black rooster was strutting about grandly, followed by a flock of a dozen or so hens.

The rooster stopped near the kennel, stretched his throat up to twice its normal length, and closed his eyes.

"Cock-a-doodle-doo!" he crowed in a burst of triumph.

"That was in bad taste," Joash heard the dog say to the rooster. "You know what a sad journey our master is taking today. Must you crow at a time like this?"

"I crow when the spirit moves me," said the rooster with asperity. "Besides, I must keep in training for my early morning office. Somebody has to tell the sun when it's time for him to rise, don't you agree?"

"Yes, I suppose, you are right," the dog allowed. "I couldn't do it. I like to sleep late. In fact, your first crow at dawn often wakes me, and I can't say I like it."

"You will grant, I hope," said the rooster disdainfully, "that it's more important for the sun to rise on time than for you to sleep late."

"Will I? Well, maybe—I don't know."

And the dog tucked his muzzle in deeper between his paws, closed his eyes and appeared to doze off.

"Now, about the master," the rooster began.

"Yes? What about him?" the dog roused himself.

"I know how you feel about him. He's been very good to you. But I can't say that I have much sympathy with him."

"No heart!" said the dog sadly. "No heart at all."

"How is it possible for someone like me to feel sorry for him?" the rooster went on. "Do you know how many wives I have?"

"No," said the dog. "Do you?"

"If you think your question offends me, you are mistaken," the rooster retorted. "I'll admit I hardly know. But that only brings out my triumphs. I'm like the man who doesn't know how rich he is. At any rate, I must have at least twenty-five."

"So?"

"So! Do I have any trouble keeping them in line? Don't they come when I call them? Don't they go when I order them? Do they complain, or rail, or nag? They know what would happen if they tried it. They know who is the cock of this roost!"

"So?"

"So! How many wives has the master? One, just one! And look at him! She makes a rag out of him. She drives him to despair, to what is actually suicide. Do you call that a man? I say he deserves no better fate than what is in store for him today."

"You've got a point there," the dog admitted. "But what could he do? You know her!"

"I've had worse," the rooster boasted. "I've had all kinds, and I've known what to do."

"Well," the dog objected, "you have a sharp bill, and you can deliver quite a slap with those wings of yours. And in addition you have those wicked spikes on your legs."

"Leave my spurs out!" the rooster snapped. "Do you think I would use them on a lady? What do you take me for?"

"Beg pardon," the dog answered humbly. "But what are they for?"

"The spurs? They are for any young whippersnapper who may take it into his head to come into this yard and test the virtue of my wives."

"I see," said the dog. "They uphold your conjugal rights."

"Yes, if you want to be technical," said the rooster. "A couple of swipes with one of these spurs brings the young upstart to his senses."

"But what about the master?" the dog insisted.

"He has no bill, but he has two elbows, no? They could be very useful, especially for the ribs. He has no wings, but he has a pair of hands, powerful hands. Remember how he stopped that runaway horse! Well, in his place I would use the palms. Apply such palms in the proper area, and they will accomplish wonders."

"But the master is such a gentle soul," the dog murmured drowsily.

"A spiritless, spineless creature!" the rooster corrected. "Letting a shrew like that ruin his life! Going to his death, when a dose of simple manhood could save him! We roosters, I am proud to say, are a wholly different breed. We are the genuine master race! Cock-a-doodle-doo-oo!"

And the rooster strutted away, followed admiringly by a bevy of fluttering wives.

Joash the farmer burst into the room where his wife was waiting for him, her lips set tight in an expression of grim triumph. She glanced at him and stood up. There was something strange about him.

"Cock-a-doodle-do!" he screamed at her. She plumped back into her seat in terror.

"I'm a rooster!" he went on. "See these elbows? They are as good as bills. For picking and poking. In the ribs." And he poked Mara in her sides, not too hard, but not too gently either, hard enough, at any rate for her to scream.

"Now stand up!" he continued. "You see these palms? They

are as good as wings. I apply them in the proper area! See?" And Joash the farmer acted as he spoke.

It took a week, perhaps two, perhaps longer. But the virago was conquered and subjugated. It was not long before the elbows and palms became unnecessary. A mere glance was sufficient.

So Joash the farmer did not go back to the capital after all. He spent the rest of his life with a gentle and obedient Mara. She brought him a numerous progeny, all of whom grew up in the spirit enjoined by the Torah in the Fourth Commandment: "Honor thy father and thy mother." And may all our children grow up in the same spirit! Amen! *Selah*.

Onions and Garlic

LONG, LONG ago there lived in the Land of Israel a pious and learned man named Arye who spent all his days, and sometimes his nights also, in the study of the holy Torah. Arye's wife was a happy woman. She knew that in the World-to-come a portion of her husband's merit would be credited to her. She had brought him a large dowry when they were married, and for ten years Arye was able to devote himself to study, free from the burden of worldly cares.

But the dowry went on shrinking and by the favor of the Almighty the number of mouths to be fed kept on growing. Who doesn't know that children—blessings on their precious little heads—are always hungry? Arye's wife began to worry. Her forehead became wrinkled, and a look of anxiety brooded in her eyes.

"Arye," said she one day, "how will it all end, Arye? All I

have left are my pearl earrings. I inherited them from my mother, she from her mother, and so on back for fifty generations."

"A precious heirloom," said Arye, gazing gently upon her.

"Now, Arye, there is your good friend, Barak the merchant. He moves around in the world, and keeps on getting richer. Whatever he touches he turns to profit. Why can't you do the same, Arye? Barak doesn't come up to your ankles in learning, so why can't you also go out and trade and become rich?"

"There is wisdom in what you say," said Arye.

"So hear what I have decided, Arye. It was not an easy decision, but hard, very hard. The pearl earrings are very dear to me. But take them, Arye. Go out into the world and trade with them. You will, of course, have to interrupt your study. But it will be only for a short time. You will come back a rich man, Arye, like your friend Barak, and you will study in peace for the rest of your life."

"Your plan could not be improved upon," said Arye. "Give me the earrings and I'll start out at once, and may the Lord prosper my journey!"

"Amen!" said Arye's wife and bowed her pious head.

For many weary hours Arye plodded in the hot sun, the pearl earrings close to his bosom. Late in the day he came to a strange town and stepped into an inn to refresh himself.

"You look all weary and spent," said the innkeeper.

"And well I may be," said Arye. "I have been on the road all day, with nothing to aid me but my legs."

"You must be very poor, or you would at least have an old donkey to ride on," said the innkeeper.

"Not so poor," said Arye, taking out the earrings and holding them in his palm.

The innkeeper's eyes glittered.

"How foolish to have such jewels and travel on foot!" he exclaimed.

"What shall I do?" said Arye.

"Exchange them for a good strong beast," the innkeeper

advised. "Wait, give them to me and I'll give you—no, not a donkey! I'll give you a camel in exchange!"

"It's a good idea. You are a kind man," said Arye.

So Arye turned his back on the inn, leading an old camel by the halter. Outside the town, he managed to make the creature kneel down and mounted on its hump. But when the beast lumbered to its feet and began to amble down the road Arye had a queasy sensation in his stomach and yielded up all the refreshments which the kind innkeeper had served him.

"Stop now," said he to the camel. "Kneel down again and let me off."

The camel obeyed promptly, and when Arye looked at its ridiculous face, it seemed to him the creature was grinning.

"It's a demon, not a camel," was the thought that flashed through Arye's mind.

But he took the halter and they plodded on, he and the camel.

He came to a cluster of black tents, which he knew to be a Bedouin encampment. One of the sons of the desert came out and greeted him.

"Why don't you ride the camel instead of leading him?" he asked.

Arye explained and confided to the Bedouin what he suspected as to the true nature of the beast.

"Yes," said the Bedouin, "that's how these creatures are sometimes. You ought to get rid of him. I'll tell you what I'll do. I'll take him off your hands. I'll do more. I'll give you a goat—no, two goats, in exchange, a he-goat and a she-goat."

"You are a good man," said Arye.

"With a he-goat and a she-goat you'll soon have more goats, many of them—a great big flock."

"Thank you kindly," said Arye.

So Arye went his way, trudging between two scraggy black animals wobbling wearily beside him. The vision of the big flock of goats stood up in his fancy and beguiled him. Soon he would be back in his own city, shepherding the flock which would furnish him, his wife, and his children with milk, wool and meat for the rest of their lives. But what was that? One of the goats, the she-one, suddenly fell over and lay on the ground motionless.

"She is dead, the mother of my flock is dead!" Arye mourned. "And you," he turned to the he-goat, "what will you accomplish without her? Alas, you don't look as if there is much life in you either."

He left the she-goat where she lay, and moved on, his heart filled with sad thoughts. At the edge of the next town stood an inn and the innkeeper came out and looked intently at Arye and his pitiful companion.

"Where are you going and what will you do with this animal?" the innkeeper asked.

"Alas, I don't know," said Arye.

"Wherever you go, you'll be better off without it. Let me have it and I'll give you something in exchange."

"You are a kind man," said Arye.

The innkeeper stepped inside and reappeared with the first thing that had come to his hand in the kitchen.

"Take it," he said, "and let me have the goat."

"What is it?" Arye asked as he made the exchange.

"Look and see," said the man.

Arye looked and saw. It was a bag of onions.

Arye toiled on, holding the bag of onions close inside his ample cloak. At first a sense of wonder overcame him. His wife's earrings had become a bag of onions! How did it happen? Strange and hidden are the ways of Providence, he mused. But suddenly his mood changed. A feeling of despair swept through him. How will he return to his wife and children? To his friends and neighbors? A bag of onions! For the pearl earrings, the precious heirloom, all he would bring home was a bag of onions! Arye sat down on a stone beside the road and wept.

At this point a stranger appeared on the scene and stood facing him. He was dressed in sailor's garb and his sun-tanned features were bold but friendly. A stranger, did I say? It could have been no one else but the Prophet Elijah dressed like a sailor. It was time for Elijah to appear, was it not?

"Dry your tears and come with me," said the sailor. "My ship is in the harbor close by. I will take you aboard, and if you are hungry we'll soon take care of that. I am the ship's cook."

"To what country does your ship sail?" Arye asked.

"To-night we lift anchor and sail off for Tarshish."

Tarshish! Tarshish was the land to which the prophet Jonah sailed to escape the mission that God laid upon him. He, too, will sail to Tarshish, and if he meets with the same fate as Jonah, so much the better. Him the whale will not spew out. Why should he? And a wry thought came to his mind and brought a bitter smile to his lips. The whale might even relish his onions!

Arye followed the sailor on board the ship, always hugging his bag of onions. The same night a fresh breeze sent the craft speeding westward across the sea. But the following morning the breeze became a gale. The ship was swept off her course into waters and among islands unknown to the captain. As the day wore on the fury of the storm increased, and amid the roar of the wind, the thunder of the waves, and the shrieking of the sailors, the ship was dashed upon a rocky waste and shattered.

But you will guess, of course, that Arye did not perish in the wreck, else how would my story be a story? In fact, Arye and the sailor who befriended him were the only ones who were saved. A long time they lay unconscious on the coast, and when they revived and sat up, they saw themselves surrounded by a group of armed men.

"You must come at once to our king," said their captain, "and explain who you are and what you are doing in his country."

The king wore a huge crown of gold, studded with dazzling jewels. Beside him stood his ministers dressed in gorgeous robes shimmering with threads of gold.

"You are spies!" the king cried to Arye and the sailor.

"Spies!" echoed the ministers in chorus.

Then it was that Arye girded up his loins. He remembered how the same charge was leveled by Joseph against his brothers in Egypt, and how Judah "came near unto him," and spoke with such fervor in their defense that Joseph was moved to tears. And, indeed, Arye's solemn and learned plea also had its effect upon the king.

"You are no ordinary man," he said to Arye. "Tell me, have you saved anything from the wreck?"

"Only this!" said Arye, holding up his bag of onions.

The king opened the bag and took out an onion.

"What strange fruit is this?" the king inquired. "We have nothing like it in our land."

"Nothing like it!" the ministers echoed.

The king pealed the onion and smelt it.

"Pungent, but not unpleasant," he said.

"Not unpleasant," said each minister as he put the onion to his nose.

At this point the sailor stepped forward and addressed the king.

"Great and mighty king," he began, "may you live forever! I am only a poor sailor, but I have been a cook for many years, and since onions are unknown in your land, you must reckon this day as the most important in your history." And he went on to describe the wonderful virtues of onions, how they heighten the relish of all things that are boiled, baked or broiled. In words that made His Majesty's mouth water he told what onions do to chopped liver, chopped eggs, and chopped herring, to soups and roasts, to *pletsl* and omelets. The enthusiasm of the king and his ministers rose to the highest pitch. The king at once sent for the queen and commanded her to prepare his next meal with onions. He presented an onion to each of his ministers to give to his wife. And on the sailor's advice he saved a portion to provide future crops of onions. That sailor! Was there anything he didn't know?

A new and happy era began in the history of the kingdom, the Era of the Onion. A new zest entered into the life of the people. The men began to smile at their wives, to embrace them, even kiss them. The following year more babies were born in the kingdom than in any previous year. The king was overjoyed, for is it not written: "In a multitude of people is the glory of a king"?

Arye was anxious to return to his wife and children, but the king's love for him was so great, he would not let him go. At last, after three years, in answer to Arye's tears and prayers, the king relented. Arye and the mysterious sailor embarked on a grand ship and were sent away with the highest honors.

But before the ship sailed the king placed into Arye's hands a large sandalwood box, adorned with silver and gold.

"Here is the key to the box," said the king, "but promise me not to open it before you are back in your own home in the Land of Israel."

How, in the meantime, was Arye's faithful wife faring, she and her poor innocent brood? Alas, not so well. Kind neighbors came to her help, but Arye's long absence and the dread that he might never return was almost more than she could bear. Barak became a more frequent visitor in her home, but his words of consolation only sharpened her grief. Secretly she wished he would stay away.

At the end of a year Barak did absent himself for a month or two. With diligence and shrewdness he retraced Arye's journey up to his embarkation on the ill-fated ship in the harbor city. No, he was told, the ship never returned, was never heard of again. Barak came to Arye's wife and told her what he had learned.

"You must bow to the will of God," he said with a great show of piety. "Arye has gone to his eternal rest, and is it proper that you should remain a widow for the remainder of your life? You are in the bloom of womanhood, and many a man of substance and standing would be happy to marry you. And would you be offended if I added that I am one of them?"

So spoke Barak, Arye's good friend. What a friend! Our enemies should have such friends! But the poor woman broke into loud sobbing and turned her back on him. He went away puzzled by the manner in which his offer had been received.

Why did she weep? Why didn't she say "Thank you, Barak"? That's how it is with some people. They are so wrapped up in themselves and their importance, they don't understand what goes on in someone else's heart.

But, of course, Arye returned. He returned to his wife and children. What a day that was! The news spread through the town with the speed of lightning. Arye is back, and he brought a big beautiful box of sandalwood! He will unlock it in the presence of his neighbors that very day!

They were all there, with Barak, of course, in the forefront. Arye began by telling them all that had happened to him, then he took out the key. Every voice was hushed, every heart stood still. Arye unlocked the lid and raised it. A loud gasp broke from the gathering. The box was filled with gems and jewels, sapphires and rubies, carnelians and emeralds, diamond bracelets and brooches, strings of pearls and pearl earrings.

"Now," said Arye's wife, "you can study Torah in peace for the rest of your life."

But Arye himself was overcome with amazement.

"All this for a bag of onions!" was all he could say. He looked about for the sailor to thank him again, but the sailor was gone, nobody knew where!

Barak could have said more than Arye, but he chose to be silent. He was a deep one. He left the same day for the harbor city where he found, still riding at anchor, the ship that brought Arye back to the Land of Israel. He sought out the captain and persuaded him to take him on as a passenger on his voyage back to his country. But before embarking Barak acquired a precious possession which he carefully concealed and guarded like the apple of his eye.

What it was? It was a bag of garlic!

He was a shrewd one, this Barak. If a bag of onions, he reasoned, brought such a heap of precious jewels, what would not a bag of garlic do? Wasn't garlic more potent than onions, more pungent? He himself was devoted to garlic: he knew many others who swore by it and preferred it to onions.

The sea was calm, the winds favorable and Barak felt assured and happy. In good time the ship glided into the harbor of the faraway land, and Barak was admitted into the presence of the king.

"Great king," said Barak, "may you live forever! I have brought you a gift, a miracle fruit which I know your country lacks. It will render all your food a thousand times more delicious. It will add strength to your marrow and many years to your lives."

He was skillful with words, this Barak and well-practiced in the art of exaggerating the merits of his wares. The king and his ministers smelled the garlic and nodded approvingly.

"We welcome you," said the king. "You are our guest, our honored guest."

Barak was delighted. His venture was a sure success. Nevertheless, the longing to know how well he would be rewarded gave him no rest. He persuaded the first minister of the king to sound out his master on the subject. He was a good persuader, this Barak. The minister brought him word that the king intended to reward him handsomely. The king called him his friend and his country's benefactor. Barak glowed with pride and expectation.

The time arrived for him to embark for the return voyage. The king and his ministers accompanied him to the gangplank.

"Take this," said the king, handing him a large sandalwood box. "Here is the key, but don't open the box until you are back in your own home. You will find," he added with a gracious smile, "that we know how to reward the men we esteem."

Barak returned home and invited his friends to attend the opening of the box. Arye and his wife were, of course, among them.

"Good friends," said Barak, before inserting the key, "you will now see how a man of affairs like myself knows how to apply his knowledge and experience."

He turned the bolt, raised the lid, and everyone peered into the box. And what do you think the box contained? What! You say you know? How could you know? Right! You guessed it. A bag of onions! Just a bag of onions!

Haman in the Henhouse

It is well known that the Purim which falls a month before Passover is not the only Purim, just as the Haman of the Megillah is not the only Haman.

There was once a Prince whose domains, to be sure, were not as broad as those of King Ahasuerus, but in many ways he resembled the great monarch of Persia. He loved to wine and dine, and was an ardent devotee of the fair sex. When the affairs of the principality began to grow seedy, the lords of the realm prevailed on him to appoint a certain Bishop as his chief minister and adviser.

Now this Bishop, a man of imposing presence, was considered a paragon of wisdom and virtue, but it was not long before the Prince discovered that he was only a puffed-up balloon. So the Prince began to scorn and ridicule him, and amused his boon companions by mimicking his minister's haughty gait and pompous tone.

But there came a time when the Prince found him more annoying than amusing, and he looked about for a way of getting rid of his overbearing minister. So he ordered the Bishop to appear before him and spoke to him as follows:

"I know, of course, that you are esteemed as a man of knowledge and wisdom, but in order to be sure of it I desire to put you to the test. After three days, therefore, you will again appear before me and give me your answers to the following three questions:

"First, what am I really thinking as I look at you?

"Second, what am I, your sovereign Prince, really worth?

"Third, what is the strangest thing I have ever seen in my life?

"Go now and ponder these questions and bring me your answers. And remember it will go hard with you if your answers are not what they should be."

The Bishop went away deeply perturbed. He knew the Prince had no great love for him, and what could this test be but a device for degrading and dismissing him from his exalted station? He slumped into his chair and for a long time sat with knitted brow, his head clasped in his hands, thinking and thinking. But not a glimmer of an answer came to him to any of the three questions.

At last he stood up and mumbled, "I must go and see Motl the innkeeper. It's a bitter thing for me to do, but only he can help me." The name Motl is, of course, short and familiar for Mordecai, but no one ever thought of calling the shrewd and jolly innkeeper by the solemn name of Mordecai.

In the dead of night the Bishop put on a long robe that covered his cross and cassock, hunched his head into his shoulders, and went slinking to the inn. Motl was already asleep, and when he roused himself and discovered who his visitor was, he pronounced the two words *Shma Yisroel*, which every pious Jew utters when he faces a dire peril. For the Bishop was an implacable enemy of his people; they always spoke of him as "Our Haman."

Mordecai, that is to say, Motl the innkeeper, stood before Haman and trembled. But when the Bishop explained his mission, repeating the three questions whereon his fate hung in the balance, Motl quickly regained his composure. A full hour, even longer perhaps, the two men sat silent.

"Your Grace," said the innkeeper at last, "I am not sure I can help you, but I'll try if you promise to do exactly as I say."

"Say it and I'll do it," said the Bishop humbly.

"Then first you and I must exchange clothes," said Motl, "and I'll go to the Prince in your place. You put on my trousers and kaftn, and I'll put on your shirt, your cassock, your cross and your miter. You've brought your miter, I hope?"

"It's hidden in my bosom," said the Bishop.

"The day is breaking," said Motl.

"But what will I do until you return?" said the Bishop.

"Come with me," said Motl, and he led the Bishop to a large henhouse that stood behind the inn. He pointed to a roost where a dignified hen was sitting on a basket of eggs.

"Look," said Motl, "I'll lay these boards across the basket and you'll sit down in place of the hen. Sorry to disturb you, madam," said he to the bird, "but you must give way to someone more important than you. You sit there until I return," he admonished the Bishop, "and who knows," he added, "you may even hatch some chicks."

The same morning, Motl the innkeeper, in the Bishop's attire, stood before the Prince.

"Your Highness," he said grandly, "I am ready to answer your questions."

"Very well," said the Prince. "Question number one: What am I thinking as I look at you?"

"As you look at me, Your Highness, you are thinking that I am the Bishop."

The Prince and all his retinue were puzzled. The answer was surprisingly simple, but it was impossible to challenge it.

"Very well," said the Prince, "We'll let that pass. But now for question number two. What am I, your sovereign Prince, really worth?"

"One hundred gulden," was the prompt reply.

The Prince's face darkened and a loud murmur rose up among his retinue. "Unheard-of insolence! Treason! The man should be scourged!" they muttered.

"How dare you set my worth at a hundred gulden?" the Prince demanded.

"Behold this cross!" Motl solemnly intoned, holding it high above his head. "It cost me two hundred gulden. Now who would claim to be worth more than half the cross? No one, Your Highness. Not even the most powerful ruler in all Christendom. To be worth half the cross is glory enough for any prince or potentate."

Now the Prince and his coterie were more than surprised; they were dumbfounded.

"Can this be my own minister, that dolt?" the Prince wondered. "We'll let the answer stand," he announced. "But let us now see what you will do with the third question: what is the strangest thing I have ever seen in all my life?"

"For that, your Highness," was the answer, "you must deign to come with me to Motl the innkeeper, whose tavern, as many of your courtiers know only too well, is a short distance from the palace."

It was a bold request to make of a prince and his retinue, but by now they were all so bewildered, that it occurred to none of them to demur. So off they went in a troop, with the Prince and Motl in the lead, and the lords of the principality behind. And that alone was a strange sight for any man to see, but as you will surmise, a still stranger one awaited them.

They arrived, and Motl led them to his acre behind the tavern, straight to the henhouse. There sat the Bishop on the basket of eggs, exactly as the innkeeper had left him.

"There, Your Highness!" cried Motl. "There is the strangest sight you have ever seen, the strangest sight any man can see. A Bishop sitting on a basket of eggs in a henhouse, hatching little chicks!"

And how did it all end? In much the same way as in the Megillah. "Our Haman" was disgraced and deposed, and the Prince appointed Motl the innkeeper to be chief minister in his stead. But now everybody called him Reb Mordecai, including the Prince himself.

And may all our enemies come to no better end! Amen! *Selah.*

Share and Share Alike

THEY WERE both beggars of long standing, and they decided to "operate" together in the neighboring villages as friends and partners. They pledged each other to be loyal and faithful, and share their fortunes, good or ill, share and share alike.

"Unity!" said Zalman.

"Now and forever!" said Kalman.

In the villages there were not many of their own faith whom they could visit for alms. But they were seldom turned down and they had no cause to regret their alliance. They did, however, regret that these villagers were a rather coarse lot, crude and unrefined.

"You know, Zalman," said Kalman, "ours is a genteel profession. I like to get my alms from people of good breeding."

"Me, too," said Zalman. "But we mustn't be too snobbish."

One cold night—it happened to be the eve of Purim—they entered a house where a wedding was being celebrated. The large room, dominated by a big brick oven, was flooded with light and crowded with a gay and boisterous throng. There were good things to eat and drink, and no sooner did they disappear than the hostess brought in a fresh supply.

"Look who is here!" they cried. "Haman and Ahasuerus!"

"Unbidden guests, but welcome!" said the host. "Come and regale yourselves!"

The partners made a show of reluctance, just for the sake of good manners.

"We'll show them who is who!" whispered Kalman.

"Village boors!" whispered Zalman.

But they didn't stand off too long. The liquor, the food, the warmth weighed them down and their heads began to droop.

The host approached them with a worried expression.

"You are not planning to sleep the night here, are you?" he asked.

Zalman roused himself.

"Where would you have us go on a bitter cold night like this?" he asked.

"But the only extra bed we have is for the newlyweds!" the host explained.

"So! If a couple of young snipes get married, must two God-fearing Jews sleep in the woods?" Kalman demanded.

The host scratched his head ruefully. Then his face brightened.

"I have it!" he exclaimed. "You can sleep on top of the oven. It's not too roomy, but you'll be snug and warm."

"We have learned to accept our lot," said Kalman gravely.

"We'll retire at once," Zalman announced with hauteur.

The two clambered to the oven top and disposed themselves as well as they could. Zalman lay down on his side facing the wall and Kalman stretched out close to him with his back to the wedding guests.

"My posture," said Kalman to Zalman, "should let that riff-raff know what I think of them."

"They'll get the point," said Zalman. "Let's go to sleep." Both were soon asleep and snoring grandly.

In the meantime the wedding guests became more and more boisterous. They felt a strong desire for novel and more spicy entertainment, and one of them came forward with a bright idea.

"We'll form a line," he said, "and skip around the room. And each one of us, as he gets to the oven, will jump up and deliver a sharp smack on this beggar's rear. He deserves it, too. Just see how he has it stuck out at us."

The idea was adopted with enthusiasm and the smacks were delivered with no less enthusiasm. Kalman received them with a mixture of shock and indignation. Should he turn around and remonstrate, he asked himself? Better not, he decided. He was not likely to convince them, and after all he was getting it in the least vulnerable region. Nevertheless, it was not long before the region began to smart and tingle.

The guests got out of breath with the strenuous exercise and took an intermission.

"We'll have a little glass," they said, "and take it up where we left off."

Kalman shook Zalman roughly out of his sleep.

"Wake up," he rasped in his partner's ear, "and exchange places with me. Hurry!"

When, however, Zalman had roused himself and grasped the situation, he failed to show the alacrity that might have been expected from a faithful partner.

"Kalman," he pleaded, "don't you believe that all things are ordained from above? If it's ordained that your bottom should——"

"Share and share alike!" Kalman cut him short. "Remember, Zalman? Share and share alike!"

To this Zalman found no reply. After all, an oath is an oath, a pledge is a pledge. So with many groans and sighs, he exchanged places with his partner.

Now the wedding guests had taken their "little glass" and made ready to resume.

"Wait!" cried the one who originated the brilliant plan. "There is such a thing as justice, isn't there? We have two worthies up there on the oven, not one. The other is also entitled to his share. We'll have them exchange places before we resume."

And that is exactly what they did. Kalman's pleas and protests availed him nothing; they were drowned in roars of laughter. With Zalman they had no trouble at all.

So the round was resumed and again the smacks rained down hard on Kalman's poor "region," until the wedding guests became tired and rather bored. Every novelty, alas, sooner or later wears off. The truth will be found in the proverb about *kreplach,* that luscious dainty of ground beef fried in little bags of delicately rolled dough. A man may even reach a point, says the proverb, when he is unable to eat more *kreplach!*

When Zalman woke up in the morning his partner was already up and peering gloomily through the window.

"Kalman," said Zalman, "did you sleep well, Kalman?"

"You should sleep so well in your grave," said Kalman.

"Kalman," said Zalman, "why don't you sit down, Kalman?"

"You should be able to stand on your feet like I am able to sit down," said Kalman.

"Kalman," said Zalman, "Do you believe now that all things are ordained from above, Kalman? It was ordained that your bo—"

"It was ordained," said Kalman, "that I should have for a partner a false friend, a traitor."

"Kalman," cried Zalman, "where are you going, Kalman?"

"Back to town!"

"Wait, Kalman, we'll go together!"

"I'll find my way without you."

"But Kalman!"

But Kalman had already slammed the door behind him.

Bim-Bam and Day-Day

GETSL WAS a son-in-law.

Don't look so puzzled! I mean that was his livelihood—being a son-in-law. No, no! Not with an assortment of fathers-in-law! God forbid! Getsl was an upright young man and faithful to Rifkele, the wife of his bosom, whom he loved and cherished. What I mean is that when Getsl married Rifkele his father-in-law not only promised him a dowry of three hundred rubles, but bound himself to support him—or them, as God might will—for a period of three years.

For Getsl was no common every-day young man. Getsl had a head on his shoulders. Getsl was a keen student, and already possessed of a sizable store of learning when his father-in-law pounced on him, so to speak, and made him his son-in-law. But when a fine young man like Getsl becomes your son-in-law you don't just order him out into the hard world to grub for a living. You take him into your household and support him for a stated period—a year, three years, sometimes even ten years. And during this period a young man like Getsl continues to augment his store of learning, preparing for the career of rabbi, or *dayen,* or some other high calling. During this period, in other words, a young man like Getsl is a son-in-law.

Now the three years were drawing to a close, and what had Getsl accomplished? No small thing, if you view it from the right angle. He had succeeded in begetting two offspring, beautiful as two little angels. But his store of learning, if the full truth be told, was not greatly augmented. For Getsl had no ambition to be a rabbi or a dayen. Getsl hoped to be something else. He yearned to be a cantor.

Getsl found it hard to concentrate on the intricacies of the Talmud. In the midst of a passionate debate between two sages Getsl would stand up, pace up and down, and lose himself in a sad or solemn chant, singing bim-bam-bam, bim-bam, bim-bam, bim-bam-bam.

Nor did he hide his ambition from his father-in-law. The latter did not entirely approve, but after shrugging his shoulders, he made peace with the idea, and being not without influence in the councils of the community, he tried to have his son-in-law appointed to the post of assistant cantor as a start. But those who were charged with passing on the young man's qualifications shook their heads.

"Your son-in-law," they told him, "has a good voice. It still lacks vigor, but that should come with time. However, there is no *elan,* no thrust in his singing. It lacks the power to inspire and uplift. It's a matter of temperament, no doubt. In our opinion he could never be a really good cantor."

The verdict, as you may imagine, was a cruel blow to Getsl. He became listless and moody. He found it still harder to concentrate on the Talmud, but continued pacing up and down his study, humming mournfully: Bim-bam, bim-bam, oy, oy, oy, bim-bam, bim-bam-bam.

Just before the three years of his son-in-lawship ended his father-in-law called him in and had a heart-to-heart talk with him.

"Getsl," he said, "where will it all end? You have to make up your mind. You have to put your hand to something for a livelihood. You can't keep on bim-bamming all your life. I notice that Rifkele has a worried look in her eyes these days. So there is something I want to propose. You still have the dowry of three hundred rubles. Take the money, go out into the world and see what you can do. I know some who started with less and are now rich men. All you need to do is to get this bim-bam-bam out of your head and apply yourself to trade, to learn the value of merchandise, to understand people and be cautious in dealing with them—in a word, to business, and I'm sure you will, in short order, be able to provide for yourself, for Rifkele, and for the little angels, God bless their precious little bones."

"You are right, father-in-law, you are absolutely right," said Getsl. "Beginning tomorrow I stop being a dependent son-in-law."

So Getsl started out with the three hundred rubles next to his heart, trying to put as cheerful a face on the situation as he could. He came to the big city, sought out the people to whom his father-in-law recommended him and began the exacting labor of buying and selling. But did he do it with zeal? Was his heart really in it? In the very midst of examining some complicated transaction, his mind often wandered off, and he caught himself going: Bim-bam, bim-bam, bim-bam-bam.

He made a modest beginning with lumber and came out fifty

rubles behind. He tried grain and lost a hundred. He tried wool and earned twenty-five rubles. He was so elated he lost his balance and plunged. He entered into partnership with a new acquaintance and they bought up a large quantity of hemp. Now, I say beware of hemp. Hemp is tricky. Hemp is the graveyard of hopes and fortunes. As for partners, no warning should be necessary. Partners are worse than competitors.

They sold the hemp slowly, painfully, over a period of weeks, and when his partner's bookkeeping was over, Getsl had lost a hundred and fifty-six rubles. How much his partner lost he never found out.

"I am wiped out clean," said he to himself. "What shall I do? Where shall I turn?"

He had enough left for the return trip to his town, but he had no heart to face the reception that awaited him. He even lacked the spirit to seek solace in his bim-bam. He wandered aimlessly in the streets of the city and stopped in front of a music shop, gazing at the instruments on display. For no reason at all, he went inside and put down the greater part of the little he still had for a flute.

With the flute tucked under his arm Getsl walked on and came to a field on the outskirts of the city. There, under a tree, he sat down and played the instrument. Getsl, it should be noted, had a way with any musical instrument. He was so moved by the sweet, piercing notes, that he broke off, covered his face with his hands and wept.

When he looked up again someone stood facing him. When and how did this stranger get there? Getsl remembered hearing no footsteps. The stranger was a short individual with broad shoulders, a broad ruddy face and a broad black beard.

"Good, good!" said he in a soft but cheerful voice. "You did the right thing, having a good cry. Now come with me and we'll go to my hut."

Without a word Getsl did as the man told him. The hut was near enough—right there on the edge of the city.

The two ate together and Getsl stayed on. He felt a peculiar lightness of spirit, as if all his cares had been suddenly lifted off his shoulders. He talked and talked and his host listened.

"So you wanted to be a cantor, did you?" said he at last. "Let me hear something from you. Let me hear your voice."

Getsl leaned back and sang: Bim-bam-bam, bim-bam-bam, bim-bam, bim-bom-bam.

The little man listened, smiled benignly, but shook his head. "No," said he, "this won't do. You'll never get anywhere with bim-bam."

"No?" said Getsl.

"Bim-bam," said the stranger, "is for students and scholars. Bim-bam is for men who ponder and meditate, who speculate and wonder. Bim-bam is for men who knit their brows, who are shut in, who are oppressed by the weight of the world. Now, I don't say: Down with Bim-bam! God forbid! There are times when I myself go bim-bam. But what does bim-bam do to uplift the soul? At most it helps you stroke your beard when you are wrestling with a Talmudic problem, or snap your fingers lightly when you have found the solution. But can you fling up your arms and stamp your feet with bim-bam? Will it make men leap towards their Father in Heaven, or exult in Him or long for Him? For, after all, does it not say: 'Serve the Lord with joy, come before him with rejoicing?' What, then, can a cantor accomplish with bim-bam? Isn't he the bellwether of the holy flock in their ascent to the Higher World! No! Bim-bam is not for a cantor, not for a real cantor!"

"What must I do then?" Getsl pleaded.

"I'll show you," said the strange little man.

He stood up and began singing in a soft but tense voice:

Day-day-day, day-day-day, day-day, day-day, day!

He continued and his day-day went crescendo. It gathered strength, became fervent, jubilant, ecstatic. Then, by slow gradations, the mood changed. Now it was tender, appealing, yearning. But it was still in the pitch of day-day, charged though it was with emotions of a different order.

Getsl listened enthralled, his heart responding to every

change in the mood of the singer's day-day. Gradually the mood reverted to its original fervor. The little man flung out his arms and stamped his feet. Then he planted his hands on his hips and began to dance.

Before he knew what he was doing Getsl was on his feet, dancing with his strange host and joining in his triumphant day-day.

The man stopped singing and smiled blissfully at Getsl, and Getsl smiled back at him with understanding and a sudden flood of joy.

There is little more to relate. Getsl stayed on with his host for a week or so, and then returned to his own town, bankrupt and happy. All day long his joyous day-day resounded through his father-in-law's house. Again he appeared before the committee and was engaged at once as associate cantor of the congregation. It was not long before his fame spread far and wide. To show their admiration and affection, people called him Getsele instead of Getsl. Who hasn't heard of Cantor Getsele?

Getsl and Rifkele lived happily for many years and their flock of angels continued to grow. I often wonder why these angels come down from heaven to dwell on this earth of ours. Heaven, I am sure, must be a more delightful place. It's a riddle I can't answer, any more than I can answer the riddle of the little man with the ruddy face and broad beard who taught Getsl to go day-day. Who was he? I mean who was he, really and truly? I leave you to your own guesses. As for the sweet little angels, whatever their reason for making the journey from heaven, the Lord bless them and keep them. Amen! *Selah!*

Once There Were Two Brothers

Once upon a time in a certain town there lived two brothers, one rich, the other poor. The rich brother lived like a lord, in a grand house with fine furniture, the best food, servants and everything the heart could desire. He had plenty of gold and silver, but he wanted more and more. He was, in fact, a hard-hearted man, a miser, and his servants were under strict orders to turn away from his door any beggar who might appear and ask for charity.

The other brother lived in a hut that was almost a hovel, but he never turned away anyone who was hungry, even if it meant sharing his pittance with the needy one. He had few worldly goods, this poor brother, but he did have one thing with which he refused to part, no matter how hard-pressed he was. This was a silver spoon, an heirloom, which he received from a granduncle of his.

"Keep this spoon," said the saintly man just before he died, "and do not sell or pawn it. Some day it will prove to be your salvation."

But whenever this poor brother entertained a beggar at his meager board who seemed to him to be especially deserving, he took out his silver spoon and permitted his guest to use it.

Now one day who should appear in this town, but Elijah the Prophet! No one, of course, recognized him because, as everybody knows, Elijah always travels in disguise. This time he was disguised as a beggar. He wore a shabby *kaftn* with a rope around the waist for a girdle. In one hand he carried a staff and with the other he held on to his beggar's sack which was slung over his shoulder. No one in the town took any notice of him, but if anyone had watched this beggar carefully, he would have discovered a strange thing about him: the dogs never barked at him!

The beggar came to the door of the rich brother's house, but a servant appeared promptly and ordered him to go.

"Tell your master I am hungry," said the beggar, "and he should know that it is a sin to turn away a hungry man."

The servant went inside but soon returned.

"My master wants me to tell you," he said, "that it is written: 'In the sweat of thy face shalt thou eat bread,' so go away at once."

The impudence of that miser! To attempt to cover up his sin with the words of the Holy Book! That, of course, compounded the sin and made it very grave indeed.

So Elijah wandered off and before long he stopped at the hut of the poor brother, who welcomed him and seated him at his table and laid before him whatever he could find in his larder. He also fetched out his silver spoon and urged him to use it with some chopped herring that he served him, for it seemed to him this beggar was entitled to the special honor. So the beggar ate and chanted the grace, and before departing he blessed his host, saying:

"Whatever you do, may you continue to do it!"

The poor brother was a little puzzled by the blessing, but before trying to unravel its meaning he polished his precious spoon and laid it in its coffer. He returned to clear his table, and lo and behold, there lay the silver spoon! He rubbed his eyes, tapped his forehead, and took the spoon to the coffer. There in the coffer lay the first silver spoon! Trembling with excitement, he returned to the table, and sure enough there was another silver spoon on it, just like the two that were already in the coffer.

Then the poor brother understood! He understood the beggar's blessing. And he realized who the beggar was. He continued taking silver spoons to his coffer, and when it was full he said "Enough!" He was a modest man, not greedy, not covetous.

But he really did have enough. He was no longer a poor man. He bought a decent house to live in, a new dress, a new wig and new candlesticks for his wife, new shoes and clothes for his children, and he had enough left to enable him to study Torah without being oppressed by worldly cares.

But, of course, it was impossible for this great wonder to remain secret. Everybody in town soon knew about it, including the rich brother. It brought him no pleasure that his brother was no longer a pauper, as is written "He raiseth up the poor out of the dust, and lifteth up the needy from the dunghill." Instead, he was devoured by envy and chagrin.

"Why, oh why, did I send the beggar away?" he moaned all day. And he ordered his servant to be on the lookout for that beggar and when he found him to lead him into his parlor and treat him like a prince. And, sure enough, the servant found the same beggar, for he was still tarrying in the town, and conducted him to his master's home.

"Toybe!" said the rich brother to his wife when he saw the beggar heading towards his door. "Bring me your gold bracelet with the pendants, Toybe!"

"Why all of a sudden my gold bracelet with the pendants, why?" Toybe demanded.

"If you know too much, you'll get old before your time," he sneered at her. "Do as I tell you, and if you are worried about your bracelet, let me assure you that soon I'll give you two bracelets for your one, three, or ten or twenty."

"I was afraid there was something wrong with you," she answered. "You haven't been yourself lately. But now I am sure you have gone out of your mind."

Nevertheless, she brought him her gold bracelet with the pendants: first, because she thought it best to humor him; and second, because he tyrannized over her.

"Come in, come in, my honored guest!" the rich brother cried when the servant conducted the beggar into his parlor.

"Sit down and refresh yourself. Motke!" he ordered his servant, "bring a bottle of my best wine, bring two drumsticks from the roast goose, bring and bring and bring!"

But the beggar just smiled benignly and said: "All I want is a piece of bread and some water."

"Did you hear, Motke?" said the miser. "Bring!"

The beggar ate his bread and drank his water and rose to go. The miser felt his heart palpitate. But before he left the beggar turned to him and said:

"Whatever you do, may you continue to do it!"

"Aha!" said the rich brother to himself, and his heart stopped palpitating.

So now the rich brother was alone in his parlor and was about to pick up his wife's bracelet with the pendants. But a sudden thought struck him. He must be able to continue for, say, five hours without being interrupted. He must make sure he will not have to interrupt himself. So he decided to take a simple hygienic precaution. He stepped out to relieve his bladder.

He is still relieving it, the wicked miser!

The Effronteries of Kopl Kabtsn

This story would never be a story if people didn't die. Why shake your head over it? It could be shown that the entire world wouldn't be a world for the same reason. That's the way the One Above created it and found it good. Good, did I say? When he ended His work He found it "very good." And our sages, bless their memory, explain it and say: "*Very good*—that means death."

It happened in my little town Baranka. A *shtetl* like hundreds of others. Tumble-down houses, a *shul*, a bathhouse, a market-place where goats roamed at will. And outside the *shtetl*, but not too far away, the House of Eternity, where people, good, bad and middling, were taken for their eternal rest.

Now Baranka was an old *shtetl* and gradually, with God's help, the House of Eternity became crowded and overcrowded.

"There is no way out," said the *rov* and the trustees. "We'll have to buy and lay out a new House." And so they did. The ground was leveled and set out, a good fence was built around it, and the people gathered and dedicated it with prayer and thanksgiving—and, of course with tarts and brandy—and there it was, ready to receive guests.

Easy to say, receive guests. But the guests were not anxious to go there. No one, at any rate, was willing to be the first guest. Either he himself, prior to his departure, or those who had authority to speak for him after the event, denied the trustees the right to accommodate him as the first guest. Is it so hard to understand why? The prospect of being all alone in a House so big, for who can say how long a period, is forbidding if not frightening. Our people, God bless them and keep them, like to be among people—relatives, friends, even enemies. That's the way they are and you won't change them.

So the new House stood there, or if you like, lay there, unoccupied, and the trustees grew more and more worried. For the old House was getting so overcrowded, it would soon be impossible to find room for another arrival. What was to be done? The trustees met with the *rov* and it was decided to offer a reward to the town denizen who would consent to be the first occupant of the new House. Not an insignificant reward, mind you, and yet it failed to have the hoped-for effect. There are some things in life more important than money.

But now it's time to introduce our hero, Kopl Kabtsn. After two score years and more, the second name which proclaimed him a pauper, and was given him as a nickname, clung to him with the dignity of a family name. And was he an ill-starred *kabtsn*, this Kopl, the Lord shield us and preserve us! They said of him that if he were to pick up a gold coin from the ground, it would immediately turn to lead. Yet he could be proud and stubborn, this Kopl. The luxuries a *kabtsn* will afford himself!

So it happened on the day before a certain Passover that Kopl and his wizened old wife found their home only half prepared for the holy festival. That is to say, the home had been carefully scoured and cleansed of leaven, but none of the things prescribed for the feast had yet been brought in. No matse, no wine, no fish or fowl, or eggs or nuts. The woman sat in a corner weeping, and Kopl paced up and down in desperation. Suddenly he turned and faced her.

"Neshe," he announced, "We have to do it, there is nothing else we can do!"

Neshe just stared at him.

"It's a ruse," he said, "and some people will condemn me. But I'll make it good. It won't be long before I'll make it good. I know it."

Neshe continued to stare.

"This is what I want you to do," Kopl explained. "Go to the head trustee and tell him I have just died. Tell him it was my last wish to be laid in the new ground, and collect the reward. They'll come for me, and I'll be ready for them, and they'll take me away. You will then go to market and buy everything we need for Passover. And you may as well redeem the candlesticks, don't forget."

Neshe stared harder than ever.

"You are wondering what they'll do to me?" said Kopl. "Don't wonder and don't worry. The One Above will look after me. Be sure I'll be back tonight for the *seyder*.

The woman did what her man told her: she always did what he told her.

The trustee was so overjoyed he forgot to offer condolences. He handed the woman the reward, and without losing any time he dispatched two sturdy draymen to perform the necessary rites and tasks with the remains of Kopl Kabtsn.

Off they went, with Kopl stretched out on a covered bier in the bottom of the vehicle. They came to a tavern on the edge of the town and decided to go in and fortify themselves before proceeding with the arduous part of their mission. No sooner were they gone than Kopl threw off the covers, and after rearranging them on the bier, made off as fast as he could and returned home. Neshe had not yet returned from market so Kopl first rehearsed the order of the *seyder* with the help of his *agode*, then lay down and fell asleep.

The draymen came out of the tavern, feeling flushed and important. They had stayed longer than they intended: doesn't every man do the same when he steps into a tavern? In short order they reached their destination and lifted the bier out of the cart.

"You know what I'll tell you," said one to the other. "There is nothing like a couple of little glasses to lighten a man's toil."

"Right you are, on my faith as a Jew," replied the other. "This Kopl of ours has grown light as a feather."

But when they uncovered the bier they fell into each other's arms, clinging tight, trembling and blubbering with terror. They rushed back to town lashing their horse without pity, and pulled up before the trustee's house. The stupefied official hastened to Kopl's hut.

"He is still sleeping," his wife, who had now returned from market and was absorbed in her Passover preparations, informed him. "It's been a hard day for him and I mustn't wake him."

The frantic trustee ran to the *rov*. The *rov* sat back, closed his eyes and furrowed his high forehead.

"Nothing," he said, opening his eyes. "We must do nothing to mar the holy festival. After Passover we'll have him up before the Tribunal. He will not go unpunished, you may be sure."

Never will Baranka forget the trial of Kopl Kabtsn. It seemed as if the whole town was there, and those who were unable to get inside pushed and crowded around the door. It was a warm spring day and the windows were open. Those up front could hear nearly all that went on and relayed it to those behind them.

For weeks and weeks nothing else was talked about in the town, and the one thing that people couldn't stop marveling at was the arrogant speech Kopl made in his defense. Such effrontery! No one suspected he had it in him.

"My masters!" he began. "You have heard what the trustee had to say. You have also heard what the two honest men who drove me as far as the tavern had to say. But what can I say? Nothing. Nothing at all. I am a humble man and I have dashed the hopes of an entire town, a holy congregation. I have sinned. But not wilfully, not defiantly. I took the reward, but only as advance payment for a service which I am solemnly resolved to perform. I was driven by despair, thinking of the oncoming *seyder* night, seeing my poor spouse sitting in the corner with folded hands and weeping. Weeping on the eve of the holy and joyous festival of Passover! My Neshele weeping when every other housewife was busy and happy!

"But what am I saying, my masters? Do I sound as if I am defending myself? I have no wish to defend myself. I am guilty. Let the trustee go to my home and take the pillow off my bed. Let him take my Neshe's candlesticks which she has just redeemed. Let him take whatever else of value he can find. Alas, he will find very little! My clothes are in tatters, even my Sabbath *kaftn* is nearly in shreds.

"So, then, I stand before you and await your sentence. And I have only one more thing to say. There is one sentence which you may hesitate to impose on me. So I say to you: don't hesitate. Order me to carry out the obligation I assumed, and to do it immediately. I will accept your verdict. I will lay hands on myself this very day, right now, in your presence, if you—"

At this point the *rov* rose from his seat and cried: "Enough! It is enough!" And in a softer voice he said: "Go home, Kopl. Go home to your wife." And addressing the other members of the court, he said: "This case is unique. There is nothing in Talmudic law that covers it. We can only do as our hearts prompt us. The Tribunal is adjourned."

And that was the end of the trial of Kopl Kabtsn. As to the outcome, opinion in the town was divided; in Baranka opinion is always divided; that's the kind of town we are. A minority shook their heads, saying "Poor Kopl! What could the Tribunal do? Order him to do away with himself to make the trustees happy?" But the majority was indignant. They couldn't forget the man's outrageous effrontery.

But wait. In the matter of Kopl's effrontery, you have only heard the beginning.

A fairly long time passed during which there was no occasion for the trustees to worry. The angel with the drawn sword and thousand eyes passed us by. "It's all for the sake of Kopl," said the town wag. "The Lord is giving him a chance to redeem himself." But one Friday, just before sunset, it became known that Berke, the town idiot, was no more. And since the necessary rites could not be performed on the Sabbath, Berke could not be brought to his eternal rest until the following Sunday.

Soon enough something else became known. The trustees intended to accord Berke the honor of inaugurating the new House. No longer any need for them to be so anxious about Kopl's health. The town idiot had solved their problem. In life, poor Berke, who had no kith or kin, was only a minor nuisance and an object of pity; now he became a person of distinction, entitled to the gratitude of the whole town. Everyone seemed to approve of the trustees' decision.

The following morning the Sabbath services in *shul* proceeded as usual. The first half was over, and the cantor, the *gabay* and the *shames* made their way to open the Ark and take out the scrolls for the reading of the Torah portion. Suddenly a well-known figure took his stand before the doors of the Ark and glared at the congregation. It was Kopl Kabtsn.

"I do not permit the reading!" he cried in a loud and angry voice.

The congregation was stunned. Had Kopl gone mad? The right not to permit the reading of the Torah on the Sabbath may, of course, be exercised by any man in Israel. Its purpose, as everyone knows, is to enable a man who feels wronged to air his grievance in public and obtain a promise of redress. But did he, Kopl, have a grievance? Didn't the whole town have a valid grievance against him?

In the silence that followed Kopl's rasping voice was heard again.

"They are going to lay Berke in the new and empty cemetery!" he cried. "It's a shame and a scandal!"

It took the congregation a few moments to absorb the import of these words. Then the storm broke. People stood up, shouted and shook their fists at him. The effect on others was exactly opposite. They laughed. Their laughter was loud and uncontrolled, with a touch of hysterics in it. Before long the merriment gained the upper hand. Those who began by shouting joined in the laughter, which grew louder and louder.

The *rov* made his way to the Ark beside Kopl and faced his congregation. Not a word issued from his lips. But slowly at first, then at a faster rate, the laughter subsided, until the silence became heavy and oppressive.

"Enough!" said the *rov* in a soft and sad voice. "Enough of desecrating the holy Sabbath. You will now listen to what Kopl has to say."

And did Kopl have much to say? He did. He spoke about Berke, of his strange, unhappy life. He reminded them that Berke was a gentle and harmless person, and how everyone in town felt it was a good deed, especially pleasing to Him Above, to give Berke food and rescue him from the children who always tormented him. He even reminded them of the way Berke smiled; how it wrung the heart to see him smile.

"And now," he continued, his voice growing louder, "Berke has left this world, he is on his way to a better world. No kith or kin will follow his bier, no one will shed a tear as they lower him into his grave. But our trustees will rejoice. They will take advantage of his loneliness to do with him what they didn't dare do with any one else. Is this justice? Is this in keeping with our holy Torah? I am an ignorant man, God forgive me, but there is something I remember. Somewhere in the Torah it is written: Don't put a stumbling-block before the blind. And my *rebe*, Paradise should be lighted up for him, said this means more than the bare words. It means don't take advantage of anyone who is helpless, who is friendless and alone in this bitter world."

Kopl stopped, unable to go on, and in the *shul* you could have heard a pin drop. The *rov* took a step forward.

"We have heard why Kopl didn't permit the reading of the Torah," he said. "I want to assure him, in the name of this holy congregation, that his grievance will receive careful consideration. And now let us go forward with the Opening of the Ark."

What more is there to tell? But perhaps you have some questions to ask?

First, was Berke laid in the new House? The answer is No. They managed somehow to find room for him in the old one.

Second, who, then, was the first to be laid in the new House? The answer is Kopl Kabtsn. No, it didn't happen so soon. A few years later. And during those years—you won't believe it if I tell you—the town had no need for either House. Some people said the town owed it to Kopl's merit. But others just scoffed at the notion. In our town opinion is always divided.

Oh yes! Something I forgot to tell you. When the *rov* returned to his seat that Sabbath morning those near him heard him say: "What a people you have, dear God, what a people!" The *rov's* words got around, and the town wondered just what he meant. Some were sure he meant the congregation, the unseemly way they behaved when Kopl stood up before the Ark. But those who were near the *rov* at the time said No. There was no anger in his voice, no sorrow. On the contrary, they said. His eyes shone, they said, and there was pride and wonder in his voice. And some came right out and said he meant Kopl Kabtsn! What peculiar ideas some people get!

But that's the way it is in our town. If one says it's day, another says it's night. That's the kind of town we are.

The Visitor from Over There

A SIMPLE VILLAGE housewife, what would Bashke know about the special Sabbaths that come in the course of the year, like, say, the Great Sabbath that occurs just before Passover, the Sabbath of Repentance between Rosh Hashona and Yom Kippur, or the Sabbath of Consolation? People who have the good fortune to live in cities and towns know that the Sabbath of Consolation comes right after the Fast of the Ninth Day of Ab when pious folk mourn the destruction of the Temple. The Sabbath of Consolation is to comfort the mourners, for on that day they read the healing words of the prophet Isaiah, *nachmu, nachmu ami,* "Comfort, comfort My people." That is why, as those fortunate people know, that special Sabbath is called "Shabes Nachmu."

But Bashke, the wife of Sholem, the keeper of the village tavern? That knowledge was never taught her, and whom was she to learn it from? The peasants who stopped to guzzle in the tavern, or their wives who came to drag them home? Of course, there was her husband Sholem. But—let it remain a secrret between us—Sholem's learning extended very little beyond her own. Sholem was a good, God-fearing man, with heavy shoulders and strong hands, and he knew how to separate the peasants when they began to brawl, and when necessary he could seize them by the scruff of the neck and throw them out of the tavern. But when it came to those black letters on white paper, Sholem, it must be confessed, was helpless.

Now it came to pass that Sholem returned one day from a visit to the town and informed his wife that he heard people say that Shabes Nachmu was on the way. Bashke in her simple innocence at once assumed that Shabes Nachmu was some person of importance, a learned scholar and wonder-worker, the prophet Elijah, or perhaps the Messiah himself! And she was all aflutter at the thought that he was on the way and, who knows? might turn up in her own village and tavern!

But Sholem forgot to tell her something else he heard in the town: that Shayke Ganev the famous rogue and thief, had been seen in those parts, and some people who never locked or barred their doors now thought it best to take those precautions.

It was a sunny afternoon in the village and Bashke was alone in the tavern when in came a worthy of remarkable appearance. He was dressed in a flowing *kaftn* that might once have been green or brown, but was now a dirty gray, held together at the waist by a broad green girdle with long fringes. His feet were shod in dilapidated boots with loose soles that slapped as he walked, and his head was covered with a sheepskin hat shaped like a cone that someone had sliced off near the top. His face was practically hidden in a profusion of crimson beard, but his small eyes had a peculiar glitter and the tip of his nose—strange to relate—appeared to move in every direction, like the feelers of an insect. Who else would it be but Shayke Ganev, that villain of many shifts and disguises?

Bashke stood up all atremble and gazed with awe at the newcomer.

"A little glass to comfort a weary wanderer," said Shayke, sitting down at the table.

Bashke brought him not a little but a big one, and marveled at the speed with which it vanished as Shayke, throwing back his head, tipped it towards the ceiling. Bashke brought him another and another. At last she found courage to ask him a few timid questions.

"You come from far away?" she inquired.

Shayke waved his hand grandly to indicate great distance.

"Have you seen Shabes Nachmu? Do you know where he is now?" Bashke went on.

Shayke looked at her intently and his eyes glittered.

"I am Shabes Nachmu," he said solemnly.

Bashke was overjoyed.

"I knew you were on the way!" she cried. "And to think that you stopped in my house! What an honor!"

"The great and the lowly are all the same to me," said Shayke.

"But tell me, Reb Shabes Nachmu," Bashke fluttered on, "Where do you come from?"

"Where should I come from? From Over There." Shayke whispered mysteriously.

"From Over There? From . . . from . . ." Bashke did not dare utter the name of the place.

"Yes, from the Other World," Shayke whispered.

Bashke's face glowed.

"In that case you must have seen my dear father and mother there!"

"Indeed I saw them," said Shayke, "and that is the real reason why I have come to you."

"What is it, what is it, Reb Shabes Nachmu? Tell me about them," she pleaded.

"They sent me to bring you a message," Shayke explained. "Not a happy message. In short, they want you to know that they are destitute Over There. They have nothing to wear, nothing to eat. They beg you to help them."

"But how can I send them help?"

"With me," said Shayke. "I am going back there tonight and I'll take along whatever you give me."

The woman lost no time.

"My poor, poor father and mother," she wept as she made a bundle of all the clothes she could find, her own and her husband's, and handed it to her celestial visitor.

"Here," she said, "and give them some money also. They can use money Over There, can't they?"

"Every kopek you can spare," Shayke assured her. "But this bundle is very heavy. I don't think I can carry it so far."

"Think of my poor father and mother," she pleaded with him. "They'll fall on your neck and kiss you. Think of the great merit you will earn for this good deed. Besides, let me give you something for the kindness you will do me. Take this, dear Shabes Nachmu, it is all I have left."

Now Shayke felt sure he could obtain no more. Besides, it was advisable to decamp without delay: the innkeeper might appear and spoil everything. So he slung the bundle over his shoulder and set off.

He had already gone a good stretch on his way to the town when he heard the sound of hoofs on the road behind him. "It's the innkeeper!" his instinct warned him, and Shayke turned off the highway into a wood. After trudging a short distance on the path in the wood, he plunged into a clump of bushes, where he laid the bundle down and made certain preparations to confront the innkeeper when he appeared. "As a messenger from the Other World," said he to himself, "I did pretty well with the wife. Now let me see if I can't do the same with the husband."

Sholem the innkeeper was tearing along in pursuit of the villain who had cheated his wife when, among the trees near the highway, he beheld a sight that made him jerk at his reins in terror. There stood a man, his face almost hidden in a fiery red beard, but the rest of him as naked as Adam before he ate the forbidden apple. The man's arms encircled the trunk of a tree to which he clung as if his life depended on it.

"Who—who are you?" Sholem stammered.

"I have been sent here from the Other World." Shayke informed him.

"Why are you naked?"

"Over There we have no need for clothes."

"Why do you hold fast to the tree?"

"Because the roots of this tree wind around the earth. If I released the tree for only a moment the whole world would, God forbid, be destroyed."

By this time the man's ready and reasonable replies had restored the innkeeper from his fright. He could think again of what it was that had sent him galloping on the highway.

"Have you seen a crafty scoundrel on the way to town carrying a big bundle?" he asked the man from Over There.

"Let me try to remember," said Shayke. "Why, yes! Quite some time ago. He must be a long way from here by now! I'm sure you won't overtake him."

Sholem was convinced. Could he doubt the word of a messenger from Over There?

"Dear messenger," he prayed. "Be kind to me. Take my horse and go after this villain and stop him. He robbed my foolish wife of all our clothes and money."

"But I must stay here and support this tree," Shayke objected.

"Let me take your place until you return," the innkeeper answered, brandishing his stout arms.

"But I am naked," said Shayke. "How can I show myself on the highway?"

Again the smart innkeeper came forward with a solution.

"Here," he said, stripping off his *kaftn,* his trousers, and everything he had between them and his skin. "Let me have the tree. Put on my clothes, mount my horse, and bring me back that liar and thief. And don't worry, in my hands the world will be safe."

Shayke did as the innkeeper told him, but before entering upon the highway, he stopped and picked up his own clothes and the bundle. Then he galloped away, leaving the naked innkeeper with his arms tight around the tree, but full of glee at the thought of what he would do to the brigand when the man from Over There returned and delivered him into his hands.

Exactly how long he stood there is not recorded, but it was a long time before someone found and rescued him. His strength was exhausted and some people thought he was delirious. He mumbled things they couldn't understand. "The world," he babbled. "Be careful, be careful! The world!"

And may Heaven preserve and protect us all from the wiles of blackguards like Shayke Ganev! Amen!

Zanvl and the King

THERE WAS once a king who was different from the ordinary run of kings. The ordinary king, as is well known, is not distinguished for wit and wisdom. He is devoted to the pleasures of the body, not to those of the mind: to eating and drinking, to horses and dogs, to wives and concubines. But this king was shrewd and sharp. If he chose, he could speak in riddles, so that only the wisest of the wise understood him. The Jews of his realm even suspected that at one time or another, when he was young, he had sharpened his wits on the whetstone of the Talmud.

It happened one day that this king went out walking in the market place of his capital, accompanied, of course, by two generals as aides-de-camp, one on each side of him. They kept close, but slightly behind him, as is proper. The king's attire was simple and modest, but the two generals wore brilliant uniforms, blazing with ribbons and medals, and strutted proudly through the market place like roosters in a barnyard.

Suddenly the king stopped.

"Do you see that Jew over there in the long shabby *kaftn* and cap down over his ears, standing there with his hands in his pockets and dreaming of his yesterdays? Bring him over to me!"

In less than a minute the Jew, whose name was Zanvl, stood before the king. The king looked him up and down and said: "A seven-story *kabtsn*."

"Yes, Your Majesty," Zanvl agreed.

"Tell me," the king went on, "why didn't you let the five take care of the seven?"

Zanvl's eyes began to twinkle.

"My ten," he answered, "are unable to keep pace with my thirty-two."

The king looked pleased.

"I suppose," he said, "you have already been wrung out?"

"I have been wrung out three times, Your Majesty," Zanvl answered, "but I have to get wrung out twice more."

"I know what you are up against," said the king. "I'll tell you what I'll do. I'll send you two roosters and you can pluck them."

"I'll pluck them, Your Majesty, and not just once," Zanvl replied.

The king and his two generals moved on and Zanvl got lost in the crowd. But the two bemedaled flunkeys were writhing with curiosity. What did the strange talk between the king and the pauper signify? They eyed each other, and each one jerked his head towards the king as much as to say, "Ask him, why don't you?" But neither of them dared. Finally they couldn't contain themselves, and both blurted out together:

"Your Majesty, won't you graciously tell us—"

The king silenced them with a long stare.

"You want to know?" he said. "Go find the Jew and ask him."

It was not easy to find him. They pushed through the crowd this way and that way, forcing people to get out of their way, but at last they found him.

"You there!" they snapped. "Stand still and tell us what you and the king spoke about. He ordered us to find you."

"If he sent you to find me," Zanvl answered coolly, "it's not because *he* wants to know, but because *you* want to know."

"Very well, then," they said. "We want to know, so tell us!"

"You want to know, but why should I tell you?" Zanvl replied. "We had a private conversation, the king and I."

By this time the generals realized that they must change their tune. Arrogance and threats would get them nowhere. So they said very humbly:

"Please, do us a favor and tell us."

"A favor?" said Zanvl. "Why not? I like favors. I live from favors. So, then, this is what we said to each other, the king and I. But wait. You see this pocket? Just place a thousand gilders in it. There is plenty of room."

The generals looked at each other, but they didn't hesitate long. It'll be worth the money, they were sure. So they did as they were told.

"The king asked me why didn't I let the five take care of the seven," Zanvl resumed. "That meant why didn't I provide in the five warm months for the seven cold months. So I told him my ten can't keep pace with my thirty-two. And what could that mean but that my ten fingers can't provide for my thirty-two teeth? Then he wanted to know had I already been wrung out. That meant had I married off a daughter. Because, you know, nothing wrings you out like marrying off a daughter. The king himself married off a daughter, so he must know all about it. You heard what I told him: I have already been wrung out three times and I have to get wrung out twice more. For you must know that my wife—she should live and be well—is an obstinate woman and took it into her head to have only girls. So now you know."

"But wait!" the generals objected. "What about the roosters?"

"The roosters?" Zanvl repeated. "That too? You don't have to know everything. If you try to know too much your hair will turn gray and you'll be old before your time. Besides, His Majesty must be pining for you."

Well, they really did learn a great deal. They were both sure of it. The king would certainly be impressed.

They found the king and told him, but he was not impressed. In fact, he treated them with contempt.

"So you went away without getting an answer to your last question," he scoffed at them. "Well, you are blessed with clever heads, both of you. When you get bald your heads will be good for cracking nuts. Go out and find the Jew, and don't come back without the answer, or it will go hard with you!"

What could the poor generals do? The king commanded, so they went. This time it was not so hard to find Zanvl. There he was in the same spot where they had left him. He seemed to be waiting for them.

"Please," they implored him, "tell us about the roosters. Our careers, even our lives depend on it." Such humble generals, adorned with ribbons and medals, were never seen before!

"It's plain," said Zanvl, "that you are in trouble and I am not so heartless as to refuse my help. A thousand gilders, please, right here," he interposed, spreading open the pocket of his *kaftn*. The generals promptly complied.

"Now then," Zanvl resumed, "I'll tell you what you want to know. It's a secret that I would not entrust to anyone else. You yourselves are the roosters. The king said he would send you to me to pluck. I said I would pluck you, and not just once. He did what *he* said. I did what *I* said. We are both men of our word."

Now the generals knew. Their education was complete. As for Zanvl he turned homeward, saying to himself: "You never had so much money in your life, Zanvl. You are ready for the wringer."

The Emperor and the Tailor

Yudl the tailor sat cross-legged on his haunches, stitching away on a new patch he was laying on a pair of patched up trousers. What was Yudl thinking of? Not, you may be sure, of the patch, nor of such trivial things as the quarrels and conflicts between kings and emperors. For the days were the days of the great Napoleon and of the huge army which he took across Russia and which, people were saying, had shriveled up in the Russian winter and was now trying to get out and return to where it came from.

No, Yudl was thinking of more important matters: of the feast of Purim which had just been celebrated; of the mud which made the streets of his *shtetl* impassable; of the approaching Passover and the heavy demands it made on your lean purse; of the sun that was beginning to caress the earth. "A wonderful tailor, the Almighty," said Yudl to himself. "What beautiful new clothes He is making for His world in honor of the holy festival." And Yudl hummed a little song as he stitched away, a well-known song about a tree by the road, old and bent, and a weary old Jew on his way to the Land of Israel, and what great joy there would be when he reached his goal.

But suddenly his door was flung open and a curious individual burst into the room. He was short and paunchy, and dressed in a dazzling uniform that sparkled with gold medals.

"Quick!" he snapped at Yudl. "Show me where I can hide! They are after me, a whole troop of Russian soldiers with spears!"

The fiery gleam in the little man's eyes and the commanding ring in his voice struck terror into the heart of Yudl the tailor, and he sat and stared as if paralyzed.

"Don't you hear me?" the little man screamed. "I am the Emperor Napoleon, and they will kill me if they find me here!"

Yudl roused himself. A human life in imminent danger! It was no time to sit and stare.

"Come with me, Your Majesty," he said. "I'll hide you and if you lie still they'll never find you."

He led Napoleon to a neighboring room almost entirely occupied by a bed.

"Get in there and stretch out," said Yudl pointing to the bed.

Napoleon did as he was told and Yudl spread a heavy featherbed on him, then threw another featherbed over the first, a third over the second and a fourth over the third. Napoleon had been in many a hot place before, but never had he perspired as he did now.

Napoleon's bedtime was not a minute too early. Three Russians stamped into the tailor's workroom.

"Has anyone come into your house?" they demanded. "The truth, now, or we'll lift you up on our spears!"

"Into my house?" said Yudl. "Who should come into my house?"

The Russians looked here, there and everywhere, and before leaving, just to make sure, they plunged their spears a number of times through the featherbeds. Then, not to lose time in vain search, they clattered away.

How lucky Napoleon was! Twice lucky. First, because he was such a little man. Second, because Yudl's featherbeds were high and well-stuffed.

In a little while Napoleon stuck his head out from under the featherbeds. He was still trembling and his face was as white as a sheet. But he recovered quickly. After all, he was Napoleon!

"Are they gone?" he asked.

"Yes," said Yudl. "You can come out now."

Napoleon jumped off the bed, smoothed out his uniform, straightened out his medals, and stood up straight before Yudl the tailor, like an emperor!

"You have saved me from certain death," he declared, "and I am going to reward you. I give you leave to ask me for three things and they will be granted. Now ask—and remember: any three things, no matter how expensive."

What should Yudl ask for? Was there ever a tailor in such a dilemma? He thought and thought and finally said:

"Your Majesty, my roof has been leaking for two years. Please have it mended for me."

Napoleon eyed the tailor with hard contempt.

"Is that all you can think of asking me?" he sneered. "Very well! Your roof shall be repaired. Now ask again. And this time let it be something worth-while, something a monarch will be proud to grant."

The tailor twisted his beard and thought and thought. What in the world should he ask for? What did he need? Then he saw a great light!

"Your Majesty," he said, "my wife and I have been married twenty years and she is still wearing the same wig she got on her wedding day. I suppose," Yudl stopped to explain, "you know that among our people modesty forbids a married woman to wear her own hair, don't you?"

"Of course, I do," said Napoleon loftily. "Some years ago I stopped in the Land of Israel on my way home from Egypt and they told me all about it. Now go on with your request!"

"Well, Your Majesty, she wants a new wig. She nags me to death about it. And between you and me, she is entitled to it. The old one looks like a tuft of old flax."

"So?"

"So won't you please order a new wig for my wife?"

Napoleon laughed a short, bitter laugh.

"I ought to consider myself insulted," he said, "but it's plain to me that you have no understanding of life's real values. Very well, then. Your roof shall be repaired and your wife shall have a new wig. But remember, tailor, I am the great Napoleon and you can ask me one thing more. Now let it be something really grand and memorable, something which my historians will not fail to record."

Yudl the tailor was at the end of his wits. He twisted his beard, he even chewed it, but he could think of nothing. He just didn't need anything! At the same time the awe and dread which Napoleon first inspired in him began to wear off. Now he saw before him a little man who, instead of being majestic, was only pompous, a little man putting on airs. "What a funny little *goy!*" said Yudl to himself.

"Must I really ask for something?" he smiled at Napoleon.

"You must!"

"Well, if I must," said Yudl, "I will ask you to tell me how you felt when the Russians drove their spears through the featherbeds."

Napoleon glared at the tailor, amazed and indignant.

"How dare you ask me such a question?" he stormed. "How dare you become familiar with me, the conqueror of Europe? Have you never heard of *lèse majesté?* I will order you to be shot!"

He called in a troop of his soldiers who happened to be passing by, and Yudl the tailor was cast into irons and taken away.

"Where are you taking me?" he begged.

"Never mind where," they told him. "Early tomorrow morning you will be shot. Those are the Emperor's orders."

All night long the tailor wept and prayed and beat his breast. "What will become of my wife, my little ones?" he moaned.

A little before dawn he was taken out and tied to a tree. Three soldiers with loaded guns took their stand in front of him. An officer stood near them with a watch in his hand.

Yudl was already more dead than alive. He shook in every limb and the perspiration flowed down his body in streams. One second he was hot, the next he was cold. Is it necessary to describe in detail how a tailor would feel in such a situation?

"Now then," said the officer to his soldiers, "The moment has arrived. When I say three you will fire!"

The soldiers raised their guns and aimed.

"One!" said the officer.

"Two!" said the officer.

But before he could say "three," the sound of galloping hoofs was heard and an imposing general on horseback with medals on his chest, burst upon the scene.

"Don't shoot!" he cried to the soldiers; and to Yudl he said: "The Emperor pardons you, and he ordered me to give you this letter."

"I pledged my imperial word to grant your requests," Napoleon wrote. "I have repaired your roof and I have bought your wife a new wig. And now you know how I felt when the

Russians drove their spears through the featherbeds. I have fulfilled my pledge."

Two Frogs

The way was long and the road hot and dusty. With heavy heart a poor *melamed* urged on his goat. He was taking him to the nearest town in order to sell him.

Before setting out the *melamed* discovered that he was fond of the silly creature. But what alternative had he? Could he let his wife and children starve for bread and refuse to sell the goat? So man and beast plodded wearily along, the man giving vent to his sorrows in frequent groans.

A beggar appeared from nowhere and began following the man and the goat. The beggar looked even more woebegone than the *melamed,* and his groans were louder.

"What insolence!" said the *melamed.* And turning to the beggar he demanded:

"What right have you to groan so loud? Are your troubles greater than mine?"

"You have a goat," said the beggar, "and I have nothing!"

"Yes, I have a goat!" said the *melamed* bitterly. "I'm a happy man! Yes, I'm a happy man!"

Just then a small frog appeared from the roadside and jumped on in front of the wayfarers.

"Look here!" the *melamed* turned suddenly on the beggar. "I'll give you the goat! Just catch that frog and swallow it, and I'll give you my goat!"

The beggar ran forward, caught the frog and swallowed it.

"Give me the goat," said he.

"Take it!" said the *melamed*.

Now the beggar was urging the beast along the road, the *melamed* following a short distance behind.

"What have I done?" said the *melamed* to himself, and his heart sank. "What will my wife say? What will I bring home for my children to eat?" And groan after groan broke from his bosom as he plodded on after the beggar and the goat.

But very soon a series of nasty sensations started up in the beggar's inwards. The sweat broke on his forehead and his knees sagged. He turned fiercely on the *melamed*.

"What right have you to groan like that?" he demanded. "Do you consider your lot worse than mine?"

"You have the goat," said the *melamed*, "and I have nothing!"

"Indeed!" cried the beggar. "So you think I am a happy man! Oh, my belly, my belly!"

And just then another frog appeared from the side of the road and jumped on in front of the wayfarers.

"Look!" the beggar cried. "Do you see that frog? Catch it and swallow it, and you can have your goat again!"

The *melamed* at once caught the frog and swallowed it.

"Now give me the goat!" he cried.

"Take it," said the beggar.

The *melamed* had his goat again and urged it on along the hot and dusty road. Behind him walked the beggar, still groaning: "My belly, my belly!"

But now came the turn of the *melamed*'s inwards, where the frog produced a fierce commotion. Neither now resented the other's groans: now they understood each other.

At last they came to the town and halted. The two looked at each other, pained and bewildered.

"Friend!" said the *melamed* to the beggar. "Tell me, I pray you, why did you and I have to swallow frogs?"

"Why, indeed?" the beggar replied.

And the two walked on together and groaned.

The Monumental Wisdom of Chelm

Foreword

Chelm is not a figment, but a real town in Poland, some forty miles east of Lublin. In the first decade of this century the town was reported to have a population of about four thousand of whom more than 90 percent were Jews, its social structure typical of the small town or *shtetl*. In later decades the Jews seem to have become a minority, but until the German murder-machine destroyed them, still a sizable minority.

Why, in Jewish folklore, Chelmite became synonymous with dolt and simpleton seems to be a total mystery, but the popularity which the precious absurdities of the Chelmites achieved does not seem too difficult to explain. Chelm, we are secretly aware, is not confined to Chelm. There are Chelmites swarming all around us; there is even a little Chelmite tucked away inside each of us. For with all our confident sophistication, don't we often discover ourselves to be naive and gullible?

So in the amusement we derive from the Chelmites there is no mockery or condescension. Our laughter is not sardonic or superior. The Chelmites, we feel, are not ordinary simpletons; their simplicity is symbolic. Their helplessness is not too far removed from our own in this befuddled and befuddling world we all live in. They are caricatures, of course, but what makes a caricature effective is not so much its exaggerations and distortions, as its basic truth. The Chelmites, therefore, are not just absurd; they are also pathetic, and our laughter is laced with affection.

The Chelmites, of course, have their counterparts in other nations: in the "wise men" of Gotham and other places in England; in the fools of Schildburg in Germany; of Kampen in Holland. But the wonderful wisdom of Chelm has, of course, a rich and distinctive flavor of its own.

In his version of these tales, the author has taken liberties which, he is persuaded, have not done violence to the spirit of the Chelm saga. He has also included a number of tales not generally associated with Chelm, but which appeared to him to be fully qualified for that distinction.

Infant Prodigy

THE BIRTH OF CHELM

History loves to linger over the beginnings of memorable places, and the city of Chelm, whose people became renowned through all the earth for their incredible wisdom, is no exception. The traditions of Chelm relate that before the work of building began, the founders met in solemn assembly and deliberated a long time on the best site for their city. They decided finally to build it at the foot of a mountain.

The great day arrived and the builders began by climbing to the summit where they cut down trees for their houses. But how were the logs to be brought down, seeing the Chelmites had no vehicles or horses? Their amazing ingenuity came immediately to their aid. They lifted the logs to their shoulders and carried them down into the valley.

Now it happened that a stranger passed by and saw the Chelmites toiling and panting.

"Foolish people," said the stranger, "why do you needlessly puff and sweat?" And having spoken, he pushed one of the logs with his foot and it rolled down the mountain as if it knew exactly where to go.

The builders of Chelm stood and marveled.

"The man is a genius," they whispered to each other.

But Chelmites are quick to learn. Without losing a moment, they went down into the valley, carried the logs back to the summit, and sent them rolling in the precise manner of the stranger.

A CHELM SOLUTION

The builders of Chelm were digging for the foundation of the synagogue when one of them suddenly dropped his spade and stood still in profound meditation.

"This earth," he muttered to his neighbor who happened to be one of the seven worthies of the town, a man, in other words, of exceptional wisdom.

"Yes, this earth," the worthy repeated and joined his neighbor in contemplation.

"This earth that we are digging up—where are we going to put it?"

The worthy clasped his beard and thought and thought a very long time.

"I have it!" he declared at last. "We'll dig a pit and shovel into it all the earth we are digging up for the foundation of the synagogue!"

His neighbor nodded very slowly.

"But what," he asked, "are we going to do with the earth that we'll dig up from the pit?"

"Nothing is more simple," replied the worthy of Chelm. "We'll dig a second pit, bigger than the first, and shovel its own earth into it as well as the earth of the first pit!"

And the two men of Chelm nodded gravely to each other and resumed their digging.

RIGHT AND LEFT IN CHELM

The synagogue was duly built, but before long it was observed that the ceiling began to sag.

"We must set up a pillar to support the ceiling," said the wise men of Chelm.

They trimmed a log on top of the mountain for a pillar, but as soon as they brought it to the door of the synagogue a serious question arose and two parties sprang into existence.

"The pillar should be taken in right end first," said one.

"The pillar should be taken in left end first," said the other.

As neither side would yield, the work was brought to a stop and the ceiling was in danger of falling.

Finally one of the seven worthies of the town proposed a compromise which was adopted: to divide the log into two parts and give one to the rightists and the other to the leftists. When this, however, was done, the men of Chelm discovered that each of the parts also had two ends, a right and left. The controversy between the parties broke out afresh.

"Let each of the parts be divided again!" said the same wise worthy. But when this was done, it was found that each of the ensuing parts had a right and a left, and the controversy became even more acrid.

That day the seven worthies met with the rabbi, and the scribe was ordered to indite the following entry into the Chronicles of Chelm for the remembrance of all generations to come:

"Let all men know by these presents that our eyes have beheld a great truth. A pillar to support the ceiling of a synagogue has always two ends, a right and a left, whether the pillar be entire, or whether it be divided into halves and quarters: and as to whether it should be introduced right end first or left end first, that question we have not been able to resolve: it must stand unanswered until the advent of Elijah the Prophet, may he come speedily and in our days."

A CHELM COMPROMISE

Now, the public bathhouse also presented a grave problem. It had to do with the benches that rose up in tiers to the ceiling, on which the bathers stretched out and reveled in the steam and heat. The question was whether the planks for those benches should be smooth or rough.

Immediately two parties came into existence: smoothists and roughists. The smoothists maintained that rough planks would scratch the bodies of the bathers, not to speak of the splinters they would carry home. The roughists argued that smooth planks would make the bathers slip and fall and that some of them might be hurt, *cholile!*

The wise men of Chelm called a meeting that lasted far into the night. But each party held its ground and the assembly was deadlocked. At last the rabbi proposed a compromise which was universally acclaimed and proved over again that Torah and wisdom go together. His compromise was that the planks should be smooth on one side and rough on the other!

THEY COULDN'T BRIDGE IT

So the Chelmites overcame their differences when they built the *shul* and bathhouse, but in the case of another project no compromise, alas, could he reached. A proposal to build a bridge across the river that divided the town foundered on the rock of partisan strife.

This time there arose not two but three parties. The first maintained that the purpose of the bridge should be to enable those living on opposite sides of the river to observe the cherished custom of visiting each other on Sabbath afternoons to exchange Sabbath greetings. The second party said No. The purpose of the bridge should be to make it easier for the bearers of Purim gifts to bring them from one side of Chelm to the other. The third party insisted that both were wrong. The bridge, they declared, should have no other function than to enable the men of Chelm to catch fish for Sabbaths and holidays. The views of the parties proved irreconcilable and the bridge was never built.

To make the record complete, it should be added that a number of Chelmites, so few they could scarcely be called a party, suggested that the purpose of the bridge should be to facilitate the exchange of goods and promote trade. But all the others decried the notion, calling it sordid and frivolous.

MOVING A MOUNTAIN

The people of Chelm faithfully observed the commandments and in particular the one that ordered all living things including the human species to "be fruitful and multiply." Before long, therefore, the city was overcrowded and it became imperative to extend its area. But a serious obstacle stood in the way of expansion: namely, the mountain at the foot of which the city was built.

The wise men of Chelm met and after much and deep deliberation it was decided to move the mountain. Let skeptics hold their peace: if faith can do it, why not wisdom?

The day for moving the mountain arrived, the men of Chelm flocked to the appointed place, and began by taking off their *kaftns* and piling them together in a heap behind them. Then they rolled up their sleeves and pushed.

Now it happened that a stranger of easy conscience passed by, and seeing the Chelmites engrossed in their labor, he gathered up the *kaftns* and made off with them.

The Chelmites continued to push until they were out of breath and covered with perspiration. They stopped to rest and looking behind them, they observed that their *kaftns* had vanished.

"What does it mean?" they asked each other. "What has become of our *kaftns?*"

Whereupon one of the worthies of the town saw a great light. "Chelmites!" he cried, "don't you see what has happened? We have moved the mountain so far away, that our *kaftns* are no longer in sight!"

THE RABBI'S WISDOM

As Chelm continued to grow, the people became aware that the place of eternal rest would be insufficient for the population.

"What shall we do?" they asked each other. The cemetery must of course be enlarged, but by how much?

Finally the old rabbi provided the answer. He appointed a day and, at his command, all the inhabitants of Chelm streamed to the cemetery. When they were all there the rabbi stood up and cried.

"Lie down on the ground, every one of you side by side!"

The people obeyed, men, women and children.

"Now measure all around!" said the rabbi to the *shames*.

"What wisdom!" the Chelmites cried, "What wisdom!"

THE STOLEN MOON

It became known to the people of Chelm that in other cities the streets were lighted at night, and the Chelmites felt that their city must not be behind the times. So a meeting was called, and one of the oldest and wisest of the Chelmites stood up and spoke as follows:

"Let me give you good counsel, my masters. There are nights when the moon shines and Chelm has enough light. There are other nights when there is no moon and Chelm is dark. Why can't the moon shine for us every night? Tomorrow night the moon will be at full. Let us go out and capture the moon and keep her for nights that are dark."

The Chelmites approved: wisdom, they declared, lives in old age. Nor had they any difficulty capturing the moon. They filled a barrel with water, exposed it to the moon, and when that luminary heedlessly entered it, they covered the barrel with sackcloth held ready for the purpose, and bound it with ropes. In addition, they put the official seal of Chelm on the barrel and brought it into the synagogue.

Some weeks later the nights began to be dark. The people gathered to take the moon out of the barrel and hang it in the sky. But when they opened the barrel, alas, the moon was gone! They looked at each other ruefully and the wise old man said:

"Somebody has stolen our moon! We should have set watchmen to stand guard over her!"

USES OF A FIRE EXTINGUISHER

It also became known in Chelm that in the big cities it was the practice to put out fires with instruments made for the purpose and called extinguishers. So Chelm, not to be outdone, bought an extinguisher and placed it in the custody of the *shames*.

The good man soon discovered that the extinguisher might serve as an excellent receptacle for things worth preserving, such as clay for sealing up the mouth of the synagogue stove for the summer, horseradish for Passover, garlic for medicinal purposes and many other good things.

Now it happened shortly afterwards that fire broke out in Chelm. At once the extinguisher was brought into play, but the instrument rebelled and refused to open its mouth. The instrument was inspected and found to contain clay, horseradish, garlic, and other things.

The Chelmites were indignant and held a general meeting. A few of the young and reckless came forward and demanded that the *shames* be deprived of the custody of the extinguisher.

But the older and wiser men demurred.

"No," they said, "the custody of the extinguisher is one of his prerogatives."

Thereupon the others declared:

"Then let the *shames* swear a solemn oath that henceforth he will not keep in the extinguisher either clay for sealing up the synagogue stove, or horseradish for Passover, or garlic for medicinal purposes, or anything else."

But the older and wiser men demurred again.

"If so, where will the *shames* put away good things that need to be preserved?"

All day the two parties debated until, at last, they agreed on a compromise as follows:

"The claim of the *shames* to the custody of the extinguisher is admitted. His right to keep in it all sorts of good things that need to be preserved is also recognized. But he must swear a solemn oath that from now on he will clear everything out of the extinguisher as soon as a fire breaks out in Chelm."

A LADDER TO VIRTUE

It happened once that an abominable thing was done in Chelm: the charity box that stood near the door of the synagogue was stolen! The city was shocked and a meeting was hurriedly called to consider what action should be taken. After prolonged debate it was decided to set up a new charity box and to hang it from the ceiling so that no thief could reach it. Chelm rejoiced: the outrage would never occur again.

But several days later the *shames* stood before the rabbi.

"The box," said he, "is now beyond the reach of thieves, but it is also beyond the reach of those who might throw in their contributions."

So another meeting was called and a solution to the problem was easily found. A ladder that reached from the floor to the ceiling was set up by which the charitable were able to reach the box. And to make sure that they would not, *cholile,* be hurt, the ladder was so attached to the floor and ceiling that it could not be moved.

A FELINE IN CHELM

A large animal was once seen prowling through the streets of Chelm and the people were terrified. Two of the worthies risked their lives for the common good and captured the beast. They made careful inquiry and were informed that the animal was a feline and that its name was "cat."

The same day a solemn meeting was held and it was unanimously decided that the *shames* should take the beast to the roof of the synagogue and jump down with it to the ground. The *shames,* of course, would also be killed, but what help was there for it?

The *shames,* noble man, accepted the verdict, took the animal to the roof and jumped. He died a hero's death, but the cat was seen to run away from under him, alive and well.

Another meeting was called and it was unanimously decided to lock the animal in the synagogue and set fire to the building. The sentence was duly carried out. The synagogue was burnt to the ground, but soon afterwards the beast was seen prowling through the city, alive and well.

The town worthies bowed their heads and recorded the strange event in the Chronicles of Chelm for a memorial to the generations, concluding the entry with the following words:

"To this matter must be applied the verse in Scripture: 'There is no wisdom or understanding or counsel against the will of God.' "

A FISH IN CHELM

It is well known that not only felines but other creatures of a lower order fail to show proper respect for their betters. This is well illustrated by what befell Reb Zadok, one of the seven worthies of Chelm.

On a Friday morning, immediately after prayers, Reb Zadok went to market and bought a live and handsome fish in honor of the Sabbath. Now, having to carry his cane in one hand and the bag with his prayer-shawl and *tfilin* in the other, he slipped the fish head down into the inside pocket of his *kaftn* and went his way. But the fish was a big one and the tail projected out of his pocket.

Suddenly the fish waved his tail and slapped Reb Zadok full on the face. The fact got around and the city was in an uproar. Such impudence on the part of a fish had never been known before!

At once the worthies of Chelm came together and passed sentence of death upon the culprit. The sentence was carried out immediately. The fish was taken to the river and drowned.

PENOLOGY IN CHELM

The same assembly deliberated on a question of more general import: what to do with a thief that might be caught red-handed.

The question was referred to the rabbi and the seven worthies of the town who, after deep study, brought in a proposal which was enthusiastically adopted. Two holes, the plan provided, were to be bored in the wall of the bathhouse. The culprit was to be brought inside and made to pass his hands through the holes and keep them in that position for as long as the judge should decide. The meaning would be perfectly clear to all the good people of Chelm. It was as though the guilty man himself were to proclaim to all the inhabitants: "Behold! These hands have done the deed!"

In order, however, to make sure that the criminal would not frustrate the plan, it was further provided that rolling pins should be placed in his hands with strict orders to hold them tight.

SNOW IN CHELM

One Friday afternoon the first snowfall came down on Chelm and the people rejoiced to see the clean white blanket covering the rutted streets and dingy houses of their city. But then they thought sadly:

"The *shames* will soon be passing through the town and call on the people to close their shops and prepare for the Sabbath. What will happen to the snow when he walks over it?"

Immediately the rabbi and the seven worthies came together to see what could be done. The snow, they decided, must at all costs be kept clean. But how will the merchants know when to close their shops for the Sabbath? They might, God forbid, violate the sanctity of the holy day! Finally the rabbi issued an edict as follows:

"The *shames* is to proclaim the Sabbath as usual. But he is not to go on foot. He is to stand up on a table and be carried through the town by four of the worthies."

Wisdom Unlimited

ARITHMETIC IN CHELM

The superior mentality for which the Chelmites were famous was not, it should be noted, confined to the men. The women, too, were distinguished for it, as the following tale illustrates.

A stranger once came to Chelm and put up at the tavern. After eating a hearty meal, he asked the mistress of the inn for his account.

"The bread, the soup and the dessert come to seven kopeks," said she. "For the roast, another seven kopeks. Altogether eleven kopeks."

"Pardon me," said her guest, "two times seven are fourteen."

For a moment the woman was puzzled, but only for a moment.

"No," said she. "Two times seven are eleven. I was a widow with four children. I married a widower who also had four children, and three more children were born to us. Now each of us has seven children and altogether we have eleven. Two times seven are eleven."

The stranger paid his account, filled with admiration for the acumen of a mere woman.

SHE FOUND HER RIVAL

It was long before the good people of Chelm became familiar with the nature and uses of mirrors, and in the early days of innocence a Chelmite who was visiting the big city stepped into an emporium and picked up a bright object in which he recognized the face of his father, peace to his soul. The object was rather expensive, but out of filial piety, he bought it and took it home. But he was afraid of his wife's censure, so he hid it in the attic, and every now and then he went up there and gazed upon his father's countenance.

But his wife became suspicious. The fact is she had been having thoughts about him for a long time. In short, she suspected him of having a secret attachment for another woman, heaven shield us! Could his frequent visits to the attic have something to do with it? Did he have some memento of her up there, a picture perhaps?

She climbed up the ladder one day and made a thorough search. She found the bright object and looked into it.

"Ah," she moaned. "There she is, the wicked woman! And what an ugly old witch he picked himself!"

FULL DIRECTIONS

A stranger once came to Chelm and went looking for a man he had come to see. In the course of the quest, the stranger came upon an instance of that passion for exactness which characterized the Chelm mind and of which he had already heard.

"Grandfather," said he, approaching an old man, "can you tell me where Naphtali ben Zemach lives?"

The old man stroked his beard proudly.

"I am a Chelmite," said he, "and my ancestors were Chelmites for ten generations. Is there anyone in Chelm I don't know? I know them all, thank God, I know where they live, and I know how they live. You are looking for Naphtali ben Zemach? Do you see that house at the end of the street, the one with two stories? Naphtali ben Zemach does not live there and, as far as I know, he never lived there, neither he nor any of his ancestors. But behind that house there is another one, also of two stories. Go there and climb to the upper story. On that story you will not find the man you are seeking. He never lived there in his life. Go down to the lower story. There you may find him. Naphtali ben Zemach may be living there, but he may never have lived there in his life."

The stranger followed the directions faithfully, but as to whether he found Naphtali ben Zemach the record is silent.

BIG LOAVES AND LITTLE ONES

Later in the day the same stranger discovered the degree to which the reasoning faculty was developed among the people of Chelm.

Having bought a loaf of bread in a bakery, he observed that the loaf was bigger than those that were sold in his own city.

"Why are the loaves in your city bigger than in mine?" he asked the baker.

The baker pondered the question a long time, and at length he found the answer.

"The reason," said he, "must be that in your city the bakers take a smaller piece of dough for each loaf than we do in Chelm."

Filled with admiration, the stranger paid for the loaf and departed.

A *PROBLEM IN CONSTRUCTION*

The same keen logic stood at the service of a Chelmite who travelled to the capital to buy goods for his shop.

In a restaurant where he happened to be sitting he noticed a big table covered with green cloth. Two individuals armed with long sticks kept striking at some round colored objects that rolled like eggs all over the table.

The strange sight provoked in the mind of the Chelmite a number of puzzling questions.

"Why," he asked himself first, "are they smiting the eggs?"

But that question he promptly dismissed.

"If," he argued, "they find pleasure in it, they will no doubt pay for the damage they inflict."

The second question was not so simple.

"How," he asked himself, "did they bring the table into the building? It is plain that it could never have gotten through the door."

A long time the Chelmite sat stroking his beard, lost in thought. At length he saw light.

"How do I know," said he, "that they built the house first and brought in the table afterwards? Couldn't they have first brought in the table, then built the house around it?"

A CHELMITE RECOGNIZED

The same day this Chelmite set out to buy goods for his shop. His name, it should be noted, was Baruch. The day was hot, but he ran from one warehouse to another, panting and perspiring, his cap tilted back on his head, his *kaftn* streaming out behind him. People looked at him in amazement and at length someone stopped him.

"Reb Yankel," said the stranger, "why do you hurry in this heat? Aren't you an idiot?"

"I see," replied the Chelmite, "that you know me. But why did you have to change my name from Baruch to Yankel?"

HE CONSOLES A STRANGER

As Baruch stood on the platform of the station, a train pulled out and the next minute a man came running and stopped, his face full of despair.

"My God!" the man groaned. "My train is gone! What will I do? Everything is lost!"

Reb Baruch was touched and approached the stranger.

"By how much did you miss your train?" he asked him.

"A minute or two," the unhappy man replied.

"Is that all?" said the Chelmite. "Then why do you carry on like that? One would think you had missed it by an hour!"

THE POOR ARE HONEST

Reb Baruch was glad to be back in Chelm. He had little use for the big city and its ways. His journey made him more certain than ever that the simple and poor were in every way better than the rich. That, of course, was the opinion of all Chelmites, but they asked him if anything had happened in the big city to confirm it.

"Indeed," replied Reb Baruch, "and when I tell you, you will see the difference between the rich and the poor. All day in the big city I ran from one large establishment to another buying goods for my shop. At night I returned to my inn, and behold! I am without my cane! What could I have done with it? I must have forgotten it in one of the big places. Early the following morning I set out to look for my cane. I entered the first place: they denied it. I came to the second: they denied it. I revisited every one of those rich places and every one denied it. At night, tired and broken, I stepped into a small but poor restaurant where I had eaten the night before. Without a word, they produced the stick and returned it to me! There you have the difference between the rich and the poor!"

A LIAR IN CHELM

The town liar of Chelm was looking through his window one day, and the urge to lie came strong upon him.

"Listen!" he called down. "There is a cow flying over the roofs behind the bathhouse!"

The people heard him and ran. Those who ran told the others and soon the whole town was on its way to see the cow.

The Chelm liar got up, closed his window, and joined the rest. "Suppose," said he to himself, "there really is a cow flying over the roofs behind the bathhouse!"

NO SALE

One day a *litvak* made his appearance in Chelm, a shrewd and crafty fellow like all his breed, and there was considerable talk in town about his glibness and guile. Now it happened that a she-goat belonging to a Chelmite stopped giving milk and her poor owner didn't know what to do with her. So his wife came forward with a bright idea.

"Take her to market," she told her husband, "and sell her. But get the *litvak* to go with you. Let him do the talking. Leave it all to him."

The Chelmite and the *litvak* took the goat to the market-place. A would-be purchaser came up and looked the creature over.

"How about milk?" he inquired. "Does she give much milk?"

"This goat?" said the *litvak*, beaming with pride. "This goat is no goat, she's a wet nurse! She gives and gives! A full pail every day!"

The Chelmite, hearing what the *litvak* said, was overjoyed. "Wait, wait!" he cried. "I've changed my mind! I'll keep this goat. I'll keep her!"

IT DIDN'T BALANCE

There was a strict husband in Chelm who insisted on a full accounting of his wife's expenditures.

"You had five kopeks when you went to market this morning," he said to her, "and now you are back with an empty purse. What did you do with the money?"

"Well," the woman replied, "a kopek for this, and a kopek for that."

"That's two!" the man held up two fingers.

"A kopek here."

"Three!"

"A kopek there."

"Four!"

"Four, four," the woman puzzled. "What did I do with the fifth kopek? The fifth kopek . . ."

"Just as I thought!" said the husband sadly but sternly. "Send a woman to market! She wastes your substance and doesn't even know on what!"

A GENTLE SCHOLAR

Or take the case of Reb Pinchas the scholar and his wife. Reb Pinchas spent all his waking hours over the Talmud while the lower needs of the household were provided by the woman. Every morning she set out for the market place with a big basket of rolls which she baked the night before, and every evening she returned home to prepare food for her scholar. And always, as part of the meal, she saved two of her rolls and placed them beside his plate. Reb Pinchas had a great fondness for his wife's baking.

Now it happened once that the two perpetual rolls were missing!

"Where are the rolls?" asked Reb Pinchas gently.

The good woman answered with tears in her voice. Some drunken soldiers, she told him, passed through the market place, and made free with her rolls. They emptied the basket and disappeared.

Reb Pinchas was moved by his wife's distress.

"Don't take it so to heart," he told her. "Heaven will repay you."

He sat down to eat. The empty place where the two rolls always lay stared him in the face. A sudden change came over his mood. Reb Pinchas flushed with anger.

"Look now," he cried. "Since they were all taking rolls, why couldn't you have taken two for me?"

TRAGEDY IN CHELM

It is further on record that the wife of Reb Pinchas once came to the verge of rebellion, demanding that her husband make himself useful in the house at least. That was the time when a new infant lay in the cradle and the poor woman needed help.

So one morning before proceeding to the market place, she gave him definite instructions.

"You are to rock the cradle every time the little one wakes up, and watch the milk boiling on the stove that it doesn't run over. I'll be back soon to nurse him."

Then remembering her scholar's weakness for delicacies, she warned him as follows:

"There is something in a jar in the cupboard. Don't touch it. It's poison!"

For a while Reb Pinchas pondered on the best manner of executing his wife's commission; and being a man of learning and a Chelmite, he contrived a clever invention. He tied one end of a rope to the cradle and the other end to his ankle. And taking his stand near the stove, he was able to rock the cradle and watch the milk at the same time.

The door opened and in walked a stray dog. There was a hen in the room tranquilly pecking at the floor. The hen shrieked, flew over the stove and overturned the pot of milk. Reb Pinchas snatched at the pot in an effort to save it and gave the cradle a violent tug. The cradle overturned and the infant was thrown out.

Reb Pinchas took in the situation and became desperate. Everything, he realized, had gone wrong. Everything was lost! Dragging the cradle, he made his way to the cupboard, found the jar and ate its contents. Then, still dragging the cradle, he got to the bed, stretched out and waited.

When his wife returned she also took in the situation and burst into tears. She wept and bemoaned her fate, and said harsh things to her husband.

"*Gazlon*," said she finally, "why are you stretched out on the bed?"

"I have eaten the poison in the jar," said Reb Pinchas, "and I am waiting for death."

CAPITAL IS CONCENTRATING

There was a Chelm philosopher who visited a big city where people came together in meetings and heard fiery orators hold forth on matters of surpassing importance to mankind. At one such meeting he heard an orator exclaim: "Capital is passing into fewer and fewer hands! Capital is concentrating!"

The news that capital is concentrating made a profound impression on the philosopher, and when he returned he told all of Chelm about it. People listened and shook their heads, but no one was more disturbed than the tailor.

"Dvoshe!" he cried to his wife when he got home. "Did you hear the news, Dvoshe? Capital is concentrating!"

Dvoshe was dumbfounded. "Really!" was all she could find to say.

But the tailor, who was known as a man of action, lost no time about it. He made a bundle of his shears and pressing-iron, added needles and thread as well as his measuring tape, slung it over his shoulders and took to the road. He hurried on straight ahead, not knowing whither, not even asking himself such an absurd question.

A *STUBBORN CHELMITE*

Thus spoke the Chelm *akshn*:

Let them say I am stubborn; who cares? Let them call me *akshn*! They say it to condemn me but, believe me, I consider it a compliment. How else can a man have his way? And I—you may not believe it—I'm a man who likes to have his way. True enough, I am a Chelmite, but does every Chelmite have to be a namby-pamby, a worm?

Let me tell you something that happened not so long ago and judge for yourself if it pays to be an *akshn* or not. One morning I get up and the left side of my face is so swelled up it's terrible to look at. And a toothache—it should happen to a mad dog! But I am an *akshn,* no? So I stand it as long as I can, and since we have no dentist in Chelm—what a town, our Chelm! —I tie up my face and run to Yokl the wagoner and he takes me to Babinka where they have a dentist.

A proper young man, this dentist: white jacket, pink cheeks, pomaded hair, little mustache, thin and waxed. The moment I see him, I don't like him. I am that kind of man. I make up my mind at once and stick to it.

"Come in and sit down," he says to me. "You must have a toothache. It's the left side."

How do you like the young wizard? He made a discovery! My left side is like a melon, so he tells me it's the left side.

"I see," I say to him, "that you are a real expert. Right away you knew it's the left side."

So he looks at me down his nose and says to me: "Which tooth is it?"

Now I was really angry. I am not a man who likes to be trifled with.

"You are the expert, no? And you want me to tell you which tooth it is?" I say to him. "I see your diploma hanging on the wall, so find out for yourself which tooth it is."

"Whichever it is, I'll have to pull it," he says.

"So pull!" I say to him.

"But I'm liable to pull the wrong one," he tells me.

"That's your lookout," I tell him.

"But can't you at least tell me if it's an upper tooth or a lower one?" he argues with me.

"I'm still looking at your diploma," I answer him.

"Well," he says, "I think it's a lower tooth, and it's probably the last one."

Well, I felt like laughing right out: it was not a lower tooth at all! But I restrained myself. So he pulls the tooth he selected and holds it up for me to look at.

"Is this the one?" he says.

"What is your opinion?" I ask him.

He holds it up to the light and says: "No, I don't think it is."

"You surely know your trade," I say and I smile at him.

"It must be the next one," he says.

"Find out!" I told him.

So he pulled the next one, and the next and all the lower teeth right down to the front of my mouth.

"It must be an upper one, and this time I'll begin at the other end," he says.

"My, my!" I say. "There's nothing like having a diploma."

So he begins with the upper teeth on the left side of my mouth and pulls one after another, until he comes to the last one next to my cheek. And all the time I knew, of course, it was that one!

"Wait!" I say to him, "Don't pull that one. That one belongs to me."

"But that's the one!" he says.

"Your knowledge," I say to him, "is as deep as the ocean."

"But it's going to hurt!" he says.

"It will hurt and it will stop hurting," I say to him. "But that tooth I need."

"What for?" he says.

"For a monument," I say. "A monument to a great victory."

But maybe you don't believe what I have just told you? Maybe you think I'm one of those liars that this Chelm of ours is teeming with? Give me your finger and I'll let you feel that tooth. Don't be afraid, I won't bite it off. I couldn't if I wanted to. Don't forget I have no bottom teeth at all.

THE LOST NOTEBOOK

Chelm had a *magid* who once suffered a serious loss. The *magid* went out to preach in a nearby town. On the road he was overtaken by a peasant's wagon piled high with fodder.

"May I ride with you?" said he to the driver.

The peasant agreed, and the *magid* climbed up and made himself comfortable in the fodder. He fell asleep and slept until he came to his destination.

The *magid* stopped in the inn, and began to prepare his sermon. He looked for the little notebook in which he kept his themes and parables, but alas, the notebook was gone! Again and again he rummaged through his clothes but the precious memorandum failed to turn up.

"I lost it in the fodder!" said the *magid* to himself. "Now some horse, or ass, or cow will eat it and get to know all my sermons!"

And the *magid* of Chelm hastened to the synagogue, ascended the *bime* and smote the table for silence.

"My masters!" he proclaimed. "I solemnly declare that if some horse, or ass, or cow should come to this town to preach, the sermons will be mine and not theirs!"

A CHELMITE AT SEA

Let no one suppose that Chelm was a town of timorous stay-at-homes. Far from it. It even happened that a Chelmite once took a sea voyage!

The ship in which he sailed ran smack into a raging storm. The waves tossed it about like a little cork. Its timbers groaned and creaked and the passengers feared it would break up any moment. They chanted psalms, they wept and wailed, they cried aloud for deliverance. All of them except the Chelmite, who maintained a dignified silence.

"Don't you care what happens to the ship?" they asked him.

"Why should I?" he answered. "Is it *my* ship?"

MERCHANTS IN CHELM

This tale is one of many that might be cited as evidence of the business acumen for which the Chelmites were famous.

The story is about two of them who agreed to go into partnership and, between them, managed to find enough capital to buy a little keg of whiskey as their stock in trade.

"Berl," said Sholem to his partner, "I have seen many a business like ours ruined by credit. Let us sell for cash only."

"For cash only," Berl agreed.

They opened their business to the public and waited for customers. But no customers came and after a while Berl felt just a little bit discouraged.

"Sholem," said he to his partner, "I have five kopeks in my pocket. Pour me a little glass of whiskey. It's for cash, of course."

Sholem poured and Berl paid and drank. He felt and looked much better.

"Berl," said Sholem to his partner, "I see in your eyes that we have the right stuff. Now that I have five kopeks, I think I'll have a little also. It's for cash, of course."

Berl poured, Sholem paid and drank and he too felt and looked much better.

"Sholem," said Berl to his partner after a rather long pause. "We'll not be so foolish as to sell on credit. Pour me another little glass—for cash, of course."

Berl drank and passed the five kopeks to Sholem. Then Sholem drank again and passed the five kopeks to Berl.

Still there were no customers, but were the partners discouraged? On the contrary! They were in a state of satisfaction bordering on joy!

"Another little glass for me!" said one and paid spot cash.

"Another little glass for me!" said the other and paid spot cash.

The day passed and the contents of the little keg as well. It was time to close up for the day.

"Look, Sholem!" said Berl to his partner, hugging the keg on one side, "In one day we—we sold out our stock—all of it!"

"Yes!" said Sholem, hugging the keg on the other side, "and for—for cash only!"

The Chelm Rabbi

EAST AND WEST

Concerning the rabbi of Chelm many tales have come down, all tending to show how perfectly he and his people were suited to each other. He was a saint—gentle, kind, and, of course, wise—a genuine Chelmite. At the same time he frowned on over-clever people as the following story proves.

The rabbi was once summoned to perform the marriage ritual, and when he reached the courtyard of the synagogue where the ceremony was to take place, he found the couple under the canopy facing west. The rabbi objected:

"It is a custom in Israel for the bride and groom to stand under the canopy facing east," said he.

The *shames* came forward and turned the canopy around. But the couple still faced west. The younger men of Chelm took counsel together and changed the position of the poles. But that too proved useless: the couple still faced west.

But a stranger chanced to be present in the synagogue courtyard, and some believe that he was a *litvak*. He approached the couple, turned them around without ceremony and at once they faced east. The rabbi of Chelm was amazed.

"Where did you learn that?" he asked.

"That is how we do it in my city," replied the stranger.

The rabbi shook his head.

"Yes," he said, "apparently there are no people like those in your city for being smart and unmannerly."

NOT A SURE SIGN

One day the news spread through Chelm that the body of a slain man had been discovered within the precincts of the city. Chelm was in a state of panic, but when the rabbi issued a call for all the people to gather in order to identify the victim, they all came.

As all of them, men, women and children, stood gazing upon the corpse, a woman suddenly clapped her hands and shrieked: "Woe is me! It's my husband!"

Said the rabbi to her:

"Daughter, have you a sure sign for identification?"

The woman sobbed and said:

"Yes, rabbi, I have a true sign: my husband was a stammerer."

"It's a sure sign, a sure sign!" the Chelmites agreed.

But the old rabbi shook his head in dissent.

"You are mistaken, my daughter," said he to the poor woman, "that is not a sure sign. There are many stammerers in the world."

WHY NOT?

In other matters, too, the rabbi's knowledge was vast, while with respect to domestic animals his ideas were distinctly original. Consider, for example, the following incident:

A wagoner and a horse dealer once came to the rabbi with a serious dispute. Said the wagoner:

"This man is a swindler. I bought a horse from him and paid for it, and when I took the animal home, it bit the manger and broke its teeth. That's the kind of horse he sold me."

And the horse dealer said:

"As long as I had that horse he never bit the manger."

Finally the rabbi said:

"This is a hard case and requires a great deal of study. Come back tomorrow."

And when they returned, the rabbi said to the wagoner:

"All night I studied your case and I find the law is not on your side. What compels you to place the manger at the horse's head? Why not at his tail?"

STRANGE WAYS OF A CALF

Or take the remarkable feat of the old rabbi with his calf. When the calf was born the pious man gazed with wonder upon the creature.

"How marvelous are the ways of Heaven!" said he. "A human being is born with only two legs, but is unable to use them until a long time afterwards. This creature is born with four legs and is at once able to use them for standing and walking."

And some days later the rabbi found the calf lying in his yard asleep. He walked around it with great curiosity, and was finally taken with a desire to test the animal's strength. He seized the calf's tail and pulled it. The calf woke up frightened, and rushed out of the yard into the street, the rabbi clinging to its tail with both hands and all his strength, but unable to check it.

Realizing his desperate situation the rabbi cried aloud:

"Good people, quick, cut off the creature's tail, or it will kill me!"

AN IMPARTIAL JUDGE

What is most important in the character of a judge? All will admit that impartiality is most important. The impartiality of the rabbi of Chelm was famous for miles around.

Two litigants came to him one day to settle their dispute. After listening long and patiently to the plaintiff, he said to him:

"You are in the right."

Then he listened to the defendant and said to him:

"You are in the right."

The litigants departed highly pleased, but the rabbi's wife, who was present, was puzzled. A mere woman, what would she understand of legal matters?

"How is it possible," said she, "that they should both be in the right?"

The rabbi pondered the question long and deeply. Finally he turned to his good wife and said:

"Shall I tell you something? You are also in the right."

CERTIFICATE OF FRIENDSHIP

But it appears that the strict impartiality for which the rabbi of Chelm was noted had the effect of reducing the number of those who came to him to judge their cases. The rabbi's livelihood began to dwindle.

"We'll starve," said his wife one day. "Nobody comes here any more."

"The reason," said the rabbi, "is that the people of Chelm, God bless them, are not litigious as people in other places are."

Nevertheless he used to stand at his window and look out for possible litigants. And once he saw two men approaching who seemed to be engaged in sharp dispute. They waved their arms in violent gestures and spoke at the top of their voices. The rabbi opened his window and called them in.

"Let me adjudicate your dispute," he said to them.

"But, rabbi," they told him, "we have no dispute! We were just engaged in a friendly conversation!"

"In that case," said the rabbi, "let me give you a certificate that you have nothing against each other."

The Chelmites accepted the certificate and went away highly pleased.

CHICKEN AND LONG WALKS

There may have been hotheads in Chelm who sometimes failed to show proper respect for the rabbi, but there could be no doubt that the town as a whole was deeply concerned for his health and well-being, as the following story will prove.

It happened at one time that the rabbi began to ail. He grew pallid and lean, and it was plain that his strength was ebbing. They brought a doctor from the neighboring city who found that the rabbi was undernourished and leading a too sedentary life. The doctor ordered him to eat boiled chicken every day and take long walks.

What, then, did the good people of Chelm do? Naturally, they called a meeting, which lasted far into the night. They discussed the matter from every aspect and came to a unanimous decision. They decided there must be no delay. The rabbi should at once begin to take long walks. As for chicken, they would, as soon as possible, call another meeting.

THE INNOCENT AND GUILTY

Like any well-ordered community, Chelm had its penal institution where convicted malefactors were kept imprisoned. Not that any blood-curdling crimes were ever committed in Chelm. The inmates were guilty of offenses like making off with a chicken or a fish for the Sabbath table, or dealing out a sharp slap or two on the cheeks of a competitor in the market place. If not for the bitter problem of *parnosse*, the mice and spiders would have been the only inmates of the Chelm prison.

Now, on a certain day the rabbi of Chelm felt he should visit the prison and bring spiritual consolation to its inmates. They were happy to see him. They gathered around him and each one in turn assured him that his conviction was a miscarriage of justice. They were all innocent victims of malicious enemies who gave false testimony. They cited their distinguished lineage and honorable family connections, and wanted to know how any one could believe them guilty of deceiving, or stealing or brawling.

"My uncle is the assistant beadle of the House of Prayer. Would I do such a thing?"

"My grandfather was known throughout the province for his deeds of charity. And they have the audacity to put me in this place!"

"The chief witness against me is a liar and a thief, and I will not repeat what they say about him and his wife's servant girl."

The rabbi was bewildered and distressed. So many innocent people deprived of the light of day!

Now one of the inmates, he noticed, stood apart and said nothing.

"And you, my son," the rabbi addressed him. "You, too, must be innocent. Why did they put you here?"

"I am not innocent," the man replied.

The rabbi of Chelm was dumbfounded.

"Not innocent?" he repeated. "How is that possible?"

"I am guilty," the man declared. "I really did steal that fish—a beautiful pike."

"But how could you do such a thing?" the rabbi implored.

"I don't know what came over me. It was so many weeks since we had had fish at the Friday night meal. And that pike had such a kind look in his eyes, and his mouth was slightly open and he seemed to say: Take me. So I took him. And the fishmonger—may God punish him—set up a wild clamor, and they caught me, and here I am."

The rabbi was shocked. "You are a wicked man," he said to the hardened criminal.

On his way home, and for hours afterwards the rabbi of Chelm pondered on those innocents who languished in prison and the guilty criminal among them. He drew on his vast store of learning and concluded it was dangerous to have that criminal associate with the others. He might well be a corrupting influence. A single bad apple in a barrel of good apples—who doesn't know how true that maxim is?

So he summoned his townsmen for a solemn meeting and laid the grave problem before them.

"And now," he said in conclusion. "What shall we do? Can we release all those innocents? But they were duly convicted, and if we release them, we bring the entire judicial system of Chelm into contempt. Shall we release the wicked criminal? How can we let him go free if he is guilty by his own confession?"

So they pondered and pondered. Finally the *dayen* of Chelm stood up and spoke as follows:

"As matters now stand there is no solution for this problem. Therefore I propose that we build a new prison for the wicked criminal and for others like him who, God forbid, may be found in Chelm. In this way Chelm will have two prisons, one for the innocent and one for the guilty."

And the proposal met with universal approval.

THE RABBI AND HIS HEAD

One day, the news spread like wildfire through Chelm that the rabbi had vanished! A dreadful foreboding fell upon the town. Everybody, young and old, great and small, went out to look for him. They ranged through the forest, they searched in caves and in wells. At last they found something. They found a headless corpse!

The good people of Chelm were shocked, but at the same time they were puzzled. They were not sure it was the rabbi: they did not remember whether or not their rabbi had a head.

So they called for the *shames* and asked him if the rabbi had a head.

The *shames* pondered a long time.

"I know," said he, "that he had a beard, because he put away between the leaves of his Talmud every hair that fell from his beard. But as for a head, I don't know."

So they sent for the keeper of the bathhouse.

"Did the rabbi have a head?" they asked him.

The keeper of the bathhouse pondered a long time.

"I know," said he, "that the rabbi had earlocks, because on the day before every Sabbath and festival he washed his earlocks in hot water which I brought him. But whether or not he had a head, I cannot say."

So they sent a deputation to the rabbi's wife.

"Did the rabbi have a head?" they asked her.

A long time the good woman was silent.

"I know," said she finally, "that the rabbi had a nose because I prepared him a supply of snuff for every sabbath and festival. But whether or not he had a head, I cannot say."

And did the rabbi of Chelm have a head? To this day nobody knows.

The Chelm Melamed

A *CHELMITE PAR EXCELLENCE*

Now WITH regard to the *melamed* of Chelm it goes without saying that he was in every respect a true Chelmite. How could it be otherwise? Isn't every genuine *melamed*, no matter where he may live and labor, a Chelmite?

The *melamed* of Chelm was particularly shrewd in matters economic and financial.

"You know," said he to his wife one day, "if I were the Czar, I would be richer than the Czar."

"How so?" she asked.

"I would do a little teaching on the side," he explained.

MONEY AND CREDIT

With regard to money, the *melamed* of Chelm had his feet on the ground. He had no patience with people who exaggerate.

"More than once," he used to say, "I have had as much as three rubles all my own at the end of a semester. My father-in-law had four rubles when I married his daughter. Once I saw with my own eyes thirty-five rubles in the hand of the richest man in Chelm. But when people come and tell you they saw a hundred rubles, they either lie, or else they are the victims of hallucination, God shield us!"

And once as he sat thinking on the strange ways of the world, he arrived at a new solution of the problem of credit.

"It's a topsy-turvy world," he declared to his wife. "The rich who have plenty of money buy on credit. The poor, who haven't a copper, have to pay cash. Isn't it common sense it should be the other way: the rich to pay cash and the poor to get credit? What's that you say? A merchant who gives credit to the poor will become a poor man himself? Very well! What if he does? He'll be able to buy on credit, won't he?"

AN HONEST ANSWER

There was a foolish scoffer in Chelm who once tried to embarrass the *melamed* on the question of money.

"Melamed," said he, "if you found a million rubles in the marketplace, would you yield to the temptation to keep the money or would you return it to its owner?"

The *melamed* answered without hesitation.

"If I knew," said he, "that the money belonged to Rothschild, I fear I would not be able to overcome the temptation. If, however, I knew that the money belonged to someone like the Chelmer *shames*, I would certainly return it!"

CLASS DISTINCTIONS

The *melamed* of Chelm laid no claim to a knowledge of the latest pedogogic methods, nevertheless he had his own way of impressing his teachings on his pupils. Consider, for example, the following discourse he once held to acquaint his pupils with the differences that exist among the social classes.

"An ordinary man," said the *melamed,* "puts on a clean shirt on Friday for the Sabbath. A rich man changes his shirt every day. Rothschild changes his shirt three times a day, in the morning, at noon, and in the evening. The Czar is attended by two generals, one of whom takes off the shirt he wears and the other puts on a clean one, off and on, off and on, without interruption, night and day.

"An ordinary man takes a nap and who takes care he should not be awakened? His wife. A rich man is protected by a vestibule before his sleeping room. Rothschild has twelve men stationed before his bedroom to guard his sleep. The Czar has an army of soldiers before his door, who cry continually and all together: 'Quiet! His Majesty is sleeping!'

"An ordinary man gets up early in the morning and eats his breakfast. A rich man sleeps till ten o'clock, then he gets up and has his breakfast. Rothschild sleeps until Afternoon Prayers, and eats his breakfast towards evening. The Czar sleeps all day and all night, and has his breakfast the following day."

BIRTH CONTROL

Early in his career, the *melamed* of Chelm obtained a charge in a neighboring town and although the place was not far distant, he returned to his family only once a year, on the occasion of the Holy Days.

"You are so near," said the rabbi to him, "why don't you come in every week for the Sabbath?"

"I come in once a year," the *melamed* explained, "and every year my wife has a baby. If I came in for every Sabbath, she might, *cholile,* have a baby every week."

MY SLIPPERS, YOUR SLIPPERS

And once it happened that returning to his charge, the *melamed* forgot his slippers; and when he learned that one of the villagers was leaving for the town, he gave him a letter for his wife as follows:

"Be sure to send me your slippers with this messenger. I have put down 'your slippers,' because if I wrote 'my slippers' you would read *my* slippers, and would send me your slippers. And what would I do with your slippers? Therefore, I say plainly 'your slippers' so that you would read *your* slippers and send me my slippers."

TWO SCHOOLS OF THOUGHT

The tax collector burst into the *melamed*'s home one day and demanded immediate payment of what the poor man owed.

"I have waited long enough," he cried. "If you don't pay at once, I'll——"

By way of answer the *melamed* stood up and turned all his empty pockets inside out.

Thereupon the collector seized the *melamed*'s candlesticks, snatched the pillows from his bed and departed. The *melamed*'s wife sat down and wailed and wrung her hands, but he himself became lost in thought. A long time he sat and pondered without stirring.

Then the poor woman poured out all her bitterness on his innocent head.

"Why do you sit there looking like a chicken that has just been slaughtered?" she cried. "How will I bless my Sabbath candles? What'll we lay our heads on at night? Why don't you do something?"

"Hah? What?" the *melamed* shook himself out of his reverie.

"Is that all you are thinking of? Just like a foolish and ignorant woman! There is a more important question involved in all this —much more important, I tell you."

"Indeed? So tell me, my big breadwinner!"

"So listen! Listen carefully. There are two schools of thought on the question of why the good Lord created the night. One school maintains that the night was created for studying Torah, the other that the night was created for sleep. Now consider the tax collector. If he belongs to the first school, then why did he take away our candlesticks? How can a man study Torah at night without a light? If on the other hand, he belongs to the second school, then why did he take away our pillows?"

SHE JUST DIDN'T HAVE IT

A cow, a good milch cow—can you think of a greater blessing for a household? You come in with a pail of the life-giving fluid, rich, warm and fragrant. You pour some for your little ones, bless their precious navels. You use a portion for cooking noodles, groats, potatoes. You put away the rest and by some miracle it turns into cream, butter, cheese! Comes the dear Festival of Shevuos, when it is proper to eat all sorts of dairy foods, and they are there, ready to be served: butter-cakes, broad noodles with cheese, blintzes—whatever your heart desires!

So mused the *melamed*'s wife, and she made a solemn resolution: she would stint, she would deny herself, she would deprive herself of prime necessities. She would add copper to copper and save up enough for a cow, let it take no matter how long! He, the *melamed*, good health to him, must not know about it. She would surprise him.

And so it happened. The sum she eventually handed him was not large, but she and the delighted *melamed* agreed that it should suffice for a decent cow.

"Go," she said. "Go to the market place and come back with a good milker, and it will be a blessing for you, and me and the little ones, Amen, *selah*!"

So the *melamed* went and came back leading a cow. It was not the best cow he saw in the market place, but it was the best he could buy for the money. It was, in fact, a rather ungainly creature, with a lump at the base of its neck, big haunches and protruding ribs. But it had an udder.

"Look," said the *melamed*. "It has an udder!"

His wife looked dubiously at the cow, walked around it a few times, and without saying a word went into the house and came back with a pail and stool. Then she set to work. She squeezed and squeezed, but not a drop came out of the udder.

She stood up and let the poor *melamed* have it.

"Woe to me! Woe to both of us!" she wailed. "Where did you get this poor carcass? Who was the crafty thief in the marketplace who rejoiced when you came along? Have you no eyes in your head? You I had to send! I had to send a *melamed* to buy a cow!"

The *melamed* stood with bowed head and said not a word. What could he say? The woman was right. He deserved all the abuse he was getting. But his silence only exasperated her bitterness. She turned from him with disdain, and poured out all her wrath on the cow. She delivered a torrent of awesome curses calling down an assortment of dread diseases on the head and every other part of its poor anatomy.

But now the *melamed* was aroused. Abusing the cow—that was quite another matter!

"Woman!" he said with all the sternness he could command, "why do you rail at the poor dumb animal? You are doing a sinful thing. We are commanded to show kindness to God's dumb creatures. Besides, does she have it and refuse to give it? Don't you know, foolish woman, that she would gladly give it, if she only had it?"

HE-GOAT, SHE-GOAT

The tale must now be told of the strange transformations that befell the *melamed* of Chelm and of the wise men who by their insight into the mysteries of nature, found the answer to a baffling riddle.

"A goat," said the *melamed*'s wife one day, "is a blessing in a household. A good goat," she continued, "is no trouble or expense to her owner; she finds her own food and gives milk in abundance."

Nor did Rifkele, the *melamed*'s wife, intend her words to be merely general. After the sad experience with the cow she was prepared to settle for a goat. It was the end of the semester and she knew her husband to have some money hidden away somewhere.

"Go," said she to him, "to the neighboring town, which is famous for its goats. Go and bring home a good goat."

"A foolish woman," said the *melamed* to himself, "but this time she is right. There is merit in a good goat."

So he went to the town of goats, bought a good goat, and the same day set out with his goat for Chelm. Here and there on the way the goat stopped to browse and, although it was late, the *melamed* did nothing to prevent her. His heart went out to the gentle beast.

But twilight and darkness fell upon the earth and the *melamed* feared to continue lest robbers overtake him and steal his goat. So he stepped aside into an inn, tied the goat in the shed of the courtyard and asked the innkeeper for a bed for the night.

Now the innkeeper was a garrulous and frivolous fellow, having no decent respect for Chelmites in general and for a *melamed* of Chelm in particular. So, the *melamed* having retired for the night, the man went to the shed, untied the goat, and put a he-goat in her place.

The following morning the *melamed* resumed his journey and arrived home in triumph.

"Rifkele," he cried, "I have brought you a goat, such a year on all good and pious people. Take your pail and milk her."

But when the woman discovered what sort of a goat her *melamed* had brought her, she turned pale with anger and called down a series of strange curses impartially upon the head of the goat and that of her husband. The *melamed* listened to her meekly, but when she included his immediate ancestors in her maledictions, he roused himself and resolved to return forthwith to the man who had sold him the goat and demand satisfaction.

Without a moment's delay, the *melamed* seized the rope that was tied to the horns of the goat and set out. He travelled at a rapid pace and when he came to the inn he thought to rest a bit, and having tied the goat in the shed, he told the innkeeper of the unheard-of betrayal that had been practiced upon him. The innkeeper bided his time and at the right moment proceeded to the shed, released the he-goat, and tied the she-goat in his place.

The *melamed* came to the goat merchant and stood before him with all the dignity of injured innocence.

"How does a man permit himself," he demanded more in sorrow than in wrath, "to sell a *melamed* a he-goat instead of a she-goat?"

The merchant looked at the goat and laughed.

"Melamed!" he cried, as if the appellation connoted ridicule, instead of honor. "Can't you see it's a she-goat?"

And he called his wife, who brought a pail, and in the presence of the astonished *melamed,* milked the goat until the pail brimmed over.

The *melamed,* bewildered and crestfallen, took the goat and set out for Chelm. He spent the night in the same inn, and when he returned to his wife the following morning he brought her a he-goat instead of a she-goat. The unsuspecting woman attempted to milk the creature, her face became purple with rage, and she called down a dreadful curse upon the *melamed*'s ancestors to the tenth generation. And when the *melamed* heard it he was seized with terror, and grasping the rope that was tied to the goat's horns, he set out immediately to confront the merchant with the clear evidence of his duplicity. On the way he stopped to rest in the inn, and when he stood before the merchant the animal he led by the rope was not a he-goat but a she-goat. The merchant again laughed at the *melamed*, called his wife, who again milked the beast, filling her pail to the brim.

The *melamed* refused to believe his eyes.

"Impossible!" he cried. "I will not believe it unless the rabbi and the *dayen* attest in a written document that this animal is a she-goat and not a he-goat."

So the rabbi and the *dayen* came together, and after a thorough examination, they drew up a document which was witnessed by the seven elders and sealed with the seal of the congregation, that the animal was a she-goat in every particular.

The *melamed* took the document and the goat and set out for Chelm. On the way he stopped to rest in the same inn and when he arrived home he brought his wife a he-goat.

The woman, after innocently trying to milk it, sat down and wept. The *melamed*, dazed and desperate, took out the document and waved it.

"The animal is a she-goat!" he shouted. "Here is a document that proves it!"

The noise brought the people of Chelm to the *melamed*'s door. They swarmed about the place and presently two parties rose up among them.

"The woman is right," declared one party. "The animal is a he-goat. The signs are unmistakable."

"The *melamed* is right," maintained the other, "the animal is a she-goat. The document is not to be denied."

Finally the *melamed*, his wife and the goat, followed by all the people of Chelm, proceeded to the rabbi and laid the matter before him. The rabbi listened carefully, put on his spectacles, examined the animal thoroughly, read the document again and again and at length pronounced his verdict.

"The law," he declared, "is on the side of the *melamed*. The animal is a she-goat and the document establishes this fact beyond all doubt. But it is equally clear, and it must be ordained from on high, that the moment a she-goat is brought into Chelm, she becomes transformed into a he-goat."

And the good people of Chelm, the *melamed* and his wife included, acknowledged the wisdom of the verdict and went home in peace.

HE COMFORTS HIS WIFE

The *melamed*'s wife, all upset, came to him one day and told him with tears in her eyes that their neighbor had insulted her.

"What did she say to you?"

"She called me an old fool."

Thereupon the *melamed* proceeded to comfort her.

"You an old fool?" he cried. "Why, you are young! You are still young. And besides, Rifkele, in my eyes you will always be young. You will never be an old fool, never!"

So Rifkele was happy again.

VAGARIES OF A TRUNK

The *melamed* of Chelm and his wife had lived together for many years, a model of harmony and concord. In their old age, however, a deplorable event occurred which broke the even tenor of their common life. But since there is nothing wholly good or wholly evil, the same event led to the enactment of an ordinance which brought lasting benefit to Chelm. The event as well as the ordinance must now be recorded.

It all began with an innocent conversation between the *melamed* and his wife. It was in the evening when his labors were over and the good woman was knitting a stocking.

"Rifkele," said the *melamed*. "Here am I nearly seventy years old and never have I eaten a cake stuffed with cheese and kneaded with butter. And the holy festival of Shevuos is at hand, when it is a great *mitsve* to partake of such pastry."

The woman stopped her knitting, her eyes became wistful and her mouth watered. She sighed and said:

"Alas! I can say the same for myself."

For a long time the *melamed* stroked his beard lost in thought.

"I have a good idea," said he at length. "Do you remember the big trunk you brought as part of your dowry? We haven't used it all these years. Let us cut two openings in the cover, and every day I'll throw a little coin out of my earnings into one and you'll throw a little coin out of your allowance into the other. The day before Shevuos we'll open the trunk and there will be enough for flour and eggs and cream and cheese. We'll have a cake befitting the holy festival."

"So be it," the good woman replied.

But in his heart the *melamed* thought deceitfully.

"How is it possible," said he to himself, "for me to spare anything from my wretched earnings? Let her deposit her mite and it will be enough."

And in her heart she too thought deceitfully.

"It's impossible for me to spare anything," said she to herself. "He will throw in his coins and they will suffice."

At last came the spring and the lovely festival of Shevuos. With beating hearts the *melamed* and his wife unlocked the trunk, lifted the cover and looked in. The trunk was empty!

The good woman flew into a rage.

"Where are your coins?" she screamed and dug her hands into his beard.

The *melamed* was outraged.

"Woman of evil, where are your coins?" he thundered and buried his hands in her wig.

And as they struggled back and forth they both fell into the trunk. The cover came down with a crash, and the lock snapped shut.

Now, the trunk, it must be told, was very big and, to move it more easily, it was furnished with four wheels, one in each corner. Moreover, the day being warm, the door of the house was ajar and—a circumstance of grave importance—the doorway had no threshold. And because the *melamed* and his wife, both transported with rage, still struggled within it, the trunk began to move. It made for the open door, and, with no threshold to arrest its progress, it rolled out into the street.

On the same street stood the synagogue. The trunk continued its journey and came to a halt inside the holy place.

People saw the trunk rolling solitary down the street, but no one dared touch it, so astonished were they all and terrified by the sight. And when finally they saw it inside the house of worship, skipping, veering, and pitching, and heard muffled sounds, strange and unearthly, issue from its entrails, they were seized with panic and ran to the rabbi and the seven worthies.

The rabbi and the worthies of Chelm came together and took immediate action. They adopted a solemn resolution that for the sake of the common weal, the *shames* must risk his life and open the trunk. The *shames,* noble man, accepted the charge. He performed special ablutions, prayed devoutly and put on his burial robes. Then he entered the synagogue, opened the trunk and found the *melamed* and his wife clasped in desperate struggle, her hands still in his beard and his in her wig.

Again the rabbi and the seven worthies came together and spent a long time in profound deliberation. The outcome was an ordinance in four sections which brought untold benefit to the town of Chelm for all time:

One: Every door in Chelm must have a threshold.

Two: A *melamed* must not live on the street where the synagogue stands.

Three: It is not seemly for an old *melamed,* whose wife knits stockings, to hanker after Shevuos pastry.

Four: A trunk that is brought as part of a dowry must not be furnished with wheels.

L'ENVOI FOR THE MELAMED

Once the *melamed* of Chelm was discovered by an acquaintance at a fair in a neighboring town.

"Melamed," said the acquaintance, "what business have you at the fair?"

"I came," the *melamed* replied, "because I had an idea I would find a driver who would give me a lift back to Chelm."

Tanchum and Yokl

TANCHUM GOES TO MARKET

For a proper understanding of Chelm, it should be instructive to consider some of its undistinguished citizens, say, Tanchum the water carrier and his friend and neighbor Yokl the wagoner. For even the ordinary Chelmite is not ordinary.

The Chelm in Tanchum came out early in life. His mother once sent him to market to buy a chicken and he came back with a pitcher of water!

"Woe is me!" cried his mother. "Where is the chicken?"

"I went to the woman who sells chickens," Tanchum explained. "The woman said her chickens were wonderful; they were so fat. 'Oho!' said I, 'fat is better than chickens!' I went to the butcher to buy fat. The butcher said his fat was wonderful; it was like oil. 'Oho!' said I, 'oil is better than fat!' I went to the grocer to buy oil. The grocer said his oil was wonderful; it was as pure as water. 'Oho!' said I, 'water is better than oil!' So here I am with a pitcher of water!"

HE TRIES THE MATCHES

On another occasion his mother sent him to buy matches. "Be sure to try them," she warned him. "Make sure they light."

Tanchum came back with the matches and his mother tried them. She tried one, two, three; they refused to light.

"Didn't I tell you to try them before you buy them?" she cried.

"I did," said Tanchum, "I tried them all. They were all good."

HE HAS HIS PRIDE

Even when he was still young, Tanchum was noted for his pride. His mother found him in the kitchen one day, and the dog was standing over a bowl of milk lapping it up.

"Tanchum!" she cried. "Why don't you chase the dog away?"

"I don't talk to him," Tanchum explained. "He ripped my pants yesterday."

HIS CAREER AS SHOEMAKER

For a number of years, Tanchum was a shoemaker, and this is his own account of it.

"My father and mother were at odds," he explained. "She wanted me to be a tailor and he wanted me to be a shoemaker. In the end he had his way. And let me tell you, it was fortunate for me that he did, for otherwise I would be starving. I have been following my trade now for four years and it hasn't happened yet that anyone who comes to me should order clothes. They all order shoes!"

HE GOES TO TOWN

In a spirit of enterprise Tanchum made his way to the big city and strange as it may sound, he tried his hand at business. Out of his brief career in that field, the following incident is remembered:

His employer once sent him to a neighboring town to collect from a customer whose account was in arrears.

"Tanchum," said his employer before sending him off, "when you get to the town go about your business very subtly. Begin by visiting the market place. Step into a restaurant and order a cup of coffee. Look around, start a conversation with your neighbor. Inquire casually about our customer. Find out if he is still solvent. Then drop in on him, be courteous but firm, and try to collect as much as possible. As soon as you know definitely how much he is ready to pay, send me a telegram."

The following day, Tanchum sent his employer a telegram as follows:

"No coffee in this town. What shall I do?"

HE GETS SLAPPED

When the train on which Tanchum returned pulled into the station a tall person was seen striding up and down the platform and calling, "Yeruchem! Yeruchem!"

Tanchum put his head out of the window and looked inquiringly at the tall person. The latter ran forward and slapped Tanchum twice in the face.

The other passengers laughed and Tanchum also laughed.

"Why are you laughing?" they asked him. "You are the one who got slapped."

"Yes," said Tanchum, "but my name isn't Yeruchem, it's Tanchum!"

HE FINDS HIS TRUE VOCATION

In the big city Tanchum took a wife—things like that always happen. Soon Tanchum returned to Chelm with his wife and he became a water carrier.

Tanchum was satisfied with his lot and happy. Sometimes his work brought him unexpected pleasures. Once when he went down to the river to fill his pails, he saw his wife on the bank downstream washing his clothes. On a flat stone before her lay his drawers, and she was beating them with a heavy wooden implement. Tanchum watched the operation and a wave of gratitude swept over him. There and then he made up a new blessing.

"Blessed art thou, O Lord," said he, "who gavest me understanding to get out of my drawers in time."

HE TRIUMPHS OVER HIS WIFE

Tanchum's wife, it must be confessed, was not so easily satisfied. It mustn't be forgotten that she came from the big city. After living in certain quarters for ten years, she insisted on moving to better ones.

What did Tanchum do? He yielded. Is it possible to make head against a wife who always tells you about the luxury she enjoyed before she married you?

She went out and found new quarters. Shortly after they installed themselves, a fire broke out in the neighborhood. Tanchum and his wife stood at the window and looked out. The next minute they saw the house next to theirs in flames.

"Do you see?" said Tanchum to his wife gleefully, "you always tell me that I am a *tipesh*. But who was it that rented a place right next to a burning house? Was it you or I?

HE TRIUMPHS AGAIN

In her heart of hearts, Tanchum's wife was fond of him, but she was also ashamed of him. "You're such a *tipesh*," she used to say to him. Moreover, she began to hanker for the big city. That's how they are, the women who come from the grand places! She decided to get a divorce and took him to the rabbi.

"What have you against him?" asked the rabbi.

"He's a *tipesh*," she answered.

"How long have you lived together?" asked the rabbi.

"Fifteen years."

"Fifteen years and you've only now discovered that he is a *tipesh?*"

At this point Tanchum could no longer contain himself. "She is not telling the truth, rabbi," he cried. "She has known it all along!"

The rabbi of Chelm refused to divorce them and they lived happily ever afterwards.

HIS ROLE AS LORD AND MASTER

Tanchum knew that Holy Writ made it plain that he, not his wife, was to wear the trousers. "And he," it says, meaning the husband, of course, "shall rule over thee," meaning the wife.

He was big and strong and might have had no difficulty in fulfilling the command, were it not that his wife, though small and skinny, had sharp features and a still sharper tongue. Her tongue, it was said, was mightier than his brawny hands; and it was even whispered that in moments of abandon she didn't scruple to use her own hands on his face in a manner that pained and confounded him. At such moments, Tanchum the water-carrier had recourse to the nuptial bed, not however in order to lie on it, but to take refuge beneath it.

To Tanchum, however, this maneuver meant no surrender of his prerogative. Once, as he lay under the bed, his long legs projecting across the room, a knock was heard on the door.

"Come out from under the bed and open the door!" said his wife who was standing over him.

"I will not!" Tanchum replied.

"Will you open the door?" she repeated and a grim note sounded in her voice.

But—was Tanchum dismayed?

"No!" he cried from under the bed. "You can't order me around! Who do you think is the master of this house?"

TANCHUM INTERVENES

This happened when the French under Napoleon were invading Russia. They were approaching Chelm when Tanchum was walking home with two pails of water which he had drawn at the river. He lifted up his eyes, and behold, the French were coming! Now, it is well known that if you meet someone on the road who is carrying full pails you are going to have good luck.

"These soldiers," said Tanchum to himself, "are coming against my king, and am I going to help them?"

So he poured the water out of his pails on the road before the enemy. When he came home, his wife saw the pails and asked why they were empty. Tanchum told her, but instead of approving she railed at him.

"If two powers fall out," she snapped, "do you have to interfere?"

PLUMS IN AND OUT OF THE POT

Tanchum's wife was really no virago, appearances to the contrary notwithstanding. She was, in fact, a kindly soul. Together with her own children she brought up an orphan boy, the child of a distant relative. The boy was always hungry, nor would it be just to blame the woman, for aren't all growing boys always hungry?

Now one day Tanchum's wife put up a pot of plums on the stove and went away. When she returned the pot was half empty. She didn't have to guess how it happened, and as soon as she was able to lay hands on the boy she let him have it.

The boy raised a loud and bitter outcry, so loud, indeed, that all the neighbors came together and there was much indignation among them.

"To treat a child like that!" cried one.

"And an orphan! Think of it, a poor orphan!" cried another.

"And what is he guilty of?" cried another. "He ate a few plums, the poor child! Was such a thing ever heard of?"

Tanchum's wife listened to the clamor with every appearance of contrition.

"Do you think?" said she finally, "that I begrudge him the few plums he ate? *Cholile!* But don't you see? Every time he takes one plum and another plum and another, there is less and less in the pot?"

The Chelmites stopped their clamor.

"If that is so," said they, "then, of course, it's different."

SLAPPER AND SLAPPEE

It was a Friday afternoon, the Chelm bathhouse was crowded, and all backs being bare, it was hard to distinguish who was who. But Tanchum was sure he recognized the back of his friend Yokl the wagoner, so he came close and gave the naked back a resounding slap.

The slappee faced the slapper and it was not Yokl. "What's the meaning of this?" he demanded.

Tanchum explained and apologized profusely. But a stinging back is not easily appeased.

"So you made a mistake!" the man bristled. "You thought I was your friend Yokl!"

"Forgive me," said Tanchum humbly.

"And suppose it really was Yokl, did you have to give him such a fiery slap?" the other cried.

Tanchum's face flushed with anger.

"If I want to slap my friend Yokl," he replied, "do I have to ask you or any other man in Chelm how to do it? You should learn to mind your own business!"

YOKL HAS A SUGGESTION

Yokl, the wagoner, was a man of short temper who found relief in dispensing floods of picturesque curses. But he was really a good and pious soul, and was especially fond of horses.

He was not among the wisest of his townsmen, but, being a Chelmite, he could not altogether escape the effects of the wisdom with which the very air of the town was impregnated. Consider, for example, the following bit which has been recorded as having dropped from his lips:

"Blessed be the Holy One," said the wagoner, "who ordained

the Sabbath for His people Israel! Without the day of rest a hard-working man like me would go under. It's only a pity that He didn't establish the Sabbath for the middle of the week. At the end of the week I am too tired to enjoy it properly."

DELAY FULLY EXPLAINED

There was a merchant in Chelm who had business in a neighboring town and he sent word to Yokl on a Sunday to call for him on Monday. The wagoner came exactly a week later. The merchant was indignant and ordered him out of his house.

"Please," said the wagoner, "it's not my fault, and I did the best I could. Sunday you told me to come on Monday. Tuesday I forgot about it, and when I saw on Wednesday that I won't be able to come on Thursday, and Friday night I couldn't come on account of the Sabbath, and Sunday I mustn't come because you told me to come on Monday, I came today! So how am I to blame?"

THE SILLY HORSE

There was a time when Yokl was so poor and oats came so dear that he decided to wean his horse away from the habit of eating. He began by cutting down his allowance of oats. Then he omitted his meals altogether one day a week, then two days a week, then three. Yokl saw his experiment succeeding and rejoiced. In the midst of it all, the silly horse spoiled everything by dying. Yokl refused to be consoled. He stood over the beast, wept and cried:

"Another week or two, and all my worries would have been over, so you go and die!"

HE SCOFFS AT THE RAILROAD

When the railroad came to Chelm, Yokl remained incredulous to the end. He scoffed even as people stood at the station to see the first train depart.

"Now we shall see the big wagons ride without horses," said they.

"Impossible," said Yokl, "wagons don't move without horses."

A shrill whistle was heard, but the train stood still.

"Whistle away!" said the wagoner, "but if you want to move you'll have to get horses."

Again the whistle sounded, but the train didn't stir.

"What did I tell you?" said the wagoner. "I ought to know something about it. I've been a wagoner for twenty years!"

The whistle sounded a third time and, wonder of wonders! The wheels began to grind, the big wagons began to move, and the train bounded away.

A moment Yokl was dumb with amazement; then he recovered.

"How are you going to stop it?" he cried. "It will never stop! Never!"

HIS CAREER AS A BRIGAND

Now, the Chelmites were not given to travelling and the wagoner's business was never in a flourishing state. Why, indeed, should Chelmites go gadding about? Did other cities have anything to teach them? But the railroad made Yokl's lot still more bitter. He came to the end of his resources.

He even tried other callings, but with no better success. So, in desperation, he decided to become a brigand.

He found his opportunity and slipped the kitchen knife into his pocket. Then he made off for the forest where he sat down beside a road and waited. He waited a long time and the sun began to set.

"Time for *Minche,*" said he to himself.

He chanted the "Happy Are They," then faced east and began the Eighteen Benedictions. He was only half-through when someone came up the road. The wagoner signaled to the man to wait, for, as everybody knows, the Eighteen Benedictions cannot be interrupted for anyone or anything. The man waited.

The wagoner ended the Benedictions, went three steps backward as the ritual requires, and chanted the *Oleynu,* which closes the Afternoon Prayer. And then, without losing a moment, he approached the man and seized him by the lapels of his coat.

"Money or your life!" he cried.

The man was dumbfounded.

"Have you gone crazy?" he cried, for he knew the wagoner very well.

But the brigand knew no pity.

"I am not crazy," he shouted. "I am a *gazlon,* do you understand?"

And with that he whipped the knife out of his pocket and brandished it over the head of his victim.

But suddenly the wagoner lowered his hand and turned pale.

"My God," he moaned, "I took the *milchige* knife instead of the *fleyshige.*" *

Yokl took to his heels and disappeared in the forest. He spent the night beneath the stars and decided to try again on the morrow. The knife, he realized, was useless, but he would have recourse to another method, the simple method of intimidation.

The day happened to be Lag B'Omer, the only day in the seven weeks that follow Passover when festivities are not forbidden. On that day it is customary for teachers and pupils to go to the woods for an outing.

And sure enough, as the *gazlon* trudged through the woods he came upon a group of jolly, shouting children and their *melamed.*

Yokl burst upon the scene and shouted, "Hands up!"

Every pair of hands shot up into the air, except the *melamed's.*

The *gazlon* turned fiercely upon the poor man.

"Hands up, *melamed!*" he thundered. "I'm a brigand, can't you see?"

"I—I can't lift my hands," the *melamed* stammered. "I have a terrible pain in my shoulder!"

* The dietary laws require different utensils for "milk" dishes (*milchige*) and "meat" dishes (*fleyshige*).

"A pain in your shoulder?" exclaimed the *gazlon*. "Ay, ay, ay! Have you tried iodine? Sometimes hot compresses are very good. Try them, try them!"

And the *gazlon* disappeared.

He went his way deeper into the forest and before long the sound of footsteps reached his ear. He stepped aside, and when the wayfarer came in sight, he barred his way.

"Money or your life!'" he cried.

"What?" said the man. "Do I look like Rothschild to you? I'm a pauper. I beg for alms from door to door. What can I give you?"

"Well," said the brigand more quietly, "it doesn't have to be much. A small coin will do, say ten kopeks."

"Ten kopeks! I have to knock on thirty doors before I collect so much."

"Well then, can you spare a cigarette? I haven't smoked all day."

"But I don't smoke!"

"Oh! It's too bad. In that case, give me a pinch of snuff. There is nothing like a good pinch of snuff to set a man up!"

The wayfarer took out his snuffbox, opened and extended it to the brigand, who helped himself to a large pinch. He inhaled the snuff and sneezed three times in quick succession.

"Good health to you and long life!" said the stranger.

"Long life and good health to you!" replied the brigand.

And the two shook hands and went their separate ways.

And after that the *balagole* returned to his wife and children and to his horse and wagon.

TANCHUM ASSERTS HIMSELF

It was the night before Purim and Tanchum was unable to sleep. Questions kept grinding in his head like a Purim rattle. "How will I manage tomorrow? How will I get around? How will I trudge all day in my leaky shoes through the mud of the Chelm streets?" For on Purim the water carrier became the bearer of the Purim gifts which the people exchanged, even as the Book of Esther enjoined. That day brought him not only substantial revenue but honor as well.

But the thaw had set in early and the mud in the streets of Chelm was more than ankle-deep. It would fill his tattered shoes and he would bring it squirting and oozing into the best homes of the town. The housewives would glower at him and all their generous impulses would be squelched in the mud. There would be no honor and no revenue.

A deep groan began rumbling in his bronchi, but before it could break through he remembered something which brought him up with a start. Only the previous week Yokl the wagoner, his friend and neighbor, had come home from a distant town with a new pair of boots. Shining boots that came up above the knees, and tight as a drum about the feet. With such boots who would worry about mud? So early tomorrow morning, Tanchum resolved, he would talk to Yokl and his friend and neighbor would surely let him wear his boots for his Purim rounds.

With a happy sigh Tanchum lay down again, but a new worry began to nag him. Yokl his friend and neighbor? Neighbor—yes; but friend—he wasn't so sure. Who can be sure of anyone? Every man has something hidden away in his heart that doesn't show in his face. New boots, brand new! Is Yokl the sort of man who would let me drag them all day through the mud of Chelm? He is no lover of his fellow men, this wagoner. He is crude and selfish. He only loves his horse. He cares more for his horse than for his wife. Will he let me have those boots or not? If he was any sort of man he would say, "Take them, Tanchum, wear them all day, and come back at night with your pockets full of coins, white silver coins." Why not? Don't I help him out? How often does he come to me to lend him a gilden to buy oats for that precious horse of his? "I am just short of one gilden, Tanchum, my friend. Would you want to see my eagle starve?" A flatterer, that's what he is, and a hypocrite. And of all the people in Chelm, he and no one else has to have a new pair of boots, and mine have to be in ruins! Is this justice?

And who came to his help that day when his wagon broke down on the road? Crack! went the axle, and off came both front wheels. And I took the yoke of pails off my shoulders, and got down under the wagon, and nailed two slats across the crack and bound up the axle and put the wheels in place. Do you remember that, Yokl, you good-for-nothing hypocrite? "Such shoulders, Tanchum, my friend; every Jew should have such shoulders!" That's what he said to me. And now what do I ask you, Yokl? Just to let me wear your boots on Purim, the day that means so much for my wife and children, poor things. And what is your answer, you scoundrel, you———you! But I'll show you! I'll let you know who you are, I'll tell you what you can do with those fine boots of yours, I'll———"

And swiftly the water carrier jumped out of bed, and without stopping to put something over his night shirt, he glided out into the night.

The cold air startled him. He halted, stood still and wavered. Then he went on and knocked on his neighbor's shutter. A shaggy arm appeared as the shutter was pushed open, and Yokl's eyes peered into his.

"Yokl," said the water carrier. "Be so kind Yokl, and forgive me. I mean——what I mean is——the boots. Not mine, Yokl. Yours, your boots. I mean your new boots, Yokl. No, Yokl, you don't have to lend them to me. Why should you? Wear them yourself, in good health."

And the water carrier returned quickly to his home and bed, and fell promptly asleep.

And what does the foregoing prove? It proves that a Chelmite, be his station ever so humble, is not a man to be trifled with.

The Wisest of the Wise

HORSES AND OXEN

It is well known that there are degrees of wisdom as there are degrees of piety, humility, benevolence, and all other virtues. The wise men of Chelm were not all equally wise. There were some among them who were supremely wise: philosophers, thinkers, illuminated spirits. They made up a group that held meetings every Sabbath afternoon in the synagogue, and delved boldly into the secrets of nature, the mysteries of life, the problems of society, and other questions that baffle lesser minds.

"Everybody knows," said one of them once, "that oxen are killed for meat and horses are not. Nevertheless, there are always more oxen than horses. How does that happen?"

"It's because," replied another, "horses are stolen and oxen are not."

"Then why is it," rejoined the first, "that in those places to which the stolen horses are taken, there are also more oxen than horses?"

"That's because," replied the other, "horses are stolen from those places also."

And thus a difficult question found a simple answer.

THREE QUESTIONS, THREE ANSWERS

The same philosopher hit upon the answers to three other difficult questions.

"Why," he was asked, "does a dog wag his tail?"

"Because," he answered without hesitation, "the dog is stronger than the tail. Were it the other way, the tail would wag the dog."

Again he was asked why the hair on a man's head turns gray sooner than his beard.

"It's because," he replied, "the hair on his head is twenty years older than his beard."

"And why," he was further asked, "are the waters of the seas salty?"

"Don't you know?" he said. "It's because of the thousands of herring that live there."

ALL IS VANITY

Among the philosophers of Chelm, the matter of illusions was a frequent subject of discourse. One Sabbath afternoon in winter they talked about the vanity of all things, and one of them even went so far as to maintain that all things were nothing but illusions—mirages of the senses, and that nothing exists in reality.

That night one of the group was unable to sleep. He got up and paced his room in the dark.

"Yes, indeed," he said to himself. "All things are only an illusion—an empty dream. There is no heaven and no earth, no light and no darkness, no me and no you."

And as he walked he ran into the stove and barked his shins. The pain was formidable.

"It seems," said he to himself sadly, "that there is such a thing as a stove after all!"

HEREDITY

Nor was the science of genetics and heredity a terra incognita to the Chelm philosophers as the following conversation, fully authenticated, proves.

Said one to another:

"Strange that my beard is so thin. My grandfather, may he rest in peace, had a long thick beard like a forest."

"May it not be," replied the other, "that you take after your grandmother and not after your grandfather?"

The first pondered the question deeply.

"You are right," said he finally, "I distinctly remember that my grandmother did have a very thin beard."

OF LIFE AND DEATH

This gloomy philosopher pondered deeply on the subject of life and death. He came to the conclusion that in view of life's tribulations, death was no great misfortune.

"Of course," he pointed out, "Some of our sages held that it's better for a man not to have been born. But how many are fortunate enough to enjoy this advantage? Maybe one in ten thousand."

OFFSPRING AND OMELETS

"I am thinking," a Chelm philosopher once said to another, "that I have found a flaw in the order of creation. In my opinion it would have been better if the way of the woman in bearing offspring were the same as the way of the hen."

"Indeed!" said the second philosopher.

"Yes," continued the first, "I would have ordered it that a woman should also lay eggs."

"But why?" asked the other.

"Why, you ask? Because that way would be much better for us—the men."

"Really?" the second philosopher wondered.

"Yes, indeed!" said the first. "Sometimes a man wants to beget sons and daughters. So he says to his wife: 'Take your eggs and hatch them!' Another time a man—well, a man is just hungry. So he says to his wife: 'Take your eggs and make me an omelet!' "

TWO WORDS UNSPOKEN

There was one among the philosophers of Chelm who was a fatalist, and he often drew on his own experience to prove his contention that a man's destiny was fixed and immutable.

"Listen to what happened to me today," he once reported to his fellow thinkers. "For no reason that I can explain, I walked into the bank. Behind the windows sat individuals with piles of papers before them. They didn't even look at me. At one of the windows stood a man with a heap of money which he was counting, and this man did look at me. I began to feel very strange—hot and cold at the same time. 'Something wonderful is about to happen to you,' said I to myself, 'your destiny is upon you.' And I realized that everything depended on two words, two words which the man at the window might utter, two words which might raise me up and remove all burdens from me for the rest of my life. But did the man at the window say those two words? He did not! It was not ordained that he should. Alas, it was not to be!"

"And what could the man have said?" the philosopher was asked.

"What could he have said?" the fatalist replied. "Two words—no more! He could have said: 'Yankl, take!' "

ESTABLISHING IDENTITY

Who will deny that philosophy is a real friend to man? But everything real, no matter how good, is dogged by a shadow, and the shadow that dogs philosophy is skepticism.

A disturbing thought once assailed the mind of one of the thinkers of Chelm.

"How is a man known in the market place?" he asked himself.

"By his clothes," he straightway answered.

"But in the bathhouse," he continued. "In the bathhouse

everybody is naked. There is danger, therefore, that a man may lose his identity!"

On Friday, when every man of Chelm went to the bathhouse in preparation for the Sabbath, the philosopher was afraid to go. But the holy Sabbath! How can a man fail in his ablutions for the Sabbath? So he took a red thread, tied it to his foot, and proceeded to the bathhouse.

"Now I am safe!" he assured himself. "Now I cannot be mistaken for another."

He rubbed himself with more than usual energy and failed to note that during the process the thread slipped from his foot, and was picked up by his neighbor. The latter, recognizing the virtue of the red thread, tied it to his own foot.

The philosopher, having completed his ablutions, looked down, and behold! his thread was gone! And looking around he saw a red thread on the foot of his neighbor.

"Friend," said the unhappy philosopher, "I have never seen you before, but I know who you are. You are I. And now that I have told you who you are, would you not be good enough to tell me who I am?"

IRREPARABLE LOSS

The same philosopher once stepped into a shop to buy himself a new hat for Passover. He stood before the merchant, rummaging into one pocket after another.

"What is it?" the merchant asked. "You've lost something?"

"I took the measurements of my head before I left home and wrote them down on paper," said the thinker, "and now, alas, the paper is lost!"

HE ONCE WAS BEAUTIFUL

It is reported of the same philosopher that his features were singularly ungainly, and when the *shadchn* brought him before the maiden whom he was to wed, she looked at his features with an expression of incredulity.

"You look at me thus," said he, "because I am so ugly. But let it be known to you that I was not born ugly. In fact, I was born very beautiful. But I was put into the hands of a mean and envious nurse who exchanged me for another."

The maiden's sympathies, it should be noted, were deeply touched and she agreed to marry him.

GROWTH OF MAN

This philosopher had a way of startling his fellow thinkers with unexpected questions.

"From which of his extremities does a man grow?" he once asked them. "From his feet down or from his head up?"

After a long and deep silence one of them ventured a reply.

"I remember," said he, "when I was a boy my father bought me a pair of trousers. When I first put them on they dragged on the floor. Two years later they only reached to my ankles. That proves that a man grows from his feet down."

"Not so," replied the other. "I was in the market place yesterday and a company of soldiers marched through. I looked carefully and saw that their feet were all on a level, but their heads were not. Some heads came high, others were low, and it became clear to me that a man grows from his head up."

And the wise men of Chelm nodded in agreement.

WHAT A SPLASH!

It was noted once that for several days one of the deep thinkers failed to appear among his companions. When they inquired about him they were alarmed to learn that he was refusing food and drink and spending his nights without sleep or rest. He was in the throes of some profound speculation.

So they came to him and begged him to unburden himself to them.

"Perhaps," said they, "this will bring you relief."

For a long time he made no answer, but finally, when they implored him again and again, he yielded.

"This," said he, "is the thought that torments me. If all men now on the face of the earth became one man; if all the trees in all the forests became one tree; if all the seas on the earth became one ocean; if all the axes in the world became one ax; and the man arose and took the ax, and cut down the tree and it fell into the ocean—"

He halted and his listeners drew a deep breath.

"Then what? Then what?" they whispered.

"Then, then," he whispered in reply, "how loud would that splash be?"

GOOD TIDINGS FOR THE POOR

It was once observed that the countenance of this sage became as though illumined, and his brother philosophers realized he had made a new discovery.

"What is it? What is it?" they asked.

"Thank Heaven!" he answered. "From now on every poor man will eat cream and every rich man will drink sour milk. I've discovered how to do it."

"It's very simple," he continued solemnly as they crowded around him. "Let a decree be issued in Chelm that from now on sour milk shall be called cream, and cream sour milk!"

OPTICAL ILLUSION

The philosophers of Chelm could hold their own in any field of human knowledge, including the realm of political economy. Such complicated subjects as the monetary systems of nations held no terrors for them.

"It has been definitely established," said one of the thinkers "that there is only one large gold piece in the country and it constantly changes hands. This process is called circulation."

"It's not so," objected one of his audience. "I once saw two gold pieces in the hands of two individuals at the same time."

The deep thinker wrinkled his brow.

"That," he declared finally, "was an optical illusion, produced by the speed of the circulation," a reply which convinced even the skeptic.

THE CLINCHING ARGUMENT

The controversy that raged in Chelm over the relative importance of the sun and the moon will long be remembered. As usual the town was divided into two camps, sunists and moonists, and neither side would yield an iota to the other. Don't ask me to give you the grounds on which each side based its stand. They are too subtle and involved, and, besides, since the controversy is now happily settled, they have become unimportant.

How was it settled? By the wisdom of one of the Chelm philosophers, of course. "How can there be any doubt that the moon is more important than the sun?" he asserted. "Without the moon our nights would be pitch-dark. But does the sun do anything for us? The sun shines by day when there is already plenty of light."

CHELM FOUND SAFE

A stranger once came to Chelm and reported that the river that flowed through his city had overrun its banks and flooded half the town. When the Chelmites heard this they feared for their own city. What if they too should be flooded? So great was the anxiety in Chelm that some of the people lost all desire for food.

"There is no ground for fear!" a Chelm philosopher declared. "Our town is safe."

"How do you know?" asked the stranger.

"We have so many fish in our river that they drink up all the excess water," the philosopher explained.

And with that the anxiety that weighed on Chelm was lifted.

A TAILOR IS RENDERED HAPPY

There was a tailor in Chelm whose affairs were not going well at all. It looked very much as if competition, honored as the life of trade, would prove to be his death. There just wasn't enough work to go around.

After long and deep thought the tailor concluded there was only one hope for him. The Messiah must come! Then the dead would be resurrected and they would all need clothes. What a rush there would be on the tailors of Chelm!

It was not long, however, before another thought came and cast a shadow on his bright hope. The tailors would also be resurrected! What a host of tailors there must be waiting for resurrection! Again competition, worse perhaps than it was at present. The tailor became moody and despondent.

His wife went to one of Chelm's deep thinkers and begged for help. Without losing a minute the philosopher came to the tailor and spoke to him as follows:

"Your fears are groundless. It's true, of course, that the tailors will also be resurrected, but do they know anything about the latest fashions? How, then, will they be able to compete with you?"

Lemach and Lekish

BUTTER DOWN, BUTTER UP

Of the deep thinkers of Chelm the two deepest were Lemach and Lekish, and the Chelmites never stopped debating which of the two was the deeper. But being true philosophers, they themselves stood above the controversy. Indeed, Lemach and Lekish were fast friends.

The two met one day and a single glance at his friend's countenance revealed to Lemach that Lekish was deeply disturbed.

"Tell me what it is that weighs on your mind," said Lemach.

"Lemach," said Lekish, "is it not an established fact that whenever a poor man, like you or me, drops his bread it always falls butter-side down?"

"It is so indeed," Lemach replied.

"This morning," Lekish continued, "I dropped my bread and it fell butter-side up."

"Ah!" Lemach exclaimed, as he realized fully the strangeness of the event.

"All day," Lekish continued, "I have thought about it, and I am unable to explain it."

"Mmm!" Lemach mused as his intellect began to grapple with the problem. But he struggled in vain. Sunk in silent meditation, the two sat together a long time and when darkness fell they separated and sighed deeply as they bade each other good night.

At a small hour of the morning, Lekish was awakened by a gentle knocking on his window. He opened the door and Lemach stood on the threshold in the moonlight.

"I have the explanation!" Lemach whispered. "It's because you buttered your bread on the wrong side!"

And the two philosophers, clad in their nightrobes, embraced ecstatically beneath the moon.

BIRDS AND COWS

It is related that one day Lemach and Lekish were strolling outside the town of Chelm discoursing on the wonders of creation. It was a pleasant day in summer; above them the birds darted and twittered, and the cows grazed lazily in the meadows.

One of the philosophers stopped and became lost in thought.

"The ways of Heaven are mysterious," said he finally. "Consider the birds and the cows. The bird is small and his needs are modest. Nevertheless he has been given wings and he has access to the sky as well as the earth. The cow is big and her needs are much greater. Nevertheless she is held down to the earth."

Now, as the speaker looked up towards the sky, a flock of birds flew by and something fell on his nose. Hastily he turned aside and wiped his face with his sleeve.

"What is it?" asked his companion.

"I have found the solution to the mystery!" declared the other joyfully.

"Indeed! What have you found?" asked the other thinker.

"I have been shown the reason why the Lord in His wisdom and mercy thought it best not to give wings to the cow."

THE TELEGRAPH

Two large vehicles arrived in Chelm one day, laden with long spiked logs, rolls of wire, ladders and tools. There were men in the vehicles who set to work at once, planting the logs at regular intervals along the road, and stringing the wire from one log to another.

The people of Chelm were thrown into a furor, bordering on panic.

"What are they doing?" was the whispered question that ran from mouth to ear.

But no one knew, and all eyes turned to Lemach who answered without hesitation.

"They are putting up a telegraph system for Chelm," he told them.

"And what is that?" they demanded.

"Suppose," Lemach explained, "your wife has gone to visit her aunt in the big city a hundred miles away and you want her to come home at once. So you send her a telegram and in one hour she is on the way to Chelm."

"In one hour!" they marvelled.

"That is all it takes," Lemach assured them.

"But how? How is it done?" they insisted.

Lemach became lost in thought.

"It's very simple," said he. "You touch the wire in Chelm and something sounds in the big city, and that's how they know."

But one skeptic knitted his brow.

"My head," he declared, "doesn't take it in."

But just then a stray dog appeared, and seeing the crowd, he was about to make off, when Lemach whistled to him. The dog stopped in amazement: there was a kindly note in Lemach's call to which he was unaccustomed. He hesitated and then, in somewhat gingerly fashion, approached the philosopher.

"Look," said Lemach solemnly. "Here is the dog's rear: that's Chelm. Here is his head: that's the big city. And here is his tail: that's the telegraph. Now see what I do!"

And Lemach gave the dog's tail a violent pull. The dog uttered a shrill yelp and ran away.

"That's how the telegraph works," Lemach concluded. "You pull it in Chelm and you hear it in the big city a hundred miles away!"

And everybody understood and marveled.

HOW TO STAY SOLVENT

A stroll through the market place of Chelm brought deep furrows to the brow of Lemach and when, in the dusk between Afternoon and Evening Prayers, his faithful companions gathered around him in *shul,* there were deep sighs when he told them what he had seen and heard.

"Yes," he reported, "our merchants are in a bad way. There are too few customers and too many competitors. They all sell for less than it cost them. They lose money on everything: the dry goods merchant on every yard of calico; the grocer on every pound of onions; the market women on every apple and *beygl.* The longer they continue the more impoverished they become. Alas it has always been so, it was never any better."

A chorus of deep-felt "Oys" rose up from the circle. But one of the younger ones, somewhat bolder than the others, ventured a question.

"Forgive me, I beg you," said he, "but if every day they lose money, how do they stay in business?"

In the silence that followed you could almost hear the sage ponder. The disciples waited hopefully, but as the silence continued some of them began to shuffle and whisper, and the sage's countenance became more and more somber. Then the clouds lifted and he turned to the questioner with his customary gentle smile.

"My son," said he, "your question is a question, but you forget one thing."

"Aha!" cried the disciples, "Aha!"

"You forget," the sage continued, "that on Sabbaths and holidays the market is shut down, so they manage to stay solvent."

HOW DO THEY LIVE?

Lekish spoke up in support of his colleague's findings, setting the matter in a larger framework.

"It has to do with the science called political economy," he announced, "and I can give you another illustration. Consider the men in our town who look after our communal needs—the *rov,* the *shames,* the *dayen*—pious and learned men, all of them. Do we pay them enough to live on? Certainly not. How then do they live? They are kept alive by their piety. They fast on Mondays and Thursdays. If not for these fasts, I hate to think what would happen to them. They would, *cholile,* starve to death."

A PHILOSOPHER ABROAD

It happened once that Lemach fell into a mood of melancholy. For days and nights he had pondered on the higher mysteries, on life and death, on things that "eye hath not seen nor ear ever heard," and many were the questions that even he was unable to answer. And early one morning he said to his wife:

"Gitele, I have come to the limit of my wisdom. I will now go to foreign lands. I will seek out the wisest of the wise and lay my questions before them."

"How will you travel to foreign lands?" asked Gitele. "You have no passport."

Lemach wrinkled his brow and found the answer.

"My good friend Lekish," said he, "has a passport. I will use his."

Gitele wept profusely, but in the end she accepted her husband's resolve as an edict from on high. Lemach obtained his friend's passport and set out for the frontier.

"Remember," was Gitele's last admonition. "Your name is not Lemach, but Lekish."

"The name, yes, of course," said Lemach with the absent air that marks every genuine thinker, "Lemach no, not Lemach, of course not!"

And realizing the gravity of the matter, he kept reiterating in his mind as he travelled towards the border:

"Lemach—no! Not Lemach, of course not!"

He reached the frontier, and a guard stood there and ordered him to stop. The man had a fierce up-curling mustache, and in his hand he held an instrument which Lemach knew was capable of dealing death.

"Passport!" the guard snapped.

Lemach produced the document.

"Your name!" the man demanded.

"My name—yes—my name. Lemach—certainly not!" Lemach replied.

THE WATCHMAN

Lemach came to the capital of the foreign land and in one of the squares he saw a great building. Never in his life had he seen such an immense structure!

"Good friend," said he to a passer-by, "what building is that?"

"It's the government bank," said the man.

"And it's full of money?" asked Lemach.

"Every nook and corner of it—millions and millions!"

"And who is the soldier with the gun near the door?"

"He keeps watch over the money."

"Isn't there danger that the soldier himself will steal the money?" asked Lemach.

"It's all put away in big iron boxes and double-locked and bolted with iron bars. No thief could open them."

"In that case," said Lemach, "what need is there for the soldier?"

But the man had become impatient.

"I don't know," he declared, "perhaps you can answer the questions yourself."

Lemach looked hard at the soldier and thought very deeply.

"It's clear," said he finally, "that this soldier is really a thief, and he is stationed here to keep him from robbing other places."

HAT AND GLOVES

Nor did Lemach return to Chelm empty-handed. He brought a variety of things that bespoke the greatness of the capital, and among them a newspaper. The thing in the newspaper that aroused most curiosity was a big advertisement of a clothing store showing the picture of a man wearing a straw hat and gloves.

"This is strange," said the philosophers of Chelm. "If the season of the year is winter, why is he wearing a straw hat? If it's summer, why is he wearing gloves?"

At last Lemach himself found the answer!

"It's summer!" he declared. "And why is he wearing gloves? Because he is going out to pluck nettles!"

THE MELAMED *AND THE* CZAR

In the chronicles of Chelm there is proof that the town was once visited by the Czar himself! And to silence all skeptics let the following be cited from the record concerning the *melamed* of Chelm, and his friend the philosopher, Lemach.

The *melamed*, it appears, made it a practice to put away a small part of his earnings and in time he was able to build himself a little house. But soon enough he learned how true are the words of the sage who said: "The more property, the more anxiety."

Into the humble abode of the *melamed* once strode a huge official in uniform who took a stamped paper out of a portfolio and in a loud voice proclaimed:

"His Majesty, the Czar, commands you to pay one ruble!"

The terrified *melamed* searched in a hidden nook, found the sum demanded and gave it to the man who pocketed it and departed. A little later the *melamed* recovered from his daze, and wondered greatly over what had befallen him. Unable to answer the questions that pounded on his brain, he went to his friend Lemach.

He found Lemach sunk in meditation and, after rousing him, related the strange visit of the official.

"I understand everything," said the *melamed*, "but there are three questions that I am unable to answer. First: How does the Czar know my name? Second: What need has the Czar of my ruble? Isn't he rich enough without it? Third: In order to collect my ruble the Czar sends a man from the capital to Chelm. Doesn't it cost more than a ruble to ride from the capital to Chelm and from Chelm back to the capital?"

Lemach didn't answer at once. It was not his way. He meditated a long time in silence, then turned to his friend with the assurance of a man who knows he is standing on firm ground.

"Three questions, three answers," he began in the terse style of the true thinker. "First: How does the Czar know your name? The answer is simple enough. Do you remember the Czar's visit to Chelm last year? You and I stood together by the side of the road, waiting for the Czar's carriage to pass. 'Motl Melamed,' I said to you, 'here comes the carriage of the Czar!' No doubt, the Czar heard me say it and wrote your name down in his notebook. Now for the second question: Why does the Czar need your ruble? The answer to that is also simple. There is a correspondence between the Kingdom of earth and the Kingdom of Heaven. The Talmud says: "The governance of the earth is like the governance of Heaven.' The King of Heaven, blessed be He, is holiness itself; nevertheless He is glad to hear you say 'Holy, holy, holy!' In the same way the Czar is glad to have your ruble. And now we come to your third question. You are mistaken if you think the man came to Chelm just for your ruble. You have no understanding of state matters. Listen and learn. That man, you should know, was a soldier in the capital; and when his period of service was over he went to say good-by to the Czar. In the course of conversation the man mentioned the fact that he was going to Chelm. 'To Chelm?' said the Czar. 'In that case, do me a favor. There is a *melamed* in Chelm who owes me a ruble. Collect the ruble from him and send it to me.' "

"Lemach," said the *melamed,* "all that men say about you is only half the truth. You are the ornament of Chelm. You are wisdom itself."

FRESH AIR

Lemach and Lekish often recall the memorable journey they took to the neighboring town of Babinka with Yokl the wagoner and his horse, Old Cholera. Originally Yokl himself employed the two words as a term of abuse, but in time they became the name by which the old worn-out nag was identified.

Both sages went to Babinka on important missions: Lemach to pay his annual visit of homage to a retired old teacher; and Lekish to attend a circumcision feast where he would be accorded the high honor of holding the infant in his lap during the operation—to serve, in other words, as the *sandek*. It was a bright autumn morning when they set out, and both philosophers felt invigorated and grateful to the Lord of the Universe for every breath of the crisp air they inhaled.

Now the distance from Chelm to Babinka was not great, but the road was out of the ordinary. It consisted of a series of inclines, some gentle, some steep, with only short level intervals between them.

"Start moving, a plague in your inwards!" Yokl encouraged his horse, and cracked his whip. The wagon began to grind and they were off.

"What do you say to my Old Cholera, my lion, my eagle?" Yokl smiled to his passengers. "Not bad for an old bundle of bones, hey? I've had him myself for fifteen years, and he was no prancing colt when he fell into my hands."

The animal was certainly not an impressive sight. His head hung low, his middle was sunk deep, his ribs begged to be counted and the bones of his crop and haunches nearly burst out of his skin.

"You are fortunate to have a horse like that," said Lemach solemnly. "He gives you an opportunity to earn great merit by practising the command to have compassion for God's dumb creatures."

"And it is not right to curse him the way you do," Lekish added.

"He doesn't mind in the least," said Yokl with assurance. "He knows I don't mean it. And do you see this whip? It never touches his skin. I just crack it over him and he likes the sound."

They came to the first incline and Yokl pulled Old Cholera to a stop.

"Here you will kindly step out," said Yokl ingratiatingly, "and the three of us will push the wagon up the slope. My eagle will also help out a little."

The two sages and the wagoner applied their shoulders, and

without too much effort they pushed the wagon to the top of the incline. Before them the road dropped down at a rather steep angle.

"Don't bother to return to the wagon," said Yokl. "We must hold it back or it will go hurtling down and scatter our bones on the road, not to speak of Old Cholera who is sure to get his hocks cracked. He might even, God forbid, hit the ground with his teeth."

The sages grasped the spokes of the hind wheels, Yokl held on to the tailpiece with all his strength, and the horse and wagon came safely to the bottom.

"Now," said Yokl proudly, "we have a level stretch of road, and you can climb back into my chariot."

"Show what you can do, old carcass, an epilepsy in your ribs!" Yokl cried to his horse, as he cracked the whip over him.

But all too soon, and in spite of Old Cholera's magisterial pace, the level stretch came to an end and the road took a winding turn up the shoulder of a hill.

Again the passengers got down and pushed, and when they came to the top of the hill they again labored to restrain it from tumbling headlong down the slope together with the horse. When they sat down in the wagon, their breath was coming short.

It came still shorter when they went through the same procedure a third time and a fourth. But at the end of the fifth bout they saw the first houses of the ramshackle town of Babinka and sighed with relief. The wagon ground to a halt before a tavern, and the two sages entered for nourishment and rest.

"Lemach," said Lekish when they felt restored, "there is a question pounding in my head and I can't answer it. No one will deny that for all things in heaven and earth there is a reason, and a philosopher must probe until he finds it. I know the reason why you have taken this journey to Babinka and the reason why I have taken it. I also know why Yokl the wagoner has done it: he has a wife and children to feed. But the horse, Lemach, why did that poor beast have to take this weary journey? Why couldn't he have stayed in his stall in Chelm chewing his straw and resting his old bones?"

For a time Lemach pondered in silence.

"You are right, Lekish," he finally said. "It was a sin for Yokl to make the horse come also, and it is only proper he should know it and atone for it."

So they sent for Yokl, who had already unharnessed Old Cholera and taken him to the stable for his midday ration of oats. Yokl was now regaling himself in the kitchen with scraps from the pots and pans, and bits of conversation with the innkeeper.

Yokl came and stood before Lekish and Lemach, who looked as stern as it is possible for Chelm philosophers to look. The wagoner was frightened. Why did they send for him except to give him a dressing-down for what they endured on the road? But instead they demanded to know what need there was for him to take his horse on the hard journey, and accused him of violating the command that enjoins compassion for God's dumb creatures.

But Yokl himself was also dumb. He was bewildered and said not a word.

"Do you confess your sin?" said Lemach.

"Will you do penance for it?" said Lekish.

"No!" the wagoner finally blurted. "No sin! No penance!"

"So hardened you are?" said Lemach.

"You have no regard for your soul?" said Lekish.

"But I—I had to take him along," Yokl pleaded.

"Why?" said Lemach and Lekish in unison.

"How could I leave him behind, in his dark and nasty stall? Isn't he too entitled to look upon God's bright and beautiful world? And besides, he needs——"

"What? What does he need?"

"He needs," said Yokl, almost in a whisper. "He needs the fresh air."

The Chelm philosophers sat silent. Then each one in turn stood up and pressed the wagoner's hand.

LEKISH AND HIS STRANGE JOURNEY

It was well-known in Chelm that there was something peculiar about Lekish. He lived with his wife and children, to all appearances like any other Chelmite, but in reality Lekish waited. He waited for the real head of his household to arrive. Yes, the real head, as though he himself were not the head of his household. Every day Lekish expected his arrival.

Lekish, it should be said at the outset, was inordinately proud of his native city, Chelm. He was convinced that no other city, not even the capital, was superior to it. He had no patience with those who sang the praises of other cities, belittling Chelm expressly or by implication. Whenever such frivolous talk was heard in the circle of deep thinkers around the synagogue stove, a little smile would curl up from the beard of Lekish which everybody understood. And it happened one fateful day that Getsl the *shadchn,* who had visited the capital and was brimming over with what he had seen there, was annoyed by that smile, and turning on Lekish, he said:

"Why don't you go there and see for yourself?"

"I will," said Lekish, nor did he realize how those two words were going to affect the course of his life.

The following day Lekish set out for the big city. He tightened the belt of his breeches, tied his girdle around his waist and slung over his shoulder a little bundle containing his *tales* and *tfilin* as well as a scant supply of bread and cheese, for it is well known that the material needs of the genuine philosopher are modest. It was a pilgrimage in reverse that Lekish embarked upon, for its purpose was to vindicate the shrine from which he departed rather than to worship at the goal for which he was bound.

The day was hot and heavy, but his heart was light and his step springy. For a good distance the road was level, then as it turned and sloped gently downward, the city of Chelem became lost to view. Lekish trudged on. The sun mounted higher and it became still hotter. Peasant carts rumbled by and raised clouds of dust on the road.

Now the sun stood overhead and Lekish came to a crossroad. Near it rose a broad sycamore and a little brook gurgled over gray and golden pebbles. It was an alluring spot, and the same moment Lekish became aware that he was hungry. He washed his hands in the brook, pronounced the blessing, and ate of his bread and cheese. Then he drank from the brook and chanted grace.

"It's only right that I should rest here a little," said Lekish. He sat down in the shade of the tree, his back against the trunk, pervaded by a drowsy sense of well-being. His eyelids drooped and his thoughts wandered off into the haze of sleep.

Suddenly Lekish roused himself. A disquieting thought smote upon his mind.

"If I fall asleep, how will I know what direction to follow when I wake up?" he asked himself.

Now Lekish was wide awake, and sat beneath the tree and pondered. The solution he found was exceedingly simple, as indeed all great inventions are. Lekish took off his shoes, and put them down on the road with the toes pointing toward the big city for which he was bound.

"Now, I'm safe," said he with that vast complacency which sometimes comes over a philosopher. "When I wake up I'll know what direction to take!" And Lekish sat down again beneath the tree, and almost immediately fell asleep.

Lekish slept, but all around him the world was teeming with wakeful life. The ants at his feet were heaving and struggling with the burdens they carried to their lairs; the birds darted about seeking subsistence in the air, in the trees and on the ground; and wagons and carts rolled by in both directions, bearing the good fruits of the farms to the cities and the ingenious devices of the cities to the farms. And it happened that a wagon going to Chelm, heaped high with stalks of green peas, rolled past near the philosopher's shoes. And some of the stalks that hung down low swept the road and, as the wagon moved slowly by, they caught the philosopher's shoes and turned them completely around. Such was the strange thing that leaped from the lap of destiny while Lekish slept.

Lekish woke up refreshed and a happy smile lay hidden deep in his beard. He saw his shoes standing where he left them, took careful note of the direction in which they pointed, and put them back on his feet.

"Many uses," he mused, "are hidden in things, of which the simple are not aware. But the man to whom God has granted wisdom, discovers them."

Lekish tightened his belt, looked to the knot in his girdle, took up his bundle, and resumed his journey. He hoped to reach the capital by nightfall, but great was his surprise when, as the road took a turn, he saw it plainly in the distance and not far off.

"So that's the capital!" said Lekish to himself viewing it from the road. "It's not so big. In fact, it's not any bigger than Chelm. But that's how men are. The thing that is not theirs always appears to them bigger and better and finer."

Lekish walked on and came to the first straggling houses of the outskirts.

"What is there about these houses," said he, "that makes them better than the houses on the outskirts of Chelm? It seems to me they are no better!"

Now he entered the city itself and looked around at the streets and houses.

"I swear," said he, "I have seen streets and houses like these in Chelm also! The streets are narrow and crooked and the houses need new roofs. And even the goats nibbling at the fences are like the goats in Chelm!"

He reached the market place and what he saw there filled him with wonder and triumph.

"Blessed art thou, O Chelm!" he cried. "Not even the capital can boast a better market place than yours. Everything here may also be found in yours! The same stalls, the same stands, the same well in the center, the same hollow log where the goats and chickens quench their thirst. Chelm, my Chelm, you are vindicated."

But Lekish was still unsatisfied. He was thirsty for some more draughts of triumph.

"Friend!" he cried to one who ran towards him, his coattails flying and perspiration dripping from his forehead, "tell me, are there any synagogues in this city?"

The man stopped in amazement and Lekish had to repeat the question.

"How then?" the man answered. "Everywhere! Everywhere!"

"Take me to the biggest!" said Lekish.

The man who had been rushing and sweating but really had nothing to do, took Lekish to the place he desired to see.

"Now blessed be the name of the Lord of Hosts for ever and ever!" Lekish exclaimed. "The biggest synagogue of the capital is no bigger and finer than the Great Synagogue of Chelm!"

Lekish went out and continued his journey through the streets of the city. Towards nightfall he came upon a street that was strangely like his own. He went on and came to a house that was also like his own. He entered the house and sat down to rest, feeling tired and bewildered.

"Where is the master of this house?" said he to a woman who came in carrying a market bag.

"Is this the best joke you can think up, philosopher mine?" the woman asked.

She set food before him, children came into the house, and they all ate.

"Everything in this city is exactly as in Chelm," he mused. "It's not true that there is a finer city in the world than Chelm. But where is the master of this house?"

"He is sure to come soon," said Lekish to himself after eating and chanting grace. "I want very much to see him. I'll stay here and wait for him."

But that night the master of the house failed to come. Nor did he come on the morrow, nor on the days that followed.

And Lekish continues to live in that house with the woman and the children. Lekish is happy and contented, for Chelm, the city of his pride and love, triumphed against her traducers. But every now and then he turns to the woman who brings him his food and says:

"When will the master of the house come home? Isn't he ever going to come?"

The Quips and Pranks of Hershele Ostropolyer

Foreword

HERSHELE OSTROPOLYER was not a mythical figure. He lived and laughed in the Eastern Europe of the second half of the eighteenth century, committing bold pranks, telling stupendous lies, inventing droll conceits, quipping and clowning to the joy of his own and succeeding generations. Sometimes subtle, sometimes broad and coarse, his shifts and devices were never dull.

Hershele played a variety of roles, including even that of a Robin Hood of sorts. He did not, *cholile*, rob the rich, not even to give to the poor, but he represented the poor man's vengeance against the rich, especially the miserly rich. The rich miser ranks with the grasping peasant and ignorant villager as a favorite butt of his pranks. And since, as in every society, the positions of authority were usually held by the more affluent, Hershele became the champion of the humble against the exalted. He owes his popularity, therefore, as much to the gratification he brought to the poor and lowly as to the brilliance of his wit and the daring of his inventions.

Hershele Ostropolyer was the foremost of a goodly company of wags and pranksters—Motke Chabad, Froym Greidiker, Shayke Fayfer and others, and his greater renown absorbed many an exploit of his confreres. For who but Hershele was bold enough or ingenious enough to perform this or that feat? Even some of the escapades of illustrious non-Jewish pranksters have been credited to him. There has been, indeed, a sort of "cultural exchange" among the wags of different nations, including Till Eulenspiegel the German, and Mulla Nasreddin, claimed by the Iranians, the Turks, and the Arabs.

The Quips and Pranks of Hershele Ostropolyer

A *ONE-LEGGED* GOOSE

HERSHELE BECAME acquainted with hunger when he was still a child in the home of his widowed mother and her large brood, and he soon developed a knack for finding ways to appropriate food. But the most he could do was to keep the enemy at bay, so when, while still in his teens, he was invited by a well-to-do uncle to spend some weeks in his home, Hershele did not wait for the invitation to be repeated.

Now, habits acquired in early life have a way of clinging fast. Early one morning Hershele stole into the kitchen, and seeing a baked goose on a big platter, he ripped off one of the drumsticks and consumed it. When the meal was served his uncle eyed the one-legged goose sternly.

"Who ate the other drumstick?" he asked with a glance at Hershele.

"This goose," Hershele replied innocently, "must have had only one leg."

"Have you ever seen a one-legged goose?" asked his aunt.

"Oh, yes," said Hershele. "Many times."

That afternoon they all went walking and there, at the edge of a pond, stood a goose on one leg!

"Look, Uncle!" cried Hershele, "There's one of those one-legged geese!"

The man approached the goose and clicked his tongue at it.

Immediately the other leg appeared. He looked scornfully at Hershele.

"But, Uncle," said Hershele with the wide-eyed expression of innocence for which he became famous, "why didn't you click your tongue at the goose on the table? We could have had two drumsticks instead of one."

HERSHELE A PERSISTENT GUEST

This uncle was a rather timid soul, and Hershele, of course, took full advantage of his diffidence. He stayed on and on. But there comes a time when even a worm will turn, and the poor host began to throw out hints that became more and more pointed.

"In this city," he told Hershele, "prices keep going up all the time. A meal that cost two gilden only a short time ago now costs three."

"Yes," Hershele agreed, "in a big city the cost of living is high. In my town you can get an excellent meal for only two gilden."

"In that case," said his host eagerly, "why don't you go back to your town?"

"My town?" Hershele opened his eyes wide. "What are you saying, Uncle? Who in my town has two gilden?"

Things got worse and finally his worried uncle offered to pay Hershele a lump sum if he would leave.

"A hundred gilden," said Hershele.

"A hundred gilden!" the host jumped. "In no time a ne'er-do-well like you would run through the money and you'd come back here. No, I'll send you, instead, ten gilden every month."

"No, Uncle," said Hershele. "What will an unlucky devil like me do if before paying me the full sum you go bankrupt?"

After another week his uncle surrendered. He gave Hershele the hundred gilden and said to him:

"Let there be no hard feeling between us. I want you to know that you'll be welcome to come here at times, especially when we celebrate some happy occasion."

In the morning Hershele went away and just before the dinner hour he was back.

"I was deeply touched by what you told me when we parted," he said, "and suddenly I said to myself: What happier occasion could there be for my uncle than my departure? No doubt he is celebrating right now, I said to myself. So I've come to celebrate with you."

NO PLAGUE, BUT—

Hershele felt no inclination to return to his oversized and underfed family, so he decided to go out and see the world. He came upon many towns and stopped in many inns, but the ancient problem remained unsolved: he was nearly always hungry.

What a wonderful world this would be, thought Hershele, gazing at the blue sky and green fields, if not for this accursed hunger! And he remembered ruefully one of the many proverbs for which his grandmother, peace unto her, was famous. "If the belly," she used to say, "lay in the grave, the head would wear a crown of gold."

He came once to a certain town and after several vain applications, he was received by a benevolent housewife who recognized in him a deserving starveling. She invited him in, and placed before him a large bowl of steaming boiled potatoes. Hershele didn't waste a moment, but he hadn't swallowed more than three when the master of the house appeared and sat down opposite him. The man was fascinated by the speed with which Hershele caused the potatoes to disappear. Finally he spoke:

"From what town," he asked, "does a young man come?"

"Kazanka," said Hershele, naming the first town that came to his head.

"Kazanka!" the man nearly jumped. "Why, that's my town! I was born there!"

"My luck!" said Hershele to himself. "Now I have to be careful."

"How long is it," he asked his host, "that you've been away from Kazanka?"

"From Kazanka?" the man mused. "Let me see . . . it must be at least twenty-five years."

"God be praised!" thought Hershele, and resumed his onslaught on the potatoes.

"But I remember Kazanka very well," his host assured him. "I remember many of the people who lived in Kazanka. Tell me, how is Reb Feivl, the lumber merchant?"

"Dead," said Hershele.

"Blessed be the Righteous Judge!" the host spoke piously. "I suppose," he went on, "the business is now in the hands of Ruvn, the eldest son. How is Ruvn?"

"Dead," said Hershele.

"Ay, ay, ay!" the man mourned. "He had a kind heart, Ruvn. But let me see. How is the *shames* of the new *shul*? He was a young man when I left."

"Dead," said Hershele.

"He too? How sad! And his brother-in-law, Velvl? We used to be good friends."

"Dead," said Hershele.

The sorrowful host mentioned a number of other people he knew in Kazanka. They were all dead.

By this time Hershele had liquidated the contents of the bowl, and he sat back and sighed.

The host looked at him quizzically.

"Tell me, young man," he said. "What happened in Kazanka? Was the town swept by a plague?"

"A plague?" Hershele replied, wiping his lips. "God forbid! Kazanka is a good healthy town. Only——"

"Only what?"

"You see, sir," Hershele explained. "It's I who am not quite healthy. I suffer from a sickness known as hunger. The doctors don't know very much about it. They are never hungry. Let me tell you about one of my symptoms. When the sickness attacks me and someone places a bowl of hot potatoes in front of me, I become dead to the world, and all the people in the world, including those in Kazanka, are dead to me."

IN HIS FATHER'S FOOTSTEPS

It was late one night when Hershele, after a long trek, came to an inn and ordered the landlady to give him a nice room and a good supper. The woman eyed him sharply, and his appearance as well as the fact that he had arrived on foot, led her to conclude that he was either a beggar or a tramp.

"I'm sorry," she told him. "There isn't a morsel in the house. My guests have eaten up everything."

Hershele looked down with a woebegone expression, then jumped up and paced furiously up and down the room.

"I have no choice," he muttered. "I'll have to do what my father did."

The woman became frightened.

"Tell me," she stammered, "what was it—what did your father do?"

But Hershele seemed unaware of her presence. He approached the table and struck it a mighty blow.

"I have no choice," he cried, "I'll have to do it!"

Now the woman was terrified.

"Young man," she implored. "Don't, I beg you! I'll bring you something to eat. At once, at once!"

Hershele ate and ate well. He wiped his lips, sat back, and heaved a deep satisfied sigh.

"Now, young man," said the landlady, "won't you please tell me what it was your father did and you were going to do?"

"Certainly," Hershele replied. "You see," he said confidentially, "whenever my father, may he rest in peace, found no supper he used to go to bed hungry."

HERSHELE FINDS A FRIEND

On the road one day Hershele picked up a boon companion and the two travelled on together. Avreml was a good sort, not too clever, but faithful.

They came to a town where they had the good fortune to be received by a generous citizen who invited them to sit down and join him in a meal which was being served to him.

"Two plates of good chicken broth for our young guests!" he ordered the servant girl.

The plates arrived and the sight made the eyes of the two guests sparkle and their mouths water. The surface was golden and covered with rich eyelets that permitted not a whiff of steam to rise up and suggest that the broth beneath might be very hot.

Hershele took a good spoonful into his mouth. He put down the spoon, sat back, and his eyes filled with tears that rolled over his cheeks.

"Why do you weep?" asked the host.

"Why shouldn't I weep?" Hershele answered. "I just remembered that a year ago today my uncle Moyshe fell to the bottom of the well."

Avreml took a spoonful of the broth and he too winced and wept.

"You too?" the host queried. "What happened to *your* uncle?"

"I have no uncle," Avreml answered. "I weep because the uncle of this dear friend of mine didn't take him along when he went to the bottom of the well."

The treacherous broth was followed by two slices of succulent fish, but the fish only added to the rift between the two comrades.

They were not of equal size, those two slices, and Hershele acted with speed and possessed himself of the bigger one. Avreml was indignant.

"Where are your manners?" he demanded. "Where were you brought up? In the woods?"

"And you?" Hershele retorted. "What would you have done? Would you have taken the smaller slice?"

"I certainly would," said Avreml proudly.

"Well, there it is! It's yours. Take it and be happy!" said Hershele.

HERSHELE AND HIS CREDITORS

Hershele returned to his native town and shifted as well as he could. One of his shifts was to borrow money. Now, borrowing money, as is well known, is an art, but not paying it back is an even greater art. Hershele became adept in both.

Having wheedled a small loan from a neighbor, the latter wanted to know when it would be returned.

"Do I know?" answered Hershele. "Am I a prophet or a fortuneteller?"

Time passed and the lender claimed his money.

"This month," said Hershele, "I am unable to pay it back."

"But you told me the same, last month!"

"Well," said Hershele with triumph, "didn't I keep my word?"

Another acquaintance whom he asked for a loan denied knowing him.

"Bad," said Hershele, shaking his head. "It's a bad sign. I'm sorry for you."

"What do you mean?" the man demanded.

"A friend of mine," explained Hershele, "became very sick. If your friend doesn't know you, the doctor told me, it means that the next day he will die. And that is exactly what happened," Hershele concluded, wiping a tear from the corner of his eye.

It appears that Hershele's acquaintance was so moved by the story that he became one of his creditors.

Another creditor became tired of Hershele's frequent requests and gave him an abrupt and final "no" for an answer. Thereupon Hershele stood up in front of him and began to recite the "Magnified and Sanctified," the prayer for the dead.

"What are you doing?" the man cried in alarm. "I am not dead yet!"

"For me," answered Hershele, "you are!"

But once, in order to obtain money, he was compelled to pawn his watch.

Late one night he knocked on the shutter of the pawnshop. The proprietor, clad in nightshirt and cap, stuck out his frightened face.

"What time is it?" Hershele asked him.

The man was furious.

"For this . . . for this . . . you come and———" he spluttered.

"I don't trust any watch but my own," Hershele informed him.

On another occasion he had to resort to a usurer whose demands were much harder to withstand.

One cold winter day he came to Hershele and insisted that he accompany him to the judge. "I can't make you pay, but he will," the man gloated.

"How many overcoats have you?" asked Hershele.

"Is this a new trick?" the usurer replied.

"Trick?" answered Hershele innocently. "How can I go out in this cold without an overcoat? Bring me an overcoat and I'll go with you to the judge."

The man returned with an overcoat and the two proceeded to the judge. The latter listened to the moneylender and then called on Hershele to reply.

"Your Honor," said Hershele, "I hesitate to say anything about this unfortunate man. But I am compelled to inform you that he is not in his right mind. He lays claim to everything he sees. He can't help it, poor man. To prove what I say, ask him, for example, to whom this overcoat I am wearing belongs."

The usurer didn't wait to be asked.

"To me, of course!" he declared. "I loaned it to you to wear before we left to come here."

The judge peered closely at the claimant. "Go home, my man," he said. "Go home and try to calm down. Tell your wife to give you some hot milk. It's good for the nerves."

HERSHELE KNOWS BETTER

In those days Hershele was so poor he had to use his floor for a bed and his fist for a pillow. Nevertheless, he still visited the tavern and managed to pay in cash, his credit having run out long before.

"Hershele," they said to him once, "why don't you stop wasting your substance on drink and buy yourself at least a pillow to lay your head on?"

"Not I," said Hershele. "I know all about your pillows. Once, just to convince myself, I placed a feather under my head before falling asleep. I got up the next morning with a stiff neck and a headache. So I reasoned: if a single feather can play so much havoc, what will a whole pillow do?"

POOR THIEVES!

Hershele, trusting in Providence, took a wife and set up a home of a sort. And strange as it may appear, his domicile was visited by thieves, and not once but twice.

"Get up!" his wife whispered in his ear. "There are thieves in the house!"

"I know it," Hershele replied, "but I can't get up. I'm burning with shame. There isn't a thing in the house worth taking!"

The second time, Hershele jumped up and seized the intruder. The thief tried to escape.

"Don't try to run away!" said Hershele. "Let me join you in your search. Perhaps your luck is better than mine!"

A GOOD BEGINNING

"Hershele," a neighbor asked him one day before the Passover feast, "how far have you gone with your Passover preparations?"

"Half of them are done," said Hershele.

"How do you mean that?" asked the neighbor.

"The leaven," Hershele explained, "has been removed from the house. All I have to do now is to bring in the matse and the other Passover provisions."

THE IRONY OF IT!

Hershele resolved to become a merchant and go for the higher brackets, but he realized that his beginning must be modest. So he acquired a rickety old cart and a broken-down plug and rode about among the neighboring villages and farmhouses, picking up merchandise for disposal in the town market. In the matter of fodder for the horse, Hershele did the best he could.

"Old chap," said he to his sad-looking steed. "I know that the straw I give you is not entirely to your taste. You are dreaming of oats, you old gourmet! But believe me, I, and my wife and my children are not pampering ourselves either. When things take a turn for the better I won't forget you, you may be sure."

Things refused to take a turn for the better. But one day he did manage to buy a bag of oats from a peasant, and took it to market. "A bag of oats!" thought Hershele. "The irony of it! This old plug of mine has to pull a bag of oats to market."

In the market he was approached by a dapper looking customer.

"You have something in that bag?" he asked. "What's in it?"

Hershele took the man a little distance away from the cart.

"Oats!" he whispered in his ear.

"Oats?" the man cried. "So what's the big secret?"

"Sh-sh-sh!" Hershele whispered. "I don't want the horse to hear us. He hasn't had an oat for weeks."

A TURN OF LUCK

In his business career Hershele dealt with merchandise of many kinds, but through no fault of his own all his ventures failed.

"Luck, my friends!" he said. "The primary thing is luck. The merchandise is not important. One of these days my luck will turn and then you'll see."

And one day his luck did turn. He had decided to become a dealer in antiques. He collected a quantity of old almanacs and set out to sell them. He stepped into a restaurant and approached a man who had that solid-citizen look.

"I already have a calendar," the man told him.

"No doubt, no doubt," said Hershele, "you have a calendar, but my wife and children have no bread."

The man took a probing look at Hershele.

"Very well," he said, "but I have no small change in my pocket. Go to my home and tell my wife I want her to buy one of your calendars. She will find some small change in a little box on the second shelf of the bookcase to the left."

Hershele hurried to the door when the man called him back.

"I have just looked again and found a gilden in my pocket. Give me a calendar and you don't have to go to my home."

Nevertheless, Hershele went. His directions for finding the coins were so explicit, the woman bought a calendar for her husband.

On his way back he stepped again into the restaurant. "My heart tells me," he said to himself, "that this customer should have still another calendar."

But the customer was gone.

"Whom are you looking for?" asked the waiter.

"There was a gentleman seated at this table a little while ago. He had a thick mustache and a flower in his buttonhole."

"He's in the back room, in conference with someone. He left word not to be disturbed," the waiter told him.

"No, no!" said Hershele, "I don't want to disturb him. I only want to deliver this calendar which he ordered from me."

The waiter gave Hershele a gilden for the calendar.

"It seems to me," he said, "that this calendar is an old one."

"It is," said Hershele, "but the gentleman is a great lover of antiques. Would you believe it? He bought three of these calendars from me. Imagine his delight when he looks at all three of them at once!"

Now that his luck had turned Hershele determined to take the tide at the flood and bear on to fortune. He would open a wineshop! Wine! It rejoiceth the heart of man, as the Psalmist says, and since the heart of man is inclined toward sadness, he is ever ready to lay down his shining gilden for the precious joy-bringer.

So Hershele bought himself a little keg of wine, pasted a little sign on his door and waited for customers. In came a man in search of joy and asked for a measure of wine, but desired to taste it before paying for it. Hershele drew some from the keg; the man took a sip and made a grimace.

"Wait," said Hershele, drawing again from his keg. "Try this wine."

Same wine, same grimace.

And a third time Hershele offered a draft from the keg with the same result. But now the man observed that the samples all came from the same source.

"What is this?" he scoffed. "Do you have three kinds of wine in one keg?"

"This keg?" Hershele whispered. "It's a magic keg. I can even draw vinegar from it. Would you like to buy some vinegar?"

The man turned and hurried out, slamming the door

Some more customers came in, but after a few tastes they all left without buying.

Hershele shook the keg and listened.

"Seems to me," he said, "there's just enough left for *kidesh.*

I too can be a customer, can't I?" And he put the keg away for Friday night.

"This venture," he mused, "is not a total loss. And what does that prove? It proves," he concluded, "that my luck is still holding out."

HE SELLS A MARVELOUS PAINTING

Hershele concluded that dealing in antiques was his special field. He collected a number of dubious items and took his stand in the market place. Prominent among them was a large piece of blank paper in a cheap frame.

One of those incurable antique collectors was intrigued by it.

"That," said Hershele, in answer to his question, "is an old and famous painting."

"But," said the man, "what does it show? I don't see a thing."

"There is a mystery about this painting which I can only reveal to the purchaser. The price is one gilden," Hershele answered in a solemn voice.

The collector decided to gamble and paid the gilden.

"This picture," Hershele informed him, "shows the children of Israel crossing the Red Sea."

"I don't see them," said the purchaser. "Where are the children of Israel?"

"They have already crossed," Hershele explained.

"And where are the Egyptians?" the man asked.

"The Egyptians?" said Hershele. "They haven't arrived yet."

"But the sea! Where is the sea?"

"You forget, dear friend, that the sea was divided. Part of it went one way and part the other. Naturally, the sea wasn't there and the artist couldn't show it."

HE INVENTS A WISDOM POWDER

It was time, Hershele felt, for a new enterprise. So he shook some flour into little paper bags, and went to the market place.

"It's the genuine wisdom powder!" he cried. "Swallow a little and you'll be as wise as King Solomon. Why be foolish and ignorant?"

Up came a man whose wife had a habit of letting him know, day in, day out, that he was the biggest fool in town, and bought a little bag from Hershele.

"How will I know that the powder has made me wise?" he asked.

"You'll feel it at once," Hershele assured him. "You will know what you didn't know before."

The man left, and on the way home he tasted some of the wisdom powder.

"Strange!" said he to himself. "This is ordinary flour. The man is a swindler."

He hurried back to market and accused Hershele of cheating him.

"I cheated you?" Hershele was indignant. "As soon as you swallowed the powder didn't you know something that you didn't know before? I'll leave it to any impartial judge to say if my powder didn't make you a wiser man."

HE BEFUDDLES A POOR WAITRESS

With empty pockets and an empty but grinding stomach, Hershele walked into a restaurant and asked the waitress to bring him two sugared tarts. She set them down and he called her back.

"I think I'll have two rolls instead. Is there much difference in price?" he asked.

"No difference at all. They are both the same price."

She took away the tarts and brought two rolls. Hershele ate them and the grinding in his stomach was somewhat abated.

"If," said he to his stomach, "you think I'm doing it out of love for you, you are wrong. I'm just sick and tired of your nagging."

He was on his way out when the waitress stopped him. "You haven't paid for the rolls," she told him.

"What do you mean I haven't paid for the rolls?" Hershele replied. "Didn't I give you the tarts in exchange for them?"

"Yes, but you didn't pay for the tarts either."

"The tarts? Did I eat the tarts?" Hershele demanded, and the poor waitress was too confused to reply.

THE WAY OF SOME GOATS

Hershele's neighbor, a *melamed,* came to him one day and begged him to step into his backyard and explain a mystery that baffled him. When Hershele arrived the *melamed* showed him a dead goat that lay there and told him a sad tale.

"This goat," he explained, "is a he-goat. Some time ago I went to market to buy a she-goat. A little milk, you know—my poor wife and I wanted a little milk. But some scamp out there sold me this he-goat for a she-goat. What could I do? When my wife told me the truth about the creature, I decided to keep it over the winter, and in the spring I would exchange it for a she-goat. In the meantime the goat pestilence broke out. But, as you know, it attacked only she-goats. 'How fortunate we are, said I to my wife. 'If I had brought home a she-goat, she would now be dead! But this morning I step out into my yard, and there lies my goat, quite dead as if he were a she-goat! Now, Hershele, they say you are a wise man, can you explain it to me? As for myself, I keep on racking my brain, but I just can't understand it."

Hershele looked long and mournfully at the dead goat.

"That's how some goats are," he finally consoled the *melamed.* "When it comes to giving milk, they are he-goats. When it comes to dying they are she-goats."

NOT SO EASY TO BECOME A PAUPER

Hershele and his friends were exchanging views one day on one of their favorite topics, the poor and the rich. Whatever they said had been said many times before, by themselves and others, but it remained for Hershele to throw new light on the subject.

"Why," he asked, "do we always bemoan the poor and complain how hard it is for a pauper to become a rich man? Is it any easier for a rich man to become a pauper? Let me tell you something about a man I knew. He was rich, very rich. A big business, a palatial home, elegant furniture, the finest clothes, and jewelry—his wife just sparkled with jewels! Well, one day he went and sold his entire stock of merchandise at a loss. You think that was easy? Then he sold his beautiful home. Has anyone of you ever tried to sell a home that was like a palace? But wait, we are not through yet. He sold his furniture, his wife's jewels, even his clothes. Can you imagine what headaches he had getting rid of all those things? And all the time the unfortunate man was being hounded by all sorts of people. At last, after months and months of torment, the poor man managed to become a pauper. So you see what I mean, don't you, my friends?" Hershele concluded.

HERSHELE A DIAMOND DEALER

Having applied his talents in a variety of business ventures without success, Hershele decided to become a dealer in diamonds. He was moved to make this decision when he learned that a certain diamond merchant named Bendet enjoyed the general contempt of the community by reason of his mean and miserly disposition. A man like that, Hershele felt, deserved a little attention from him.

He began by paying a little attention to his grooming. He trimmed his earlocks and beard, gave his clothes a good scrubbing and hardly knew himself when he looked into the mirror.

"Reb Hersh," said he with a low bow to what he saw, "how can we be of service to you, Reb Hersh?"

He presented himself at the door of Reb Bendet's grand home and was informed by a grand and gloomy servant that his master was not at home and was not expected until the end of the week.

"In that case," said Hershele, "go and tell your mistress that Reb Hersh, the noted diamond dealer, is here on a highly important and urgent matter, and in the absence of her husband desires to speak to her. I know, of course, that your mistress does not concern herself with your master's transactions, but this," Hershele continued, handing the man five gilden, "will perhaps convince you that on occasion she might do so."

Without the slightest change of expression the grand and gloomy one disappeared and in short order reappeared, bringing word that his mistress will see him. Hershele found the lady sipping her afternoon tea.

"Madam," said he with all the grandeur he could muster. "Have you ever seen a diamond as big as an egg? What would you say a stone like that is worth? Of course, if it is not possible to take the matter up with your husband, I'll have to go and see Reb Sender. I know he is your biggest competitor, but what choice do I have?"

The lady became all aflutter. Allow a deal like that to go to Sender? Unthinkable!

"My husband is away," she hastened to explain, "visiting the rich gentry all around, and offering them his jewels. He won't be back until Friday, a matter of only five days. Don't go to Reb Sender or any one else. In fact," she added looking at him shrewdly, "you don't even have to leave this house. My servants will prepare the guest room for you and will provide you with every comfort. Stay with us, Reb Hersh, you will not regret it."

"Madam," said Hershele with emotion, "Your hospitality touches me deeply. I accept your invitation."

In after years Hershele looked back on those five days with genuine nostalgia. "Don't judge me by the state you find me in now," he used to say to his cronies. "There was a period in my life when I lived like a lord."

The period ended, and towards nightfall on Friday Reb Bendet came home from his travels. His good wife hastened to apprise him of everything, but he said to her: "I can do nothing now. The Sabbath is approaching. Reb Hersh and I will attend services in *shul,* then will come the Sabbath meal, and tomorrow we observe the Sabbath day as usual. We cannot, of course, take up any matter of business on the holy day. But tomorrow night we'll go into the matter and bring it off properly. A diamond as big as an egg, hey? Well, well, leave everything to me."

Thus spoke the mighty Reb Bendet and the program he outlined was carried out with precision. In *shul* Hershele sat next to him at the East Wall, at home he sat next to him at his sumptuous table. Hershele was honored and feted like a messenger from the palace of the king.

At last the Sabbath came to an end and Reb Bendet and his wife, followed by Hershele, entered his private cabinet.

"Now, Reb Hersh," said Reb Bendet, "show me the stone."

"The stone?" Hershele repeated with all the innocence he could command. "The stone I don't have yet, but I see that I owe you an explanation. I must inform you then that I visit the richest homes in town and buy up old clothes. And it occurred to me what would I do if I found a diamond as big as an egg in the pocket of an old pair of trousers? How would I know what it's worth? How would I go about selling it? Then I remembered your reputation as a diamond expert and a man of honest dealing, and I decided to consult you. So your excellent wife thought I actually had the diamond! A slight misunderstanding, Reb Bendet, just a slight misunderstanding."

Reb Bendet ordered Hershele out of his house. What more could he do? Was he going to let the whole town find out about it and make merry over him?

But the town! Was there ever a town that had any secrets?

A DOG-AND-PIG THEORY

One of the customers of the eating place that served as rendezvous for Hershele and his cronies was a certain corpulent character whom they all disliked. The table he chose was next to theirs, but he never invited any of them to share in the huge quantities of food and drink he consumed. It was time, they felt, for Hershele to pay some attention to him.

Which Hershele did.

The obese patron sat near them, swilling and guzzling as usual, and keeping his ear cocked at the same time for the clever quips that crackled at the table next to his own: his doctor had told him that laughter was good for the digestion.

"My friends," said Hershele, "there is something that's been puzzling me. Why is it when a dog chases a pig and digs his teeth into the pig's ear, both of them set up a ferocious racket? Why the pig squeals and shrieks is plain enough: it's no joke to have your ear caught between the teeth of a dog. But why, I ask you, does the dog yelp and howl?"

The cronies were silent—stumped, all of them.

"Well," Hershele continued, "I have a little theory which will perhaps explain it. With the two so close together, the dog and the pig engage in conversation. 'You are already so fat,' says the dog, 'why do you have to go on being a pig?' To which the pig replies: 'Idiot! If I weren't a pig would I be so fat?' "

It was observed that in the laughter that followed, the corpulent customer failed to join.

UNFAIR TO THE FAIR

"I don't know why it is," said Hershele to his cronies one day, "that a woman is held in such light esteem. There are people, I am sorry to say, who consider a woman lower than criminals and apostates! And if you think I am stretching it, I'll tell you what once happened to me.

"I was on my travels and came to an inn that pleased me very much. The place had everything a man of good appetite and good taste could desire. The innkeeper was a wealthy man and he had an only daughter. I had a great desire to stay at that inn as long as possible: I had been knocking around a good deal and needed a rest. So I offered to marry the innkeeper's daughter. The man was overjoyed and the virgin was also satisfied. I stayed a few months, ate and drank of the best, and was thoroughly rested.

"The day of the wedding approached and I saw that I must do something. So one day I remarked to the innkeeper:

" 'You know, there are quite a few thieves and felons in my family.'

" 'That's nothing,' said the man and waved the matter aside as though thieves and felons were of no consequence.

"The following day I said to him:

" 'You know, there are also informers and apostates in my family.'

" 'That's nothing at all,' he said.

"Can you imagine it? Informers and apostates meant nothing to him!

"The third day I said to him:

" 'There is a woman in my family—my wife.'

"The man jumped to his feet, cursing and shouting, and drove me out of the inn.

"And there you have it!" Hershele concluded.

HE DEFENDS HIS WIFE

Hershele was a loyal and devoted husband; he permitted no one to offend his wife.

She complained to him one day about the grocer. He had refused to give her any more credit; she must first pay what she owed. But that was not all. He insulted her in the presence of the other women.

"For that," she said, "I will never forgive him!"

"Don't worry," Hershele consoled her. "Never again will he insult you."

In a wee hour of the morning Hershele came and knocked on the grocer's shutter. The grocer showed his frightened face and recognized him.

"What—what is it?" he whispered.

"I want you to know," said Hershele, "that my wife will never forgive you!"

"What!" the man stormed. "For this you trouble me in the middle of the night!"

"Trouble *you?*" Hershele was indignant. "And what of the trouble I took, coming here at this hour? You may as well know that the next time it happens I won't come to you at night. I'll come by day."

HERSHELE AVENGES INSULT AND INJURY

On Thursdays the peasants from the neighboring villages came flocking to the market place of the town, bringing a variety of merchandise for sale, and some of them were not very affable to their customers. There was one in particular who became well known for his arrogance and greed. His merchandise was good, but his prices were exorbitant, and his manners execrable. It was the general opinion that something should be done about it and that Hershele was the man to do it. In this opinion Hershele concurred.

On a certain market day this peasant arrived with a sizable supply of eggs and, as usual, demanded an outrageous price for them. People came over, inquired about the price, and went away without buying, followed by insults and abuse from the peasant.

Hershele sauntered up, picked up one of the eggs, held it to the light with the air of an expert, asked for the price and promptly told the peasant he would buy ten dozen.

"Here," he said to the peasant, "button your *kaftn* down to the bottom, hold up both skirts and I will count the eggs into them."

The peasant followed Hershele's instructions and made a safe receptacle for his eggs. Hershele deposited them slowly and carefully, while the peasant stood motionless, holding up the skirts of his *kaftn* and counting. When the ten dozen were all deposited, Hershele stopped, smiled at the peasant, and immediately delivered a series of hearty slaps on his face. The peasant yelled and cursed, but what could he do? He was as helpless as a beetle on its back. A big crowd had gathered and the people roared with delight.

But wait, wait. This version of the story has been disputed by many of Hershele's admirers. Hershele, they claim, was not that sort of man. He was not given to violence. His methods, they maintain, were more subtle. He did not slap the peasant in the face.

What, then, did he do? He came close to the peasant and undid the knot in the rope that held up his trousers. And not to omit a relevant detail, it must be added that the peasants in those parts were not familiar with the uses of underwear.

It happened once, however, that a slap in the face did figure in a story about Hershele and a peasant, except that it was Hershele who got slapped. In the crowded market place one day, Hershele was jostled against this peasant, who promptly reacted in the manner indicated. At once Hershele took out a shining gilden and gave it to the peasant.

"I see you are puzzled," said Hershele to the bewildered slapper. "Step aside a moment and I'll explain. You see," he went on, "this is a special day among us. On this day when a *goy* slaps or strikes us, we are commanded to reward him. I gave you only a gilden because I am a poor man. But if you slapped one of our rich men he would give you much more. I know one who would be likely to give you fifty gilden. Would you like me to take you to him?"

The peasant's greed began boiling in him as in a cauldron. Fifty gilden!

"Take me to him at once," he said.

"One little moment," said Hershele, "it's only proper you should show appreciation for my trouble. Five gilden, please."

The peasant paid and Hershele led him to the door of the richest man in town. It so happened that the man was just leaving. The door was opened for him by a huge servant, and the peasant slapped him promptly in the face, crying, "Fifty gilden!" The servant seized the peasant, was joined by two more servants, and when they finally deposited him in the street he was a sorry sight indeed.

Hershele, who stood by to see what would happen, helped him up.

"He wouldn't—he wouldn't give me the fifty gilden!" the peasant blubbered.

"That's too bad," said Hershele. "This man is a renegade. He doesn't observe the commandments. But I know another rich man in town. Would you like to try him?"

But the peasant turned and tottered away as fast as his condition allowed him.

HERSHELE AS A TRANQUILIZER

Hershele's fame grew, but the number of his offspring did likewise, and the burden of providing for them weighed heavy upon him. But his fortunes mended when he was appointed official jester to the "court" of the prominent Chassidic leader, Rabbi Baruch of Medzibozh. The *rebe* suffered from melancholia; the plight of his people, the poverty and persecution that afflicted them, robbed him of the cheerfulness which, as a *chossid,* it was his duty to cultivate. It was Hershele's role to divert and soothe him.

He made an excellent start. On the day of his arrival the *rebe* was gloomier than usual. He shut himself up in his study, paced up and down and refused to see any one. But Hershele managed to slip past the attendant at the door and entered the study. In his hand he carried a lantern in which burnt a candle.

The *rebe* scowled at him. "What are you doing here?" he demanded.

"They told me," he murmured meekly, "that the *rebe's* face has fallen. I have come here to look for it, and if you will permit me, perhaps I'll find it."

If the *rebe* didn't laugh he at least smiled and gave orders that

Hershele should not be denied his presence and even be allowed to eat with him. But the first meal began poorly. The *rebe* was so depressed he was unable to eat. So Hershele took his teaspoon and slipped it ostentatiously into his pocket.

"What are you doing?" the *rebe* asked.

"The doctor prescribed for me and told me to take a teaspoon with every meal," Hershele answered demurely. At once, according to report, the *rebe's* appetite was restored.

But once it happened that he was summoned by the *rebe* to answer a serious charge. Hershele was seen taking food on a fast day. True, it was a minor fast, but for one who was part of the *rebe's* entourage it was a grave offense not to observe it.

"What have you to say for yourself?" said the *rebe* sternly.

"I did it," Hershele explained, "in order to help a poor daughter of Israel to obtain her dowry. I enabled her to come into a hundred gilden."

"Stop talking riddles," the *rebe* ordered.

"This is the way it happened. Early this morning I was on my way home from *shul,* wondering if I would find today's fasting hard or easy. In front of me walked two young women engaged in conversation and I overheard one of them, whom I knew to be the poor shoemaker's daughter, say to her companion, 'If I had a hundred gilden for every Jew who will not fast today, I would have a handsome dowry and would not have to be an old maid.' Hershele, I said to myself, here is your chance to do something for a worthy Jewish daughter. You can make sure that she has an additional hundred gilden. So, *rebe,* I came home and you know what I did. I performed a good deed."

HERSHELE FACES THE SUPREME TRIBUNAL

They tell that even when Hershele was in bed with his last illness his wit and good humor did not fail him.

Rabbi Baruch himself came to visit him.

"I am sure," said the *rebe,* "that with your cunning you will find a way of circumventing Satan himself."

"I haven't always managed it in this world," Hershele confessed.

"But you must have given some thought to your defense when you appear before the Supreme Tribunal. What will you say, Hershele?"

"Yes, I have thought about it. And what could a poor wight like me say? It is written, I will say, 'not of your own will were you formed, not of your own will were you born, not of your own will do you live, not of your own will do you die, not of your own will are you to give account to the Supreme King of Kings, the Holy One, blessed be He.' Five not-of-your-own-will's, I will say! Well, I will say, four of them I have already fulfilled, poor long-suffering wretch that I am. Couldn't I be spared from having to fulfill the fifth one also? And, who knows, perhaps my plea will be granted."

"I will add my prayer that it should be, Hershele. And may the gates of Paradise be opened for you!" said the *rebe*.

Pageant of the Human Comedy

Foreword

HERE, marshalled in a sort of Purim parade, are the leading characters who made up the colorful drama of East European Jewish life. Through the gay or grim humor they furnish we glimpse their serious and often tragic lives. The picture, of course, is distorted by the medium, but the whimsical and grotesque are sometimes more revealing than the strictly objective.

Into this pageant, flashes of this life as projected into the New World and modified by it, have been admitted.

A listing of some of the heroes and villains, a dramatis personae, as it were, may prove helpful. We set them down at random:

The proud beggar who never humbles himself, but lets the giver know he should feel beholden to him.

The gentle rabbi who stoops to flatter the town miser on the principle that to milk a cow you have to bend down.

The marriage broker, the biggest persuader of them all, with an uncanny gift for hitching up a mare with a mule.

The jolly pauper who scoffs at his lot, his motto being: "Rejoice, *kabtsn,* dirt is cheap."

The teacher of the young, the *melamed,* who attracts every variety of mishap, and is particularly unfortunate with goats. For some subtle reason a *melamed* and a dismal goat go together.

Those may be classed as heroes; and here are some of the villains:

The rich miser, the favorite target of the poor man's vengeance: ridicule and scorn.

The fire-and-brimstone preacher, whose frantic exhortations leave his listeners cold.

The shrew, merciless and implacable, striding along defiantly and pulling her husband by the ear.

The renegade who is "born again" at the baptismal font, and so obtains the means to provide himself with *matse* for Passover.

The glutton, the guzzler, and finally the anti-Semite who, in these pages at any rate, meets with the disgrace and defeat he deserves.

So, let the parade begin.

Rich Man, Poor Man

RICH MAN, POOR MAN

IN THE waiting room of a famous *rebe* sat a rich man and a poor man. The rich man was ushered in first and it was almost an hour before he came out. The poor man followed and was given only a few minutes.

"Rebe," said the poor man before going out, "are you not discriminating between the rich and the poor?"

"Foolish man!" said the *rebe*. "When you came in I knew you were a poor man as soon as I looked at you, but the other —I had to talk to him an hour before I knew he was as poor as you."

WEALTH AND WISDOM

There was a wise man who was asked:

"What is more important, wealth or wisdom?"

"Wisdom," he replied.

"If so, why do the wise wait on the rich? Why don't the rich wait on the wise?"

"Because," was the reply, "the wise, being wise, understand the value of riches, but the rich, being only rich, don't understand the value of wisdom."

RECIPE FOR ETERNAL LIFE

"If you want to live forever," said a wag to a rich man, "come and live in my town."

"Doesn't anybody die in your town?" asked the other.

"Yes, indeed," replied the wag. "But it has never happened yet that a rich man should die there!"

CONSOLATION FOR THE RICH

"There is no limit to the impudence of the paupers in this town!" said the wife of a rich man to her husband. "When we celebrate a happy occasion, we have to pay out to them. When they have a wedding or something, we again have to pay out!"

"Don't let it upset you, my dear," her husband consoled her. "It's true that this world belongs to the poor, but remember the World-to-come is reserved for us!"

NOW HE KNOWS

"You are courting my daughter, young man. It's quite obvious, and I don't blame you, she is a jewel. Now, we are both practical men and there are some things we want to talk over, so if you'll be good enough to take a walk with me we'll talk on the way.

"So! Fine day, isn't it? Lots of people out on a day like this. Oh, yes! I know many of them. Do you see that man in the gray suit with a flower in his lapel? Looks like a rich man, doesn't he? Well, he isn't. I owe him only a thousand rubles. The man who just passed us—did you notice him? He is a lot richer. Him I owe three thousand rubles. Not such a good creditor, presses me too hard. Wait! Take a look at the little fat man with the tall hat on the other side of the street. I owe him five thousand. Hard as nails, that little man. Had to give him a mortgage on my home. But I have an appointment tomorrow with the genuine article, a usurer of the old school—calls himself a banker. I intend to touch him for ten thousand."

"But, my dear sir, why do you tell me all that?"

"Well, since you are a practical young man and you are courting my daughter, it occurred to me that you might be expecting a handsome dowry and would wish to know how rich I am. So now you know."

HE PERSPIRED

A rich old miser became critically ill and the doctor prescribed a medicine with the following warning:

"If after taking this medicine, you perspire, it's a sign that you will get well. If you don't perspire, we can only put our trust in God."

The miser took the medicine, but failed to perspire. From mouth to mouth ran the whisper that the rich man was about to die.

"Let us call on him," said the rabbi to the worthies of the town. "Perhaps he will now repent of his ways and leave something for the needs of the community."

So they came to him, and found him indeed in a repentant mood. They brought paper and ink and the rabbi got ready to write.

"The synagogue," he said, "is badly in need of repairs."

"A hundred rubles for the synagogue," said the miser and groaned pitifully.

"The bathhouse is tumbling down," said the rabbi.

"Fifty rubles for the bathhouse," the miser groaned again and writhed.

"The widows' and orphans' fund is depleted," said the rabbi.

"A hundred—wait a minute, wait a minute!" the miser cried suddenly. "Cross it all out! I'm perspiring! I'm perspiring!"

HIGH FEVER

In another town there was also a miserly rich man who never gave to the poor or to any of the communal institutions. Once this man became dangerously ill, and the community officials felt that their opportunity had come. They called on him, spoke to him feelingly, and were successful. He promised them fifty rubles for charity!

Not long afterwards, the town learned with surprise that the man was well again. The officials paid him another visit, congratulated him on his recovery, and expressed the hope that he would pay his pledge.

"Chaye Rochl!" the man called to his wife. "Do you hear, Chaye Rochl? It's only now that I find out how sick I was. What high fever I must have had! I promised them fifty rubles!"

SUSPICIOUS

"And how are you getting on in the world?" someone was asked.

"I suspect," he replied, "that I am getting rich."

"What do you mean you suspect?"

"I can't quite make it out," was the reply. "I haven't any money yet, but I feel I am already a bit of a swine."

GOD FORBID!

It was his day, the town miser's day. His new home was finished, the furniture moved in, and the town worthies had all arrived to admire his grandeur and glory. They came in spite of their aversion for the niggard, who was as tight-fisted as he was rich. Now the man was as proud as King Ahasuerus on his feast day, "when he showed the riches of his glorious kingdom and the honor of his excellent majesty."

He took his visitors from room to room and pointed out their advantages and furnishings. Finally he led them to the dining room, a spacious room with an immense table, surrounded by elegant high-backed chairs.

"You see this table?" he beamed. "Around this table as many as fifty persons could sit down and eat!"

But suddenly his face darkened.

"God forbid!" he added.

A COMPASSIONATE MISER

This miser—I know you won't believe it—had a tender heart that overflowed with sympathy for the unfortunate, but the following true story should convince you.

It was a cold winter night and he was sitting at his fireplace in the parlor, immersed as usual in his calculations. He heard his street door open and shut, and a draft of stinging air glided into the room and made him draw his dressing gown closer about his shoulders. In came Gershn his servant and told him there was someone in the vestibule anxious to talk to him.

"Don't let him stand there and freeze," said he to the servant. "Show him in!" And to himself he said: "It must be that grain merchant come to pay his debt at last."

But the individual for whom the servant opened the door looked like anything but a merchant. His clothing was in rags, his face pinched with cold and he shivered in every limb. The story he told was brief.

"I'm a stranger in this town," he said, "I have neither friend nor relative. I have nowhere to stay the night, and I haven't eaten all day."

The miser gazed with pity upon the unfortunate, then covered his eyes with his hands.

"Gershn," he called to his servant, "I can't bear to look upon this man. He breaks my heart, Gershn. Throw him out, throw him out!"

POOR BROTHER

The committee was out collecting to help the needy prepare for Passover. They decided not to omit the rich miser. They were a little curious to hear what reason he would advance this time for not giving.

"My good friends," said the miser, "you are out for a worthy cause, a noble cause. But you all know that I have a poor brother."

"But only this morning," said one of the committee, "your brother applied for assistance and told us he gets nothing from you?"

"He did?" the miser answered. "So there you have it. A perfect instance of the inference from minor to major. You are all learned men and you know what I mean. Since I don't give anything to my own brother, how can you expect me to give to strangers?"

POOR BUT GENEROUS

A certain *melamed* used to say: "If the Holy One, blessed be He, gave me ten thousand rubles, I would at once deduct a thousand and give it away as my tithe for the poor. And I say further, if He doesn't trust me to do so, let Him deduct the tithe himself and give me the balance."

JUST A LITTLE MORE TIME

"So you've brought me my Passover clothes at last," the rich man barked at the perspiring tailor. "It certainly took you long enough! Here it is almost the eve of Passover and I was beginning to wonder if I would have to appear in *shul* in my old clothes. Don't stand at the door! Spread them out and let me see what sort of job you've done. I have to have things just right, you know."

Carefully the rich man examined the coat, the trousers, the vest. He was pleased, and his manner relented.

"If only you didn't take so long," he said in a softer voice. "The good Lord, you know," he continued with a patronizing smile, "took only six days to make this great big world of ours, and you it took two weeks to make a suit of clothes."

"Ah," said the tailor, "but look at my work, and look at the work of the Lord! Everything I have done is just right, the workmanship is without a flaw, the fit is perfect. But this world we live in! It's full of blemishes. I know that the holy books tell us the Almighty left the world imperfect on purpose. His desire is that we who live on it should finish and perfect it. Still, why must there be so much suffering in this world? So much cruelty? Why must His people Israel have to endure such a long and bitter exile? And I ask you further, why must there be so many poor people who don't deserve their poverty and so many rich who don't deserve their riches? You know what I think?" he concluded, looking hard at his customer, "I think the Almighty could have taken a little more time, just a little more time."

A MELAMED, *HIS GOAT, AND HIS CHICKENS*

Year after year the household of a certain *melamed* increased, the quarters remained the same, until at last the congestion was more than he could bear. So he went to the rabbi for advice.

"Have you a goat?" asked the old rabbi.

"How then?" said the *melamed*. "Every *melamed* has a goat!"

"Take the animal into your dwelling."

"But—but—" the *melamed* stammered.

"Will you do as I say!"

"Yes," said the *melamed*, and he brought the goat into his house.

After the first surprise, the silly animal got used to it, but the others didn't. Again the *melamed* came to the rabbi.

"I have obeyed your command," said he, "but things are worse than ever."

"Have you any chickens?" asked the old rabbi.

"A few," said the *melamed*, with a sinking of the heart.

"Bring them into your house," said the rabbi.

"Rabbi," the *melamed* began.

"Will you do as I say!" the rabbi commanded.

The *melamed* brought his chickens into his house. The birds perched on every point of vantage and felt quite at home.

The *melamed* returned to the rabbi and wept.

"Very bad, my son, isn't it?" said the old rabbi.

"It's—the end of the world!" said the *melamed.*

"Very well, then. Now go home and drive out the goat and chickens, and come to me again to-morrow."

The following day the *melamed* stood before the rabbi and his face was beaming.

"Rabbi!" said he, "my house, it's a paradise!"

NO LAUGHING MATTER

Motke Chabad was a famous *shlemiel* and a day came when all his ventures ended in failure. He went to call on the head of the community.

"If the community doesn't support me," he threatened, "I will become a hat maker!"

"And what if you will?" he was asked.

"Don't you realize what would happen?" asked Motke. "Don't you know that if I become a hat maker, every child in the town will be born without a head?"

RECIPE FOR HAPPINESS

"You ask me why I limp and groan, my friend? I'll tell you. It's because my shoes are tight. Yes, my feet are as in a vise. Why do I wear them, you ask? I'll tell you why. My business is going to the dogs, my creditors are hounding me, my rent is unpaid, my daughters are marriageable and without prospects, and my wife is an unbearable nag. I come home and my troubles sweep over me like a flood. I feel that life isn't worth living. What, then, do I do? My friend, I sit down and take off my shoes. Yes, I take these mean things off my burning feet, and what joy is mine, what happiness!"

IT WOULDN'T PAY

The rich man of the town chanced to meet the tailor and noticed that the poor man was wearing a torn and dilapidated *kaftn.* Said he to the tailor:

"I can't understand it. You are yourself a tailor. Why don't you mend your own clothes?"

"Where will I find the time?" replied the tailor. "Now I have to make a coat for the *porets,* now a pair of trousers for the rabbi, and so on. For myself I never have the time."

The rich man was moved by the tailor's words. He handed him a ruble and said:

"Here is something for your time. Take it and patch up your *kaftn.*"

Five days later he met the tailor again and in the same dilapidated *kaftn.*

"What does it mean?" said he. "Why didn't you mend your *kaftn?*"

"I'll tell you," said the tailor. "I figured out that at that price it wouldn't pay me to do it."

MELAMED'S *LUCK*

Once upon a time there was a duke who was very vain of his beard. It was indeed a handsome beard: broad and silken and brilliant black in color. This nobleman always stroked his beard and it was clear to all men that the beard was his pride and joy.

But one day the king, who was out hunting with the duke, said to him:

"You needn't be so proud of your beard. I once saw an old *melamed* in a town not far from here whose beard was handsomer than yours."

The count smiled a proud, disdainful smile.

"So you don't believe me!" the king continued. "I'll tell you what I'll do. I'll have the *melamed* brought here, but you must promise that if his beard is finer than yours, you will pay him a thousand gold pieces."

The count agreed and the same day the king sent messengers to bring the *melamed* posthaste to the capital. The king told them nothing of the reason why he wanted the *melamed,* but they had performed similar errands for the king in the past, and knew just what to do. They seized the *melamed,* put him in chains, brought him to the capital, and threw him into prison.

The chief messenger presented himself to the king.

"Have you brought the *melamed?*" the king demanded.

"Yes, Your Majesty," the man replied.

"Is he safe and secure?"

"Yes, Your Majesty."

"Bring him before me tomorrow morning," the king commanded.

Early the following morning the messenger went to the jail to execute the king's command. Accompanied by the jailer, he entered the *melamed*'s cell and looked hard at his beard. It was an extraordinary growth: it spread out in every direction almost hiding its owner's features, and reached down to his girdle. Never had they seen such a beard!

"Is it proper for anything like that to be presented to His Majesty?" said the messenger. "Jailer," he continued, "call the barber and let him remove the prisoner's beard!"

And the jailer did as he was ordered.

THE NERVOUS TWIST

Yankl the shoemaker jumped suddenly into a fortune, an inheritance or whatever it was, and became the rich man of the town. He began to receive high honors, was made a trustee of the congregation, and not only was he accorded the best portions of the Reading on the Sabbath, but he had the power to decide who was to get the other portions. Now in the same city it came to pass that a certain learned and rich man lost his wealth and, it goes without saying, everything that happened to the former shoemaker happened to the *lamdn* in reverse. Yankl, moreover, avenged himself on the fallen rich man and never gave him a portion of the Sabbath Reading. The *lamdn* was indignant and before long adopted a peculiar method of retaliation. During the Sabbath services, when Yankl, in all his grandeur, stood on the *bime* allotting the portions, the *lamdn* stood up in his place and jerked his thumb back and forth just as a shoemaker does when he pulls his thread. Yankl felt greatly humiliated, and when the *lamdn* persisted with his thumb-exercise in the sight of all the congregation, Yankl couldn't stand it and haled him before the judge. A trial took place with lawyers and all the other accessories. Now, the *lamdn*'s lawyer hit upon a shrewd device. He explained to the judge that his client suffered from a nervous condition which made him jerk his thumb in the manner that the former shoemaker found so obnoxious. The *lamdn* was acquitted. On the way home from the trial he approached the former shoemaker.

"Yankl," said he, "it's true, of course, as my lawyer explained, that I am afflicted with a nervous disease. But you, Yankl, you understand that little twist, don't you?"

A LOT OF MONEY, BUT——

He was really a good sort, this wagoner, but he liked to deliver himself of the most awesome and picturesque curses. On the least provocation or none at all, he would call down an assortment of the direst calamities or the most dread diseases on the head of this one or that one, and even on inanimate objects. After years of indulgence he seemed to have become an incurable addict.

It is told of this implacable wagoner that one morning he was seen pacing through the market place of the town, muttering: "A demon should get into your father's father. A good little cholera for you in your ribs."

"Whom are you cursing so early in the morning?" someone asked him.

"I don't know yet," he answered. "But don't worry. Someone will turn up."

He began one trip with a wagonload of passengers by informing his horse that he was an old plague and that it was time for his guts to dry up and his bones to rot. Now one of his passengers, a dignified scholar, was shocked by this tirade against a dumb creature.

"Wagoner," he said, "your language is sinful and vulgar. I'll tell you what I'll do. I'll add three rubles to my fare if you won't utter another curse the rest of the trip."

The wagoner scratched his head ruefully.

"Three rubles is a lot of money," he said. "I promise."

They set off and they had just left the town when the horse stumbled and nearly hit the ground with his muzzle.

"A sweet little cholera," the wagoner began. "Hold!" he interrupted himself. "Three rubles is a lot of money."

They rolled on and suddenly the wagon got into a rut and wouldn't move. The wagoner jumped off the box and looked daggers at his vehicle.

"Don't you think," said he to the wagon, "that it's time for you to become a heap of ———. Shut your mouth! Three rubles is a lot of money!"

The passengers got off and managed to bring the wagon out of the rut. But suddenly one of the hind wheels dropped off and everybody, including the wagoner, was shaken up.

"A jolly pestilence— No, no," the wagoner moaned. "Three rubles is a lot of money."

With the help of the passengers the wheel was put back where it belonged and for a while the wagon rolled on without incident. Then the old nag had a mild attack of temperament. Attracted by a patch of grass at the roadside, he pulled over and began munching as if he hadn't a care in the world. The wagoner leaped off his box.

"Seven hefty choleras in your belly," he yelled at the horse, "and three epilepsies in your bones! Burn up and sink into the earth!" Then he added: "Three rubles is a lot of money, but why should I drop dead from apoplexy?"

POOR BUT INTREPID

Ever hear the story of the poor little tailor? It's very short. He was out walking one day and saw a fight. He didn't hesitate a moment. He whipped off his coat, rolled up his sleeves, jumped right in, got a fiery slap in the face, and ran away. That's the whole story.

ENOUGH IS ENOUGH

"Yes, my friends," said the *melamed*, "I am rich. I am even richer than our town nabob. You know what our sages say. 'Who is rich?' they ask. And they answer: 'He who is happy with his portion!' Consider our nabob. We all know that he is stuffed with money. But is he happy? Is he content? Not he. He wants more, always more. But I? I have seven daughters, and do I want more? Not I. I have enough, thank God, quite enough."

HE WEEPS

A rich man was being taken to his eternal home and his relatives followed the bier and wept. A stranger joined them and wept with the rest.

"Are you too a relative of the deceased?" they asked him.

"No," he answered, still weeping.

"Then why do you weep?"

"That's why," he replied.

THE JOLLY KABTSN

It was a very cold day, and in the group that sat in the *shul* hugging the stove was a *kabtsn* who spoke up and said:

"In a bitter frost like we are having today I know just what to do.'

"What do you do?" he was asked.

"I shiver!" he answered.

Beggerman, Thief

BEWARE OF STIPENDS!

"My masters! Friends and brothers! We have assembled here this day to ward off a great calamity that hangs over our heads. I see a big throng before me. I am sure there is not a beggar in this town who is absent from this meeting.

"Give ear, ye heavens, and I will speak, and let the earth hear the words of my mouth. Am I too bold to use these words of Moses our Teacher? No, dear brothers! In view of the mischief that is being plotted against us, I have a right to call heaven and earth to witness. Our town worthies, our trustees, our moneybags! They are out to destroy us, to ruin our profession, to kill our self-respect. There must be no more beggars in this town, they say. They'll raise a special fund, they say, and out of this fund they'll pay each one of us a stipend. It doesn't befit their dignity, the good name of our town, they say, that we should go out with our sacks, begging from house to house.

"Was there ever such a scandal? They will give us an ample stipend, they tell us. But what about us? What are we going to do? Are we to hide and not show our faces? Must we no longer step out into the light of the world and meet our fellow men?

"Is it only what good people give us for our sacks that matters to us? And what about the things we say and the things we hear? The news we get and the news we bring? For us the chance to thank the Almighty and our fellow men. For them, to earn the great merit of giving charity.

"Shall I tell you what is really wrong with the rich? They don't understand us. They have no respect for our calling. They think it's a small thing to go begging door to door. But we must stand our ground, we must uphold our rights, the dignity of our profession! And if there are any among you who are tempted to fall into the trap and accept a stipend, I want to say to them: My enemies should receive stipends, my good friends should go begging from door to door!"

EXCELLENT SACK

"Do I know who you are? Of course, I do! You are the landlord of this inn, and this is your bill. I see, I see. The bill is very nicely made out, itemized. Last night's supper—good supper, the roast was excellent; the room—nice room, comfortable bed, and this morning's breakfast. Yes, it's all there, and the charges are reasonable. You know, my dear landlord, your establishment is really first rate. You can depend on me, I shall recommend your inn to all my friends.

"Ah, you want to be paid. Of course you do. Take my word for it, you don't have to worry about it. I am going out now and when I am back in the evening your bill will be paid in full, every last copper of it. I owe nothing to anyone. That's my rule of life. My father, bless his memory——

"What my business is? You have every right to know, my dear landlord. A little closer please, I don't want to talk too loud. You see this sack? I keep it under my coat, but it's an essential part of my trade. I am—why should I hide it from you? You are a broadminded man, every innkeeper is a broadminded man, he comes into contact with such a variety of people. So I'll not be squeamish about it and tell you very frankly. I am a beggar. I go from house to house and receive alms. Sometimes I get a copper or two, more often a slice of bread, a piece of herring, a cucumber, an apple, a pear, a plum—things you can use in your business. Everything goes into this sack. It's a good strong sack. It has served me now for many years. It was made for me by an excellent man, a tailor with a golden heart, in the town of——

"What's that you say? You'll never see me again? You don't trust me, I can see that! You have no idea how that hurts me. I am, you must know, a sensitive man. But I know how to set your mind at rest. I'll make you a generous offer. Something I've never done before. Come along with me and we'll go out begging together.

"Come, come! Don't carry on like that, Reb Innkeeper. If you don't like my offer, you don't have to get red in the face about it. I'll make you another offer. You refuse to go out with me? Well, here is my sack, go out alone!"

THOSE MONEYBAGS!

They were a coterie of beggars, old-timers, some of them now retired, who got together from time to time to exchange memories, to talk, to banter, to quarrel—to live! On one occasion the give-and-take dealt with the arrogance of some of the donors, especially the nabobs, the big moneybags, their insolence and gall.

"You remember my old friend Feitl, peace to his soul?" one of them recalled. "We were like brothers. In bad times we helped each other, in good times we rejoiced in each other's luck, and sometimes we even went out begging together. Several days before Passover we used to make our visit to Reb Simcha's counting house and receive our annual stipend—ten gilden apiece. He could have given us more, the pig, but you can't haggle too much.

"When Feitl left for the true world I came to Reb Simcha and he hands me ten gilden. So I say to him, how about the ten gilden for Feitl? So he says he heard that Feitl had gone on to the true world. So I say, 'Feitl was my best friend, he had no relatives, and he made me his heir, I can show you his will.' So he looks at me and laughs. Such insolence! So I say to him, 'do you think he'd make *you* his heir?' So he stops laughing and orders me out! It was lucky my ten gilden were already in my pocket, or he might have turned me out without a kopek. You never can tell what these swine are liable to do."

NO LUCK

"But, my good man, you don't look like a beggar!"

"I really am not, sir—not by choice or temperament. What drove me to it was one thing and one thing only. All my life, sir, I've been dogged by ill luck. You know the proverb: Without *mazl*, it's better for a man not to be born. I began with every advantage: illustrious lineage, good family background, excellent education. As for my personal traits, such as industry, integrity, humility, it would be immodest for me even to mention them. But all that was of no avail to me. I was hounded by bad luck. Whatever I tried proved unlucky."

"But you did, at one time or another, have a definite occupation, didn't you?"

"Definite occupation? Why, yes, sir. Of course, sir. At one time I was—yes I—I played in an orchestra."

"How interesting! So you are a musician! Tell me, what instrument did you play?"

"Instrument? Why yes, of course. I played an instrument. I played—the flute."

"My favorite instrument! I am something of a flutist myself—strictly amateur, of course. Wait, just let me open this drawer. Here! Here is my flute. Play something on it, won't you? Something from Gluck's *Orpheus and Eurydice*, perhaps?"

"Well, sir, here it is again. My confounded bad luck. An orchestra, mind you. So many instruments to choose from, and I had to go and choose the flute. Now, do you see what I mean?"

CAVIAR

The beggar looked so pitiful the man slipped a whole ruble into his hand. Entering a restaurant a little while later, the generous man found the beggar seated at a table eating caviar. The man was indignant.

"Aren't you ashamed of yourself?" he said. "Begging on the streets and spending the alms you get for caviar!"

The beggar became indignant in his turn.

"Look here!" he cried. "Before I got the ruble, I *couldn't* eat caviar. Now that I have the ruble, I *mustn't* eat caviar. At that rate, when on earth *will* I eat caviar?"

THE IRON BRIDGE, REB TODROS!

There was a jolly beggar who came to Reb Todros, the rich man of the town, and began by telling him that his errand involved the life or death of a human being.

"Yours?" the rich man asked.

"No, yours," the beggar replied.

Reb Todros ordered his servant to bring drinks and cookies, and the beggar, after fortifying himself generously, explained as follows:

"I listened to the *magid* this afternoon. He told us that in the end of days, two bridges will be built across the Great Sea, one of iron, the other of paper. The sinful nations will take the iron bridge, but will fall into the sea. Israel will take the paper bridge and go across it in safety. I pondered a long time over the prophecy, and I concluded finally that, as between iron and paper, in spite of what the *magid* told us, iron is to be preferred. And I thought of you, Reb Todros, and I have come to warn you: Don't rely on miracles! Take the iron bridge, do you hear, Reb Todros? The iron bridge!"

SAME ADDRESS

In the market place one day, two beggars became such a nuisance that the policeman arrested them. He took out his notebook and pencil.

"Name?' he asked one.

"Yankl ben Shmerl."

"Where do you live?"

"Nowhere. I have no home."

The policeman turned to the other.

"Name?"

"Shmerl ben Yankl."

"Address?"

"We are partners," the beggar replied, pointing to the other, "and we live together."

HE SUPPORTS HIM

It is an ancient and honorable custom for householders to bring home from the synagogue on Friday night some poor wayfarer and entertain him over the Sabbath.

In observance of this custom a man was walking home one Friday night with his Sabbath guest, when, not far from his door step, he became aware that someone was trailing them.

"Who is that?" he asked his guest.

"It's my son-in-law," the beggar explained. "I am supporting him."

WHITE BREAD

He was a meek little man, this Sabbath guest whom the proud householder took home with him after the Friday night service. In the dining room his words were few and his manner demure—almost obsequious. But the appetite he displayed during the meal filled the beholders with awe, and in the case of the host, the wonder was not untinged with a little resentment.

The white Sabbath bread—the *chale*—seemed to have a special attraction for the guest.

Now, it was the custom to eat the Sabbath fish with the weekday black bread instead of the *chale*, but the guest, showing no regard for the example set by his host, consumed an impressive quantity of white bread with his fish. Was it proper for an *orach*—an indigent guest—to flout the customs of the home whose hospitality he enjoyed?

"Reb Orach," said the host at last, "in our town we eat fish on Friday night with black bread instead of *chale*."

The guest gulped his mouthful and replied softly:

"*Chale* is better."

The host started. It seemed to him there was a touch of impertinence in the meek voice of his guest.

"You are right," he said, "but *chale* costs more!"

"I know," the guest replied, "but it's well worth the extra cost."

The host slumped in his seat. He knew when he was defeated and bided his time.

The hostess, her face glowing with pride, brought in the noodle soup, and set a big steaming plate before the guest. At once the little man revealed a way with the soup that was all his own. He began by swallowing the noodles, to the last one, then broke slices of *chale* into what was left.

The host watched gloomily as the Sabbath bread disappeared in the *orach's* plate. But suddenly his face brightened: he had an idea.

"Reb Orach," he said, "do you know that when the children of Israel stood before the Red Sea, Moses could have taken them across without a miracle?"

"How?" the *orach* asked demurely.

"It's simple," the host replied. "All he had to do was to tell the people to dip their bread into the sea and the sea would have become dry." And the host laughed at his clever notion.

"How could they do that?" the *orach* repeated.

"How?" the host followed up his victory. "Look at your own plate!"

"Not possible," the guest insisted. "It was Passover, wasn't it? The first Passover."

"So?"

"So they had no bread. Only *matse*."

TEAMWORK

There were two who worked together as follows:

They presented themselves before the wealthy man of the town and one of them, pointing to the other, said with great solemnity:

"This man is descended from saints and scholars and he is destitute."

Whereupon the rich man handed the illustrious scion a handsome gift.

"A little something for my trouble," said the first.

"Your trouble?"

"Of course," the beggar explained. "Haven't I brought him to your house?"

ROBBING THE POOR

There was a beggar who used to receive a handsome stipend every year from the banker of the town—not less than five hundred crowns. One year he received only half the amount. The beggar hastened to his patron.

"What's the meaning of this?" he asked.

"I am having unusual expenses this year," the banker explained. "My son has become engaged to an actress and it's costing me a lot of money."

"This is unheard of!" the beggar cried. "If he wants to support an actress, that's his business. But let him do it with his own money, not mine!"

NO CREDIT

The beggar told a pathetic tale and it made an impression on his hearer.

"I want to help you," said he, "but you meet me at an unfortunate moment. I am absolutely without cash. Could you come tomorrow?"

"Impossible," said the beggar.

"Why not?"

"I have lost too much already by extending credit."

PROFESSIONAL PRIDE

Seven o'clock in the morning the banker of the town was awakened by a loud knocking on the street door of his house. Quickly he opened the door and before him stood a beggar, asking for alms.

"How dare you disturb me so early in the morning?" the banker demanded.

"My dear sir," the beggar replied, "I don't question your competence in the matter of banking, but when it comes to begging, please leave it to me."

SLIGHT OBSTACLE

"I could have earned a hundred rubles yesterday," said a beggar to his cronies.

"How?" they asked him.

"A rich lady offered to pay me that sum if she could look at me."

"Just look at you?"

"That's all."

"And you refused?"

"I didn't, but she was blind in both eyes."

AN OMELET

Said a beggar to his wife:

"I want you to make me an omelet. I am curious to know what there is about it that rich people like so much."

Said his wife:

"We have no eggs."

"What of that?" said the man. "Can't you make an omelet without eggs?"

"We have no butter," said the woman.

"Listen to her!" the beggar mocked. "Butter she needs!"

"I haven't even a pan," said the woman.

"We have red coals, haven't we?" said the beggar.

The woman took some flour, poured water over it, mixed it and laid the paste on the coals. It burned to soot at the bottom and remained raw at the top. The beggar took some into his mouth and spat out.

"Those rich!" he jeered. "The things they like! Does anyone understand them?"

THE LAST POCKET

A group of people stood around a weeping beggar in the market place.

"What's wrong?" someone asked.

"I had one coin," said the beggar, "and I've lost it."

"Have you searched in all your pockets?"

"Yes."

"Look again," the beggar was told.

He obeyed. Methodically he went through his pockets and searched.

"It's gone!" he declared.

"Wait a minute," said one of the group who observed him closely. "You've skipped one of your pockets. Why don't you search that one also?"

"Oh, that one!" the beggar cried. "Oh, no! Not that one!"

"Why not?"

"Suppose," the beggar answered, "I search this last pocket and the coin isn't there!"

HARD TIMES!

"I managed to be admitted into Rothschild's home," one beggar boasted to another.

"Indeed!" said the second. "And how much did he give you?"

"Ten marks."

"That's all? I would have gotten fifty!"

"You are mistaken. I was glad enough to get the ten. Things are not so well with our friend Mr. Rothschild."

"Really? How do you know?"

"Would you believe it?" replied the other. "I saw two of his daughters playing on one piano."

A BET

Said a beggar to Rothschild:

"Don't mistake me. I am not a beggar. I have come here on business."

"Business?"

"Yes, business. I want to make a bet with you. I want to bet you a hundred francs that I can obtain something that you can not."

The banker put a hundred francs on the table. The beggar picked them up and slipped them into his pocket.

"Your Excellency," he said, "I can get a pauper's certificate from the community. Can you get one?"

STYLE

The two beggars decided to call on Rothschild. Said the older to the younger:

"You wait for me on the sidewalk. I'll deal with Rothschild alone. I know how to handle these people."

He was actually admitted into the presence of the great banker, and after listening to him, Rothschild sent him to his secretary. The secretary sent him to the almoner. The almoner sent him to the bookkeeper. The bookkeeper sent him to the porter. The porter took him by the collar and threw him out.

The beggar landed on the sidewalk near his partner.

"Nu," said the latter, "what did you get?"

"I can't say that I got anything," the beggar replied. "But shall I tell you something? The order in that establishment is simply magnificent!"

SUGAR

To a well-to-do townsman there once came a *magid* or *shames* or some such worthy and was very cordially received. After some small talk, the host asked his guest if he would like some tea and the guest said he wouldn't mind. The tea was brought and thereupon the guest did a strange thing. Instead of taking sugar from the bowl on the table, he dipped into his pocket, took out some lumps of sugar and dropped them into his tea.

"God bless you!" said the astonished host. "Why don't you take sugar from the bowl?"

"*Cholile!*" said the guest. "I never drink tea with my host's sugar. You see," he went on, "I like a lot of sugar in my tea. I can't impose upon my host, so I always carry sugar with me in my pocket."

The host was compelled to let him have his way. The guest drank a number of glasses of tea and all of them with his own sugar. The time came for him to leave and just before going he did another strange thing. He took the bowl and emptied it into his pocket.

"Mercy on us!" cried the host. "What are you doing? You insisted on drinking my tea with your own sugar, and now you take all my sugar with you!"

"The matter," replied the other, "is very simple. From here I am going to another house and there, too, I will drink tea; from that house to another and so on, and so on. Since I don't drink tea with my host's sugar, where would I take so much sugar? The only thing I can do is what you have just seen. I do it wherever I drink tea because, you understand, I don't like to drink tea with my host's sugar."

THE ROOSTER

It is a well-known fact that a *yeshuvnik* will welcome a wayfarer of his own faith who may chance to visit him. One day, Yossl the *yeshuvnik* saw on his threshold a long thin beggar with beard and earlocks. He opened his door wide and invited him to enter.

"Will you have the goodness to give me a bed for the night?" said the beggar.

"Gladly, gladly," said Yossl. "Come right in. And if you are hungry——"

"Hungry?" said the beggar with a wan smile. "There is a hole in my stomach as big as the void before creation."

"Zlate!" said Yossl, calling to his wife, "there is a hungry Jew in the house! Don't lose a minute, and remember—the best of everything!"

Never had the beggar feasted so well and Yossl stood over him, waiting on him, and deriving *naches* from the way the man ate. The beggar devoured everything with extraordinary speed, omitting to all appearances the process of mastication. And the quantity of food that he caused to vanish was astounding.

"You have, thank God, a good appetite," Yossl remarked, beaming on his guest.

"In the partition of the good things of life between the rich and the poor," the beggar managed to articulate, "the Holy One, blessed be He, observed even-handed justice. He gave the food to the rich and the appetite to the poor."

"He is wise, this beggar," said Yossl to himself. "A wise guest is an ornament to a household."

That night the beggar slept soundly and snored grandly, and

when he was up in the morning he couldn't bear the thought of going away so soon.

"Will you permit me," said he to Yossl, "to sleep another night in your house?"

That's the way he put it, the shrewd beggar: "sleep another night!" As though it wasn't the food that was uppermost in his mind!

"Yes, of course, why not?" Yossl replied.

So the beggar stayed and he ate all day as if he was under sentence not to eat again for the rest of his life afterwards. And the following morning he was reluctant to ask his host for another day. It seemed to him that the *yeshuvnik's* answer the previous morning had not been cordial enough. So he stayed without asking.

He stayed another day, and another, and another. On the fourth day he observed that the food was not so plentiful. On the fifth it was still less plentiful; on the sixth it was hardly sufficient. For the beggar's appetite, it should be made clear, suffered not the slightest diminution. This can only be stated; it cannot be explained.

"What is this?" said the beggar to his host on the seventh day. "Am I to starve here?"

"Believe me," said Yossl penitently. "It is not my fault. It's simply that the food is giving out. If you stay another day, I'll have nothing to give you. As for me and my Zlate, we are facing starvation."

"Oy *vey!*" cried the beggar. "You have nothing for tomorrow? Why didn't you tell me? Do you think I am the kind of a man who would rob people of their last morsel? Tomorrow morning I'll go!"

"Will you, really?" said Yossl and there were tears in his voice.

"Of course, I will!" declared the beggar. "Wake me up very early, before dawn. I'm a weak man and I can't walk in the heat of the sun."

"I'll be sure to wake you," Yossl promised, and so the matter was settled.

The beggar went to bed and slept like a top. Why shouldn't he? His mind and his conscience were clear. The *yeshuvnik* on the other hand was unable to sleep. To begin with, his conscience was not altogether clear: was it right to send the beggar away? In the second place, the *yeshuvnik* was afraid he might fail to wake the beggar early enough, in which case the beggar might stay on. Wasn't he a weak man, unable to walk in the heat of the sun? So Yossl lay on his bed, awake and alert all night. And as soon as the first gray glimmer of dawn appeared he got up and proceeded to wake up his guest.

The beggar was still sound asleep and his snoring was impressive. Yossl took him by the shoulder and shook him.

"What? What is it?" asked the beggar out of his sleep.

"Get up!" cried Yossl in his ear. "The rooster has crowed already!"

The beggar sat bolt upright in bed.

"What? What's that you say?" he cried. "You still have a rooster? Then I stay!"

And the beggar stayed.

THE ACROBAT

There came to a certain town a poor Jew who looked for something to do for a living. But he found nothing, so he hit upon a bright idea. He pasted up notices all over the town telling the people that at a certain hour on a certain day he would walk across the river on a rope from one bank to the other. The whole town came to see the stunt, each one paying five kopeks. And sure enough, there was a rope stretched across the river, and out came the acrobat and began to pull up on the rope. Suddenly he stopped and faced his audience.

"Good friends," said he, "I want you to know that I am not a tight rope walker and if I try to do the stunt, I will surely drown. If, however, it's all right with you that for your five kopeks, a poor Jew should drown in the river, I'll proceed!"

THE REWARD

"Once upon a time," a beggar related, "I came to a rich man's house and I don't know how it happened, but I found myself in the kitchen. In comes the mistress and asks me what I want. 'What shall I want?' I said to her. 'I am a beggar, God help me. Please give me something!' But she—would you believe it?—gave me nothing at all, and scolded me into the bargain. Unheard of *chutspe*! Then she bangs the door and I am left alone in the kitchen. Imagine, now, how I felt. It was not only that I got nothing, but the insult, you understand, the insult! As soon as I left the house, however, I had my reward. I happened to stick my hand into my pocket, and what do you think I found there? A silver spoon, as I live!"

YOSHKE TRAVELS IN STYLE

Yoshke Ganev was caught riding a horse that didn't belong to him.

"What are you doing on that horse?" he was asked.

Yoshke explained it very simply.

"Last night," he said, "I slept in the house of a peasant, and when I set off early in the morning I found the barnyard locked. Not wishing to awaken my host, I climbed the fence and jumped. And, would you believe it? I landed right on the back of this horse. He was on the other side of the fence, grazing. The animal became frightened and galloped away. And you can see I am telling the truth because—look! He is still galloping!"

YOSHKE IS GRATEFUL

After a good beating or a term in prison, Yoshke Ganev used to say:

"I am grateful to the law for beating and hounding those who follow my calling. Were it otherwise, the profession would become overcrowded and it would be impossible to make a living."

YOSHKE IS CURIOUS

Yoshke Ganev was once caught red-handed and brought to trial.

"Your Honor," said he to the judge, "will you kindly appoint a lawyer to defend me?"

"Yoshke," said the judge, "you've been caught with the goods, and what could any lawyer say in your defense?"

"Your Honor," said Yoshke, "I, too, am curious about it. What *could* a lawyer say in my defense?"

MERCY AND LOVE

Yoshke was once haled before a judge who was a convert to the Christian faith. The charge against Yoshke was serious, but he denied it.

"Your Honor," he ended his plea, "I stand here before you, and I am uncertain whether to appeal to the quality of mercy that lives in your Jewish heart or to the quality of love that lives in your Christian heart!"

TRYING A SCYTHE

"The peasants in our neighborhood," said a merchant, "come to town to buy all sorts of things and they buy very carefully. Take a scythe, for example. A scythe is an important implement and a peasant is in no hurry. He'll try it out. He tries it by throwing it on the ground to see if it has the right ring. He tries it by breathing on it to see if it has the right shine. Then he tries it on a hair to see if it has the right edge. Finally, he tries to steal it."

THINGS THAT VANISH

"We are now coming to a place," said a merchant to his driver, "that is famous for its horse thieves. They are the cleverest horse thieves in the world. When we put up at the inn, you must stay in the wagon without unharnessing and keep watch."

"Trust me, master," said the driver.

The merchant made himself comfortable in the inn, eating and drinking heartily and taking his ease. After a while he stepped outside and called to his driver.

"What are you doing, Berl?" he cried.

"I am sitting and wondering," came the answer.

"Wondering?" asked the merchant.

"Yes, I'm wondering where the hole goes when you've eaten the *beygl*."

"Ah," said the merchant. "Good, very good!"

And he went back to the inn. He sat awhile and becoming uneasy, he stepped out again.

"What are you doing now, Berl?" he called.

"I'm sitting and wondering," said Berl.

"Wondering again?" asked the merchant.

"Yes, I'm wondering where the smoke goes when I light my pipe."

"Good! Very good," said the merchant and returned to the inn.

A little while later, he stepped out a third time.

"What are you doing, Berl?" he cried.

"I'm sitting and wondering," Berl replied.

"Wondering again?" asked the merchant.

"Yes, I'm wondering," said the driver, "where our horses have gone to."

SORROWS OF A THIEF

After being robbed a number of times, a certain householder called in the police who, after examining the premises, noted with surprise that the thief had taken things of negligible worth and left untouched many valuable articles that he could easily have carried away. The police got quickly on the trail of the thief and arrested him. The prisoner was brought before the bar.

"Will you please explain," said the judge, "why you left the valuables behind and stole only a lot of trifles?"

"Please, your honor," the prisoner begged, "don't rub it in. My wife has nagged me enough about it already."

MAN AND HORSE

The peasant Mikhail came to town with a load of wood and stopped for a drink in the tavern. Two gentlemen of easy conscience who happened by looked approvingly at Mikhail's horse.

"He looks good to me," said one. "I propose that we unharness him."

"Not so fast," said the other. "I'm afraid the peasant will catch up with us."

"Leave it to me," replied the first, "we'll unharness the horse and I'll take his place between the shafts."

They did so, and when Mikhail came out of the inn he was dumbfounded to see a man harnessed to his wagon.

"What are you doing here?" he demanded, "and where is my horse?"

"I am your horse," said the man. "Years ago I committed a great sin, and for punishment it was decreed on high that I should be transformed into a horse and labor as a beast of burden until I expiated my sin. This very minute my term expired, and I have changed to my former self."

The peasant was filled with remorse that for so many years he had laid such heavy toil on a human being changed to a horse. He begged the man to forgive him for the many times he had whipped him. Then he released him from the shafts and the man went away.

Several days later, Mikhail came to the same town to visit the fair. He went to the horse mart and recognized his own horse hitched to a post. Mikhail put his arm around the horse's neck and stroked him gently.

"Alas!" said he. "Man is prone to sin. Only a few days ago your expiation ended. Why did you have to go and sin again?"

Doctor, Lawyer, Indian Chief

MONEY NO OBJECT

THE EXAMINATION over, the patient left five dollars on the table for the doctor.

"My fee," said the eminent specialist, "is twenty-five dollars."

"You see, doctor, I—I'm unable—" the patient began.

"You could have gone to someone cheaper," the doctor interrupted.

"Cheaper?" the patient was surprised. "No, doctor, when it comes to health, money is no object."

MISTAKE SOMEWHERE

The doctor looked hard at the two dollars which his patient left on the table.

"My fee," said he curtly, "is ten dollars."

"Ten dollars?" the patient repeated. "Somebody told me it was five!"

NOT SO CRAZY

The famous psychiatrist picked up the receiver.

"You are Doctor Finkel?" said the voice at the other end.

"Yes, madam."

"Doctor Finkel, the crazy doctor?"

"Yes, you might put it so, if you wish."

"I want to come to see you. How much do you charge?"

"Fifty dollars the first visit, after that——"

"Fifty dollars!" the voice gasped. "Good-by, doctor. So crazy I am not!"

SCENE: DOCTOR'S OFFICE

"In there and undress yourself!" said the doctor to the old man who had just entered.

"But, doctor—," the man began.

"I'm too busy to talk to you!" the doctor snapped. "You saw the crowd in my waiting room, didn't you?"

The old man did as he was told. The doctor made a hasty examination.

"I don't understand why you've come here," said he. "You're in perfect health."

"I'm the secretary of the synagogue," the old man explained. "I've come to see you about renewing your membership."

COMMON SENSE

The two patients lay in adjacent beds in the hospital ward, both suffering from the same affliction—a dislocated ankle. The dapper young intern came and examined the ankle of one of them, turning and twisting it with an impressive professional air. The poor fellow screamed with the pain. The doctor then turned to the other patient. He went through exactly the same procedure, but not a sound escaped from the injured man.

"I admire and envy you," said the first patient to his neighbor when the intern had left. "How can you stand so much pain without a sound?"

"It's not a matter of standing pain," said the other, "it's a matter of common sense."

"What do you mean common sense?" asked the first.

"Do you think," replied the other, "that I was foolish enough to give the young whippersnapper my injured ankle?"

WHAT IS THERE TO SEE?

"You will have to stop drinking or you may lose your eyesight," said the doctor to his patient.

The patient, who was an old man, stood up.

"Doctor," said he, "I have already passed the allotted span of threescore and ten and I don't think there is very much that I haven't already seen."

A GOOD DOCTOR

They were two stammerers and one of them, with great effort, managed to tell the other that his doctor was not doing very much for him.

"Why," said the second stammerer, "d-d-d-don't you g-g-g-go to m-m-m-my d-d-d-d-?"

But that was as far as the poor fellow could go.

THE MIRACLE

Motke Chabad fell sick and the doctor who was brought to his bedside shook his head over him.

"There is nothing I can do," said he. "We can only pray for the best."

Several days later the doctor was amazed to see his patient on the street, alive and well.

"It's a miracle," said he, "that you've recovered."

"You're mistaken," replied Motke. "It's not true that I've recovered. The fact is that I died. And the miracle happened to you, not me. This is how it came about. As soon as I died and went to heaven, I heard an angel announce: 'All doctors to Hell!' I looked and behold! you were among them. I was taken with a great pity for you. I pleaded with the angel.

" 'Spare this man!' I begged him.

" 'Why?' said the angel. 'Isn't he a doctor?'

" 'No, I can vouch for it!' I cried. 'This man is no doctor!'

"And at once they released you!"

A LADY'S AGE

The old lady, who could speak only Yiddish, was being questioned through the court interpreter.

"What is your name?"

"Malke Rabinovitch."

"How old are you?"

She replied and the interpreter translated her answer faithfully:

"Sixty-five till a hundred and twenty."

"What? What's that?" asked the judge. "Did she say she was a hundred and twenty years old?"

"She said: 'Sixty-five till a hundred and twenty,' your honor."

"I don't understand," said the judge. "Repeat the question."

The interpreter repeated the question and again delivered her answer.

"Sixty-five till a hundred and twenty."

His Honor felt annoyed.

"What on earth does she mean?" he demanded. "Can't she say how old she is? Ask her again."

And the interpreter translated her answer as follows:

" 'I told you twice already. Sixty-five till a hundred and twenty.' "

His honor mopped his learned brow, and looked bewildered and discouraged.

"Will you permit me, please," said a young lawyer to the interpreter. And turning to the lady, he said to her:

"Grandmother, till a hundred and twenty, how old are you?"

The lady answered and the interpreter translated:

" 'Sixty-five years!' "

SHOLEM ALEYCHEM A YID!

In his old age Reb Elye earned a little something now and then by helping to complete the quorum of ten that is mandatory for collective prayer; the quorum known as the *minyen.* In the witness chair Reb Elye, though slightly nervous, was a dignified figure, his black skullcap emphasizing the whiteness of his hair and beard.

"What is your occupation?" asked the lawyer.

The interpreter translated, Reb Elye answered and the interpreter translated his answer which was: "I am a *minyen* Jew."

His Honor intervened. "I don't understand," he said. "Tell him to explain what he means by a *minyen* Jew."

The interpreter did as he was told, and then delivered Reb Elye's answer as follows:

"He doesn't know what a *minyen* Jew is? Who doesn't know what a *minyen* Jew is? A *minyen* Jew is like this: if there are nine and I come in, then there are ten."

His Honor was still more puzzled. "I don't understand," he repeated. "Tell him if there are nine and *I* come in, there will also be ten."

The interpreter delivered his Honor's reply and Reb Elye's face lighted up with a happy smile. He stood up, extended his hand to the judge and said:

"Sholem Aleychem a Yid!"

INDIAN CHIEF

"No," said the skeptic, "I don't think there are any real Indians left. I've made three attempts to find some, and in each case—but let me tell you about them and you'll see what I mean.

"The first place I tried for Indians was Coney Island. There, of course, you expect to find counterfeits, and I saw through them very quickly. I mingled among them and kept my eyes and ears open. Before long, I heard one Indian say to another:

" 'Maybe you have some tobacco, maybe?'

"And the other Indian replied:

" 'Maybe you should start in smoking your own, maybe?'

"There was no mistaking the Brownsville intonation and I had enough.

"The second attempt I made in the middle west. The occasion was a county fair and the Indians were the main attraction. I looked and listened and very soon I became suspicious of the war whoops. Where, I asked myself, had I heard these sounds before? And suddenly I remembered! They were imitations of the *shofar*-blasts on Rosh Hashanah! I heard them all: *Tekiah, Shvarim, Truah!*

"But once when I was in the far west I made still another attempt. This time I was assured that I would see a famous old Indian chief—the genuine article. I went and paid admission and saw him. Black Turtle sat on a mat, his body as rigid as a stone, looking west with that last-of-the-Mohicans expression. But I refused to be convinced. I waited for him to do something, to talk, to move, to stand up—anything! And finally it happened! The chief stood up grandly and turned around. And I saw something that made me decide never to try again. I was through! Tell me, how would you feel if you saw a Yiddish paper sticking out of the back pocket of Black Turtle's trousers?"

Husbands, Wives, Children

ONE RAINY DAY

YOU WANT to know if an old bachelor like me ever came close to getting married? Yes, a number of times. But the closest call I ever had was a certain day when it was raining in torrents and I was on my way home without an umbrella. I walked as fast as I could, and I overtook a middle-aged man with a sturdy umbrella who was going my way. The circumstances, I felt, justified a measure of boldness.

"Sir," I said, "would you permit me to walk with you under your umbrella?"

The man looked long and hard at me and said: "Certainly not!"

I was stunned. But immediately the man relented and held up the umbrella over me.

We walked for a while in silence. Then he asked me where I lived and I told him.

"I'll take you home," said he curtly.

"But, my dear sir," I remonstrated, "you don't have to do that! Isn't it out of your way?"

"I insist!" he replied and we walked on. "An eccentric," said I to myself, "or—who knows?—perhaps something more serious." I decided to be on the alert.

We came to the house where I lived, but before entering I turned to my strange escort.

"I don't have to tell you, sir, how grateful I am for your umbrella. I would have been drenched to the marrow. But won't you have the goodness to explain why—"

"Why I took you home? Certainly!" he said, his manner now relaxed. "The reason is that if I didn't see you home, you would have walked with me to my home. Well, in a downpour like this, how could I have let you go on without an umbrella? I would have had to invite you into my home. Now, young man, I have a daughter. She is charming and beautiful and the apple of my eye. You are a handsome young man, and you seem to be a person of breeding. You and my daughter would have met. She would have invited you to have some tea—just to ward off a cold, you know. The two of you would have talked about poetry, music, painting—those things. You would have been fascinated by her, she would have been intrigued by you. You would have arranged to meet again and again. You would have fallen madly in love with each other. My daughter would have told me she had found her fate, her destiny, her happiness. And I? Have I ever denied her anything? I would have had to consent to the marriage. Now I ask you, young man, why should I be forced to let my daughter marry someone who doesn't even have an umbrella of his own?"

THE MOURNER

In the place of eternal rest a man with bowed head stood over a grave lamenting bitterly. An acquaintance passed by and heard him.

"Why," muttered the unhappy man, "have you gone away never to return? See what you have done to me! See to what you have condemned me!"

As the mourner walked slowly away, the acquaintance approached him.

"I saw you stand over the grave of your first wife," said he.

"No," said the man, "that was the grave of my second wife's first husband."

THE SAINT

Everybody in town knew Nochum the scribe and respected him. Not only were the Torah scrolls which he inscribed admired for their clearness and beauty, but Nochum was a man of gentle disposition, meek and soft-spoken, who was never known to complain or say an unkind word of anyone. When, therefore, his wife left him a widower with four small children, the whole town shared his sorrow and wondered how the poor man would take care of them.

It was not long, however, before Shaye the matchmaker began to cast hungry looks in his direction. Shaye allowed a decent interval to elapse, then he came to the scribe and proposed a match with—of all women in Israel—Genendl the chicken woman, the town termagant! And Shaye carried it off! Of all people Nochum was the kind who could least withstand this wily matchmaker.

For three years the poor scribe suffered in silence. He never complained and whenever he spoke of his unmerciful shrew he did it with dignity and decorum. Then came release. One morning Genendl failed to wake up. She was dead. When the rites were duly performed she was laid on a bier and deposited in the bottom of the cart of Feitl, the drayman. Nochum took his seat beside Feitl, who whipped up his nag, and they set off at a sharp clip for the cemetery.

There was a small stretch of road which was particularly rough, but the wagoners had managed to make it passable by laying logs across it, which bounced and rattled furiously whenever a vehicle passed over them. Now, just as the shaken cart was about to jolt over the last log, an unheard-of thing happened. Genendl sat up on her bier and demanded to know where they were taking her!

So Feitl turned his cart around, and took Genendl home, and Nochum's penance for sins he never committed began all over again. But his gentleness and restraint never deserted him. "A real saint," people said. "Job was an old grumbler compared to him."

But not long afterwards Genendl died again. This time there was no hurry to take her to her eternal rest. The scribe waited as long as it was permissible. Then he called in Feitl and again they set out for the cemetery.

When they approached that bad stretch of road the scribe leaned over and spoke gently to the drayman.

"Reb Feitl," he said, "be careful, Reb Feitl. Pull in your reins. Slowly, Reb Feitl. Careful, careful."

IF NOT NOW, WHEN?

He came to the rabbi and announced that he wanted to divorce his wife.

The rabbi looked up and was surprised: it was an old man who stood before him.

"How long have you been married to your wife?" he asked.

"Forty-five years."

"Are there any children?"

"Three sons and four daughters."

"And where are they?"

"All married."

"And now that you are both old, you want to divorce her?" the rabbi wondered.

"Yes," the man replied, "I want to divorce her. The match was arranged by my father and before the wedding I didn't see her. A few days after the wedding I wanted to divorce her, but my father objected. 'Wait a while and see if she isn't already with child,' said he. She was, and after the child came I wanted to divorce her. 'No,' said my father, 'she's nursing the child.' Then she became pregnant again and had to nurse the second child; then the third, the fourth, the fifth, and so on. Every time I wanted to divorce her, my father, peace unto him, objected. Then she stopped bearing and I wanted to divorce her.

'What are you thinking of?' said my father. 'Do you want your children to grow up motherless?' The children grew up and I wanted to divorce her. 'No,' said my father—and it was just before he died, peace unto him—'it will spoil your children's prospects in marriage!' Now, thank God, they are all married. And if not now, rabbi, when, I ask you?"

"YOUR HUSBAND IS RIGHT!"

The poor woman came to the rabbi and complained that her husband talked of divorcing her.

The old rabbi lifted his brows and looked up from the Talmud over which he was poring.

"Daughter," said he to the woman, "what does your husband say? Has he discovered any fault in you?"

"God forbid!" she replied. "Only he—he says—that I am ugly."

The rabbi began to turn the leaves of his folio.

"He is looking for the law in my case," said the woman to herself. "God grant he may find it to be in my favor."

At last the sage found what he sought: his spectacles. He put them carefully on his nose and looked intently at the woman.

"Daughter," said he, "your husband is right."

AND STILL THEY COME!

"How many little girls have you now?" a poor but resigned father was asked.

"Well," said he, "let's try to figure out. One of them sleeps with my wife and there are two other beds with two apiece. There are the twins who have no bed of their own; they sleep on the floor. In addition, there are the infants. One of them is in the cradle and the other—well, I don't know if the other was born yesterday or is due to arrive tomorrow."

HE PLAYS

"Rabbi," said the unhappy father, "I've just married off my daughter, but she will have to get a divorce. The young man won't do."

"What's wrong with him?" asked the rabbi.

"He can't play cards."

"What? Would to God not a single Jewish young man could play cards!"

"Yes, rabbi," said the worried father. "But he plays!"

HAPPY FATHER

"I thank God for my sons," said an elderly man. "My first-born is a doctor. The second is a lawyer, the third a chemist, the fourth an artist, and the fifth a writer."

"And what do you do?" he was asked.

"I," said the man, "have a dry goods store, not a big one, but I manage to support them all."

TOO MANY WORDS

The proud young father wired his parents: "Wife bore son—Herman."

His father-in-law took him to task.

"A telegram," said he, "should not have a single unnecessary word. Take, for example, your name, Herman. Why did you have to put that in? Would they think such a message might come to them from anybody at all? Then you say *wife*. Who else would bear you a son? Some other woman? Then what need is there for the word *bore*? They know well enough that a child doesn't drop from the sky. Finally, you put in *son*. Have you ever heard of anyone taking the trouble to wire that his wife gave birth to a daughter?"

TWO BROTHERS

Once there were two brothers, of whom one was very bright and the other very dull. The bright one was famous for his stories and witticisms and wherever he went people welcomed him. The other brother received no attention from anybody and his mother was unhappy about it.

"Avremele," said she to her bright son. "Have pity on your poor brother. Teach him some of the clever things you know. Teach him an anecdote, a riddle, anything so that people will listen to him."

And Avremele promised and took his brother aside and taught him.

"Itchikl," said he, "I'll teach you a riddle. You'll go to our neighbor's house and you'll say: 'What am I?' And they'll answer: 'You are a fool and an idiot.' So you'll say: 'Wrong! Guess again!' So they'll say: 'Tell us yourself what you are!' So you'll say: 'I am hungry!' Isn't that smart?"

Itchikl was delighted and he spent the whole day going over and over what his brother had taught him. In the evening he went to the neighbor's house and the house was full of people.

"A riddle!" he cried. "What am I?"

Everybody laughed.

"You are a fool and a donkey," they said.

"Wrong! Guess again!" cried Itchikl.

"Tell us yourself what you are!" the people cried.

"Give me something to eat!" Itchikl answered.

TALE OF TWO GRANDFATHERS

"Look, Max, it's a nice warm day. The park is green, the air is fresh, so sit down and relax. You are all upset."

"Sit down I'll sit down, Sol. But relax? I don't know if I can."

"What is it today? Your back?"

"No."

"Your sinus?"

"No."

"So what is it, Max?"

"It's Barney."

"Barney? Barney who?"

"You don't remember Barney? Barney with the fancy sports-coats and flashy shirts? Barney, the big show-off? I'll never talk to him again; never, Sol. I swear!"

"So Barney got you worked up! Better tell me about it, Max. Get it off your chest."

"You think I care what he says or what he thinks? But how does a man of his age come to act the way he acts? He's no gentleman, Sol, no gentleman!"

"Go on, Max."

"Well, I walk along, and I feel fine, and I see Barney coming. So I stop and say, 'Hello, Barney.' So he says, 'Hello, Max.' So I say, 'A long time I didn't see you.' So he says, 'I was out in California to see my married daughter.' So I say, 'I bet you have grandchildren already!' So he says, 'Yes, thank God.' So I say, 'Look, Barney, I wanna show you something. Take a look and tell me if you ever saw better merchandise in your life.' And I take out the album from my breast pocket—you know the genuine leather album with the silver buckle and my monogram on it, which my daughter gave me—and I open it and I show him my two little ones, the boy like a prince, the girl like a doll, an angel. You saw them, didn't you, Sol?"

"Of course, I did, Max. Leave your album in your pocket, Max, and go on with the story."

"For such children, Sol, Hollywood pays a million dollars! Everybody knows it. So I say to Barney, 'Well, Barney, what do you say to this line of goods? How do you like them?' So he looks and doesn't even take them in his hands, and says, 'Your grandchildren, Max?' So I say, 'All mine, Barney, all mine!' So he says, 'Nice children, very nice,' and he hands me back the album! So I say, 'That's all you have to say, Barney?—nice children, very nice? Do you know, Barney,' I say to him, 'that people stop my daughter on the street and they ask her, are those your children? They are beautiful, they say, you should send their pictures to the magazine for the prize contest!' So Barney says to me, 'Look Max, did I say there was anything the matter with those children? But if you want to see the genuine article,' he says, 'I'll show you something!' And he takes out of his breast pocket an album with a gold buckle and a monogram stamped in gold and before opening it he says, 'Top-grade leather, eighteen-carat gold buckle, a present from my daughter.' And opens it and shows me two pictures of a boy and a girl, and the pictures are all in color—you never saw such colors: red like fire, yellow like egg yolk, green more green than this grass! And he says to me, 'Now Max, you are looking at the stars of the show, the jewels of the crown!' Did you ever hear such language, Sol? Where did he learn it? 'Now, Max,' he says to me, 'take a good look and tell me if you ever saw anything like it?'

"What was there to say? I closed the album and handed it back to him and I said, 'Nice, Barney, nice children.' And it was God's honest truth! They *were* nice children. But did he think I was going to be fooled by all those colors? Mine, thank God, don't need any colors!"

"So what did he say, Max?"

"He? Well, that's the funny part of it. He got sore! Would you believe it, Sol? He is the one who gets sore! 'Max,' he says to me, 'I thought you were a good judge and a gentleman, but I see I was mistaken.' So I say to him, 'Barney,' I say, 'don't talk about a judge and a gentleman, you don't know anything about it.' So he begins to answer. So I turn around and walk away. I should stand and argue with him? So I ask you Sol, what do you say to a cheap show-off like that?"

"What should I say, Max? I would only say one thing."

"What is that, Sol?"

"I would say that when a grandfather wants to show his album he should make sure of one thing."

"What is that, Sol?"

"That the man he shows it to isn't also a grandfather. Otherwise, Max, it don't pay. The whole thing don't pay."

PROFILE OF A SMALL NUISANCE

"Benny," said his mother one morning, "are you eating green apples on an empty stomach?"

"Not empty," he replied. "I've already eaten three."

He watched as his mother, absorbed and silent, was baking cookies.

"Why don't you say something?" he asked her.

"What shall I say?"

"You could say: Take a little cookie, Benny."

He came upon his little sister one day munching a big red apple.

"Amy," said he, "let's play Adam and Eve."

"How do you play it?"

"I'll be Adam, you'll be Eve, and you must talk me into eating the apple."

The two visited their grandmother one day and she put two apples on the table, a big one and a little one.

"Now let me see which of you has the better manners," she said.

"Amy!" said Benny as he took the bigger apple.

"Benny," said his father, "your hands are filthy. Have you ever seen my hands like that?"

"No, dad, but maybe——"

"Maybe what?"

"Maybe your father did."

"Benny," said his mother, "why did you throw a stone at that boy?"

"He started up with me."

"Then why didn't you come to me?"

"Should I? You think your aim is better than mine?"

"If you don't stop being so bad," said his mother, "I'll exchange you for another boy."

"You couldn't," said Benny. "Who'd be foolish enough to give you a good boy for one like me?"

"Today," Benny reported, "teacher asked a question and nobody came up with an answer."

"What was the question?" said his father.

"Who broke the window?"

"Benny," said the teacher, "how do you manage to make so many mistakes in your homework?"

"My father helps me," Benny explained.

"Benny," said his father proudly, "who was smart in school today? Who knew the lessons, hey?"

"The teacher," Benny answered.

He confided to his father one day that his neighbor in class got his answers all wrong.

"How do you know?" asked his father.

"He copied from me," said Benny.

"How did it happen," the teacher asked Benny, "that your composition on the cat is just like Danny's, word for word?"

"We wrote about the same cat," Benny explained.

"Reptiles," the teacher told the class, "are creatures that crawl on the ground. Can you give me an example, Benny?"

"My little brother, Julius," said Benny.

"What does the crown prince become when his father dies?" the teacher asked.

"An orphan," said Benny.

"What is the first thing he does when he mounts the throne?"

"He sits down."

The teacher conjugated, "I am talking."

"I am talking," she said, "you are talking, he is talking, she is talking; we are talking, you are talking, they are talking. Now," she went on, "who can repeat this?"

Benny raised his hand.

"Yes, Benny," she said.

"Everybody is talking," said Benny.

"Benny," said the teacher, "go to the map and find America."

Benny went up and put his finger on America.

"Now, class," said the teacher, "who discovered America?"

Benny, facing the class, poked his thumb at his chest.

"Benny!" the class shouted as Benny bowed.

Nor did the teacher in Hebrew school get any further with Benny.

"Why," she asked, "did the people in the desert make a golden calf?"

"Wasn't it because they couldn't raise enough money for a cow?" Benny asked.

And once his parents took him to the opera. It was not too soon, they decided, to introduce him to the finer things in life.

"Why is the man trying to poke that lady with a stick?" Benny asked.

"Hush," said his father. "That's the conductor waving his baton. He is not trying to poke anybody."

"Then why," Benny demanded, "is the lady screaming?"

For the service in the temple Benny expressed more appreciation, but not without a reservation.

"It was a good program," he said, "and I liked the cantor and especially the choir. But why do they have to have such a long commercial?"

MAZL TOV!

There was a poor man who came to the Free Burial Society and asked them to look after the interment of his wife.

"How's that?" said the president of the society. "We buried your wife two years ago."

"That was my first wife," the man replied. "Now my second has died."

"Oh!" said the president, "I didn't know you were married again! *Mazl Tov!*"

SHE KNEW HER MAN

"When Adam came home late at night, what was the first thing Eve did?" a certain sage was asked.

"She counted his ribs," the sage replied.

Rabbis and Scholars

DAY OF GLORY

"Are we far from our destination?" the eminent rabbi asked his driver. It was the third time he asked the question.

"We are only a few miles now from the tavern at the edge of

the town," the wagoner replied. "But I understand why you are impatient."

"How do you understand it?"

"Well, in that tavern they are now sitting, waiting for you—a deputation of the foremost citizens of the community chosen to welcome an illustrious rabbi, to honor him, to—"

"You are mistaken, my good man, I am not impatient and I am not pining for honor. I confess it has become a weekday affair for me. I just wanted to make conversation."

"How can a man become indifferent to honor?" the wagoner wondered. "I can think of nothing more grand. People bowing to you, hanging on your words, speaking to you in whispers. I would give anything—I—"

He stopped. A sudden idea flashed in upon him and dazzled him.

"Rabbi," he said, "give me a chance just once to feel the joy of being honored as a famous rabbi and scholar. Let us exchange headgear and *kaftns*. We are about the same height, and our beards look very much alike. You've never been in this town before, and no one will suspect the innocent ruse."

The rabbi was amused.

"You will be taking risks just the same," he said. "Aren't you afraid?"

"You mean I may have to uphold my reputation for learning? No, I am not afraid. I'll manage one way or another. I've been in many a tight place in my life. Come, will you do it, rabbi?"

"Very well, but remember, you will have only yourself to blame."

So the rabbi put on the driver's coarse *kaftn* and faded cap, and the driver put on the rabbi's satin *kaftn* and imposing fur headpiece. The rabbi took the reins, and the wagon rolled into the front yard of the tavern.

The town worthies came out and stood humbly before the satin *kaftn* and fur hat. The wearer received their homage and said something about being fatigued and needing repose. And having rested and taken refreshments, he received the deputation formally and listened, with only an occasional nod, to their fulsome salutations.

The formal proceedings over, the atmosphere became relaxed, and two of the worthies approached the wearer of the satin *kaftn* with a question of Rabbinic law which none of the local scholars, they informed him, were able to resolve. He listened with closed eyes and when they had done, he looked at them with an expression of surprise.

"What!" he exclaimed. "You are baffled by a simple question like that? What sort of scholars have you in this town? Do they know the difference between a wheel and an axle, a colt and a filly? Let me tell you what I think of your problem. Even the wagoner who drove me to this town could solve it without difficulty. Call him in!"

The "wagoner" was called in, the worthies laid the problem before him, and he solved it promptly and to their entire satisfaction.

"Wonder of wonders!" they whispered to each other with awe. "This can mean only one thing. Learning is contagious. Some strange influence emanates from this man and enters into other people. How fortunate we are to have this monumental scholar in our midst."

"Thank you, rabbi," said the driver when the two were alone and wearing their own *kaftns* and headgear. "It felt like heaven on earth! But what I said about their local scholars was true, wasn't it, rabbi? They're not very clever, are they?"

"Compared to you, I would say, they certainly are not," the rabbi replied.

HE STOOPS TO CONQUER

A famous rabbi, who was a master in the art of getting money from the rich for the benefit of the poor, was once asked:

"How does a man of your standing prevail on himself to stoop before the rich swine of this town? Does it accord with your dignity to demean yourself before them?"

"My son," replied the sage, "it is all in the order of nature. Look now, there is no creature on earth more excellent than man, and few creatures more lowly than the cow. Nevertheless, a man has to stoop before the cow when he wants to milk her!"

IMPARTIAL

A man from a distant town once came to a young "modern" rabbi with a strange petition.

"I want you," he said, "to judge between me and the Almighty. I have a number of grievances against Him."

"Why did you come to me?" said the young clergyman. "Isn't there a rabbi in your own town?"

"There is," the stranger replied. "But the rabbi in my town is a God-fearing man, so how could he judge impartially between us? But you, I've been told, have no fear of God, so I know I can trust you."

FOR THE POOR

There was a rich miser who, it so happened, was an ardent follower of a famous *rebe*. The miser came to visit his mentor and the *rebe* enjoined him to eat only of the best meat, fish, and fowl, and to drink the best wines.

The other followers of the *rebe* thought it very strange.

"Rebe," they said, "why are you so concerned about the good cheer of that miser?"

"I'm not concerned about him," the *rebe* explained. "I'm concerned about the poor. If he himself lives on bread and water, can you expect him to think of the poor? But if he drinks the best wines and eats the best meats he may give bread to the poor."

WHAT FOR THE POOR?

Passover was at hand and the number of families lacking provisions for the festival was greater than usual. The old rabbi of the town determined to visit the well-to-do himself and solicit alms for the needy, and among those he decided to call upon was a certain rich miser, a man of surly and violent temper, whose hand never opened to the poor.

The rabbi lavished all his gifts of persuasion upon the miser without effect. He dilated on the sufferings of the poor, on the beauty and holiness of the Passover festival, on the great rewards of charity, here and in the Hereafter. The miser remained obdurate and sullen. The rabbi changed his tone. He became threatening and sarcastic. He spoke of the wrath of God and the contempt of men. He spoke of the penalties reserved for the heartless and greedy in the World-to-come.

As the miser listened his face became more and more sinister. Finally he jumped up in a rage and struck the rabbi in the face.

For a moment the old man was bewildered. Then his expression lighted up. He turned with a smile to his host.

"This that you have just given," he said, "was for me. Now what will you give for the poor?"

VENGEANCE AND LOVE

The rabbi and priest were good friends and talked of many things. The priest was an amiable man without religious prejudice, but certain things puzzled him.

"Rabbi," said he once. "You know I'm no anti-Semite. But there is something I don't understand. Why do you Jews cling to a God of vengeance? Don't you think you should rather accept the Christian God of love?"

"It may be true," said the rabbi, "that ours is a God of vengeance, yours a God of love. I'll not argue with you about it. But what does it all mean? 'Vengeance is mine, saith the Lord.' We leave vengeance to Him, and as for us, we go in for love, as it is written: 'And thou shalt love thy neighbor as thyself.' And if, on the other hand, you leave the loving to God, and you yourselves go in for vengeance, must we follow your example?"

WHY THE HURRY?

A traveller who had been to the capital returned to his own little town and the rabbi invited him to come and relate the wonders of the great city.

"There is too much to tell," said the returned native, "but something I will tell you. Take for example the elecric tramway. If a man has to go from one part of the city to another, he doesn't walk. It would take him too long. He gets on the electric tramway and in a few minutes he arrives. Then there is the railroad. In an hour you go by railroad from one city to another! Now suppose you want to talk to your friend who is a hundred miles away. You have important and urgent business and you must talk to him! Must you go to see him? No. You don't even have to lose time writing letters to him. You take up the telephone and in a few minutes you tell him whatever you wish."

"Wonder of wonders!" said the old rabbi. "But one thing is not clear to me. Why are all the people over there in such a hurry?"

A HEN AND A ROOSTER

Someone came to the rabbi of a small town with a question that baffled him.

"What shall I do?" the man asked. "I have a hen and a rooster and one of them has to go to the pot. But which one? If I take the rooster the hen raises a terrible outcry. She clucks and screams and flaps her wings. If I take the hen, the rooster shrieks so my blood curdles. What shall I do, rabbi?"

The old rabbi chewed his beard thoughtfully.

"I must look up the law on this matter," said he. "Come back in three days."

"Nu, rabbi?" said the man three days later.

"The law is to take the hen," the rabbi replied.

"But the rooster will protest!" the man cried.

"The rooster will protest?" said the rabbi. "Let him protest!"

TWO BROTHERS

There were two brothers in a town, one of whom was the rabbi and the other the bathkeeper; and the rabbi always snubbed his brother.

"Look here," said the latter one day to the rabbi. "I don't understand why you are so arrogant. If I were like that there would be a good reason for it. My brother is a rabbi! But your brother—what is he? Only a bathkeeper!"

THE PATH OF TORAH

No, it was not easy to acquire learning in the famous academies of the Old World. As soon as a smalltown youngster learned all that the local masters could teach him, he went off to continue his studies in one of those distant academies and found himself in a hard and strange world. Every day he ate the bread of charity in a different household: "eating days," they called it. And he learned how true are the words in the Talmud: "This is the path of Torah: a morsel of bread with salt shall you eat, and water by measure shall you drink, and you shall sleep upon the ground and live a life of anguish as you labor to acquire Torah."

And I remember one such youngster who not only had a keen mind, but was also quite a wag. He came home for the Passover holidays and was asked by his anxious mother where he slept and how he ate in the distant world of the academy.

"Where I sleep?" he answered. "I have a good solid bench in

the house of study, all my own, and I sleep on it like a lord. Is it hard? Well, it's not soft. And for a pillow they tell you to use your fist. And if you find it brings your head up too high, why then, you just release one of your fingers.

"And how do I eat? I eat days. The food? You want to know about the food? Well, there are only two things the matter with it. In the first place, it's dirt. Impossible to take into your mouth. In the second place, they never give you enough."

THE GIML *IN "NOAH"*

"Let me ask you a question," said one Talmud student to another.

"Ask," replied the second.

"What need is there for a *giml* in 'Noah'?"

"Where do you find a *giml* in 'Noah'?"

"Why shouldn't there be a *giml* in 'Noah'?"

"What need is there for a *giml* in 'Noah'?"

"Eh, but that is *my* question: What need is there for a *giml* in 'Noah'?"

QUESTIONS AND ANSWERS

"Kopl," said a Talmud student to his friend, "I should be the happiest man in the world."

"Really?" said Kopl. "What's happened, Chaikl? Have you drawn the big prize in the lottery?"

"A fig for your lottery, Kopl! I have something more precious. I have an answer, Kopl, a wonderful answer, a perfect answer!"

"Really? Congratulations, Chaikl!"

"But wait, Kopl. I should be happy, but I'm not. I have the answer, but I don't have the question. Tell me Kopl, my friend, where can I get the question?"

LOGIC

After a long session over his Talmud, a scholar stepped out to quench his thirst and returned to resume his study. But first he had to put on his spectacles, and they were gone! He looked for them on the table, he looked for them inside the folio, he looked for them on the floor.

"They are gone!" he declared, and stared helplessly before him.

But the next moment he summoned to his help all his powers of deduction and with the chant of the Talmud to aid him, he reasoned as follows:

"Shall I say that someone came in my absence and took my spectacles? How can I say that? If it was someone who needed spectacles he would have his own. If he didn't need them, why would he take somebody else's? Perhaps I may say that the man was a thief and stole them in order to sell them. But to whom could he sell them? If he offers to sell them to someone who needs spectacles, that person must have spectacles; if to someone who doesn't need spectacles, he won't buy them. I am compelled therefore to conclude that the spectacles were taken by someone who needs spectacles and has spectacles, but he went out in a hurry, moved his spectacles up from his nose to his forehead, forgot that he had done so, and took mine.

"And I'll go further," he continued with renewed zest. "Perhaps I myself am the man who went out in a hurry, and moved his spectacles up from his nose to his forehead and forgot that he did so?"

And thereupon the logician felt his forehead and discovered his spectacles!

ON THE NOSE

There was another scholar who was faced with a similar problem and also managed to solve it by his acute power of reasoning.

He sat down one day, opened his folio, and looked puzzled.

"Where are my spectacles?" he wondered. "Where can they be? In my pocket? No. Between the leaves? No. On the table? No. How do I know they are not on the table? I see they are not on the table! I see? If I am able to see, the spectacles must be on my nose! Ah! Thank God! They are!"

"WITH MILK"

From earliest childhood, Rabbi Jonathan of Prague was famous for his phenomenal memory. When he was five years old, a visitor from a distant city asked the boy:

"What is your favorite food?"

"Rice with—," the boy began, but at that moment his father entered, took over the visitor and the conversation ended.

Seven years later the same visitor met Jonathan again.

"With what?" he asked.

"Milk," replied the boy without a moment's hesitation.

WHAT LETTERS!

"Reb Shmerl," said an acquaintance, "what do you hear from your son? What does he write?"

"Thank you very much. Things are not so well with him. His wife died and left him with three small children, such beautiful children! His business is also bad, and it's getting worse all the time. Not long ago he had a robbery and he was left with only his shirt on his back. Things are bad, very bad. But let me tell you something. You should read his letters! It's a pleasure to read them. His style is just marvelous!"

THE LEARNED WAGONER

Yudl has been a wagoner for many years, plying with passengers and freight between his and the neighboring towns. But Yudl is no ordinary *balagole,* not an ignoramus, like other wagoners. He is no stranger to the "small print," to the Pentateuch and Rashi, to a chapter of the Psalms; he is even familiar with the famous thirteen principles of Rabbi Ishmael, the thirteen rules for expounding Holy Writ, such as the rules of *a fortiori*, "analogy," etc.

"*Balagole?*" Yudl protested. "I am no *balagole*. I happen to have a horse and wagon and drive from town to town and anyone who cares to join me is welcome. But a *balagole? Cholile!*"

Now it once happened that Yudl made a long and perilous journey and it was only his learning that saved him and his passengers from disaster. But let Yudl himself tell the story:

"Yes, it was a hard journey, the hardest I ever made. My wagon was overloaded and a fierce storm rose up on the way—a storm of wind and rain and hail, as if Satan the destroyer himself had been given a free hand with the world. And do you want to know what saved us? I can tell you in a word! The principles of Rabbi Ishmael! Just two of them. The rule of *a fortiori* and the rule of analogy. Now you know! And if you want to know it in particular, then listen and you will hear.

"The first prank that Satan played me was to take one of the wheels off the wagon. It fell right off the axle, and what could I do? Immediately I called to my aid the principle of *a fortiori*. 'Since,' I said to myself, 'there are vehicles that roll on only two wheels, my wagon should certainly be able to roll on three.' Soon afterwards, however, I was compelled to invoke the rule of analogy. We hadn't gone far when another wheel fell off! What can a man do when Satan's hand is upon him? 'Since other vehicles run on two wheels,' I argued, 'my wagon can also do it!' And I whipped up my horse and we went on. Before long, however, I had to take refuge again in *a fortiori*. The third wheel fell off the axle! Ah, my friends, where would I now be and where would my passengers be without the blessed *a foriori?* 'Since,' I said to myself, 'a sleigh moves with no wheels, my wagon should certainly be able to go on one wheel!' And believe me, we would have arrived without further mishap, were it not for Satan who was out to try us to the limit. You guess what I mean: the fourth wheel fell off the axle! 'Oho!' said I, 'so you are at it again, Reb Satan! Well, you may have the power, but I understand the principle of analogy!' And at once I reasoned as follows: 'Since a sleigh is able to proceed without wheels, my wagon can also do it!' And on we went, and since there were no more wheels to remove, the Evil One departed from us and we reached our destination safe and sound!

"Now tell me, I ask you, what would I have done without *a fortiori* and analogy?"

ANOTHER LEARNED WAGONER

The fate of a certain Jewish community lay in the hands of the *porets* who often amused himself by issuing strange and cruel edicts. But when he proclaimed the edict about the disputation, the community was thrown into a panic. It was to be a debate between a priest and a Jewish representative. The debate was to be in the Hebrew language: the priest, it appeared, was learned in the holy tongue. He boasted, in fact, that he was more deeply versed in it than the Jewish scholars.

And this was the way in which the disputation was to be conducted: the disputants were to ask each other questions, and woe betide the first who should be unable to answer! A soldier with a drawn sword would be stationed near the debaters and the unfortunate man would be immediately beheaded! And should the Jews fail to send a representative, declared the edict, the entire community, men, women, and children, would be exiled!

Imagine the despair of the community. Whom should they send and who would go? If no one went they would all be driven out! If they did send someone, they placed him in mortal danger. What if this priest really were as adept as he boasted? On the other hand, was it right for the sake of one to bring disaster upon all?

So they called a solemn assembly to decide whom to send. They waited for someone to volunteer but no one came forward. An atmosphere as of Yom Kippur hung over the gathering. Suddenly a voice made itself heard. It was the voice of Velvl the wagoner.

"Send me," he said, "and I will go!"

What an idea! Everybody knew Velvl to be a complete ignoramus. He could say his daily prayers—without, of course, understanding the meaning—and that was all! How would he stand up before the learned priest? But Velvl insisted.

"Send me," he repeated. "You have no one else. What can you lose?"

There was no alternative. Alas for the wagoner!

The day of the disputation arrived and the place was crowded with people who came from miles around to witness the event. In the center stood the priest and the wagoner, and near them the soldier with the drawn sword. The first question was to be asked by Velvl.

"What is the meaning of *eyneni yodea*?" asked the wagoner.

"I don't know," replied the priest.

Immediately the soldier acted. He rushed forward and with one blow he beheaded the poor priest.

Velvl was brought back in triumph. The people gathered in the synagogue, said the special prayer of thanks for deliverance from peril, and there was great rejoicing. But everybody was curious. How did the ignorant Velvl think of asking such a shrewd question? Had someone prompted him?

So they asked him to explain and Velvl did so without hesitation.

"The matter," he declared, "is very simple. I once had a teacher who did his best to drive something into my thick head, but it wasn't easy. One day I asked him the meaning of *eyneni yodea*. 'I don't know,' he replied. Now I remembered that, and when the affair of the disputation came up, I said to myself: 'If my teacher, peace unto him, didn't know, would it be likely that the priest would know?' And sure enough, the priest, thank God, didn't know either!"

RABBI, SULTAN, AND MONKEY

The Sultan of Morogeria was now a doddering old man, but still imperious, self-willed, and autocratic. His wives no longer attracted him, his old friends had no access to him, and affairs of state made him yawn. All his interest was now focused on one object: a monkey, to which he had become passionately attached.

One day he summoned the chief rabbi of his kingdom to appear before him.

"I have called you," said the sultan, "because you are the wisest of all my subjects. I command you, therefore, to teach my monkey to talk. I want to be able to converse with him. If you fail you know, of course, what fate awaits you."

"Yes, Your Majesty," the rabbi replied, "but to carry out your wish I need time—at least ten years."

"Not more than five!" the senile ruler commanded.

The rabbi called in the leading men of the community and informed them of the task the sultan had laid upon him.

"But how will you accomplish it? How will you teach a monkey to talk?" they asked him.

"I have five years," he answered. "In five years many things can happen. The Sultan may die, I may die, the monkey may die. And in five years—who knows?—the monkey may even be able to talk."

Cantors, Preachers, Orators

HOW IT HAPPENED

For reasons good or bad, cantors have always been the victims of scoffers and wags, and the following legend is not the worst of the jibes that have been directed against them:

At the time of Creation, every living creature, so it was decreed, was to be allotted a life-span of forty years. Whereupon the horse appeared and asked to know what his destiny would be on earth.

"Men will ride on your back," he was told.

"In that case," the horse replied, "twenty years will be enough for me."

Then came the donkey and asked the same question.

"You," he was told, "will be made to bear heavy burdens."

"In that case," said the donkey, "I'll be satisfied with twenty years."

After the donkey came the cantor.

"What am I destined to do on earth?" he asked.

"Your work," he was told, "will be most pleasant. You will do nothing but sing hymns and praises."

"In that case," said the cantor, "I would like my life-span to be doubled."

Whereupon a solemn council was held in heaven and it was decided to take away twenty years from the horse and twenty from the donkey, and add them to the life-span of the cantor.

It was so ordered; and that is why a cantor sings as he should during the first forty years of his life. The next twenty years he neighs like a horse, and the next twenty he brays like a donkey.

HE WANTS TO KNOW

For time out of memory it has been the custom of cantors to place their thumbs under their chins when scaling into the higher octaves. And once a young admirer asked a famous cantor:

"Why do you do that?"

"I've been doing it for fifty years without knowing why," the cantor replied, "and now comes a whippersnapper like you and wants to know!"

THE OIL WOULD HAVE FLOWED ON

This is a story about an ambitious cantor and an accommodating rabbi. It came to the cantor's ears that the neighboring community was looking for a cantor and he resolved to apply for the position, so he went to his rabbi and spoke as follows:

"The neighboring community is larger and richer, and it's time that I got on in the world. Help me to get the position. Give me your recommendation."

Now the rabbi who, of course, knew the cantor well, pondered the matter a long time, but finally gave him a paper on which was written the following:

"If the holder of this note had been living in the days of the Prophet Elisha, the oil would not have stopped flowing."

The cantor took the note to the neighboring town where it was read by the town worthies who, although they were rather mystified by it, were also impressed.

"This man," said they, "must be no ordinary cantor, or the rabbi would not write about him in that way."

So they engaged the applicant and it was not many weeks before they discovered the truth. They discovered that their cantor was an incompetent, an ignoramus, and a fool to boot! But they had to put up with him, for what could they do? Nevertheless, they harbored a deep grudge against the rabbi. What did he mean by saying such things about a good-for-nothing?

And it came to pass that one of the worthies visited the neighboring town and determined to call on the rabbi and ask for an explanation. He found the sage seated in his study, bent over his Talmud folio, and the visitor respectfully but firmly explained his errand.

"My son," replied the rabbi, "read over again the fourth chapter of the Seconed Book of Kings. It's the story of the oil that flowed miraculously on. Now why did the flow cease? Because there was not one empty vessel left. It follows therefore that if that cantor had been present the oil would have flowed on."

PITY THE POOR CANTOR

When it comes to cantors, there are lots of people who envy them, but very few who admire them. People envy them the prominence they enjoy and the sense of power they must have when commanding the attention and controlling the emotions of a large assembly. But candid admiration? Appreciation? Gratitude? Those things come to them very rarely. It must not be forgotten that every congregant considers himself a connoisseur of the cantorial art and looks upon every practitioner of it as fair game.

I'm a cantor myself, not one of the greats, I'll admit, but not one of the smalls either, and I say all that apropos of what happened to me the first time I officiated in a new position somewhere in Brooklyn. After the service one of the congregants, a heavy man with a broad, florid face and a huge grin, came over and said to me:

"Ours is no easy profession, I'll say."

"So you are a cantor also!" I said.

"Not I," he told me, "I'm a Coney Island barker."

PARABLE OF THE TIRED GOAT

After a long and weary journey the famous preacher known as the Dubno *magid* arrived in the town where he was to preach on the Sabbath afternoon, and was driven to the home of Reb Mendl, one of the notables, who was to entertain him during his stay in the town. Reb Mendl was proud to be the *magid*'s host. For he was not the ordinary fire-and-brimstone preacher, this *magid*. He was known far and wide for his eloquence, and especially for the parables with which he embellished his discourse. There was no one like the Dubno *magid* for apt and striking parables. What wonderful stories they were about kings and princes, merchants and beggars, saints and brigands, foxes and lions! And how readily they fell from his lips to point a moral or clinch an argument!

"I am honored, I am honored!" Reb Mendl kept repeating as he ushered the preacher into his parlor. He was eager to hear something drop from those wise lips—a new parable, perhaps, that he would be the first to circulate among his fellow townsmen. But the *magid* was silent.

"Shall I tell you something?" Reb Mendl babbled on. "It seems a little strange to me that the Dubno *magid* should sit so silent. By this time one or two parables should have issued from his teeming brain, things that I and other men would treasure in their memories."

The *magid* roused himself.

"You want a parable?" he said. "So listen and you will hear."

There was once a poor shoemaker whose thrifty wife, by dint of economy and self-denial, saved up enough to satisfy her dearest wish: to own a good, reliable milking-goat. She gave her little hoard to her husband who took it one morning to a neighboring town, famous for its fine goats, and came back in the late afternoon with one of them. The woman was all impatience. She snatched up a pail and stool and went out to milk her precious goat. She worked long and hard, but not a single drop of milk did the goat yield. She came back to her husband and showed him the empty pail. "Look," she cried, "and see the kind of goat you brought me!" Then she sat down and wept.

"Foolish woman," said he to her, "Is this a time to milk the goat? The poor creature has had a long and hard journey. She is tired and hungry. First give her food and drink, and let her rest, then you can go out and milk her, and you will come back with a full pail."

"Peshe!" cried Reb Mendl to his wife. "Do you hear me, Peshe? Set the table at once for our guest! Bring on the best things you have in the house. And listen, Peshe, put a nice big pillow on the sofa. Our guest wants to lie down and rest after he has eaten."

GRATEFUL

One Sabbath afternoon an itinerant preacher held forth in the synagogue and the following day, in accordance with custom, he went from house to house to collect his honorarium. One of the worthies of the town received him with special cordiality and gave him a handsome gratuity. The preacher was delighted.

"So you liked my sermon!" he smiled.

"Well," the other replied, "it's not exactly that. For a long time I've been suffering from insomnia, but as soon as you began I fell alseep and slept right through to the end."

TWO BEARDS

The audience was not responsive. There is something in the atmosphere of a gathering that makes every preacher and orator aware of the fact, and all his efforts to overcome it are sometimes futile. The preacher in question extended himself in every direction, but the audience remained unimpressed.

With one exception. He sat up front near the rostrum, and the preacher couldn't help noticing him. At the beginning the man's face expressed a peculiar felicity, but as the sermon continued it became overcast, and at the end the preacher saw tears run down his cheeks.

"Nu," said the preacher to himself when it was all over, "I had at least one grateful listener. Thank God for that."

So he spoke to this listener and mentioned the tears he saw on his face.

"Let me explain," was the answer. "I grew up in a small town, and I was one of a big and impoverished family. But one day we came into possession of a goat, a she-goat, a wonderful creature, who gave us a lot of milk, and we all became attached to her. It was a happy period in my life and whenever I am reminded of it, I am deeply moved. Nostalgia, they call it. Well now—would you believe it—your beard is exactly like that goat's!"

FOR SELF-CONFIDENCE

He was a famous preacher and the town to which he came received him gladly. The evening before his first sermon he visited the richest man in town and asked for a loan of ten rubles.

"I'll return the money immediately after my sermon," he promised.

The rich man hesitated, but finally granted the loan.

The preacher kept his promise. His sermon pleased the people and he was invited to preach again and again. And always before each sermon, he borrowed ten rubles from the rich man and after the sermon returned the loan.

The rich man was puzzled.

"I don't understand you," said he to the preacher finally. "If you need the money, why do you return it without using it? If you don't need the money, why do you borrow it?"

"My friend," the preacher explained, "do you realize what

self-confidence it gives a man who is facing an audience when he has ten rubles in his pocket?"

THE KEY

The preacher stood on the platform and gave his audience all he had, but to no avail. One by one, his hearers arose and left the synagogue. Finally only the sexton and the preacher remained.

Timidly the sexton approached the preacher and handed him a key.

"When you are through," he whispered, "will you be kind enough to lock the synagogue?"

A CASE OF JUSTICE

The preacher stood and held forth in his best manner, but a loud snore was heard in the audience. The preacher stopped and called the *shames*.

"Will you please wake up that man?" said he.

"It's not fair," said the *shames*, "you put him to sleep, you wake him up!"

SUCH IS LIFE!

"A human being," said a preacher in a mood of pessimism, "may be compared to a moneylender. A moneylender goes on living till he dies and the same is true of a human being."

WHAT HAVE I TO DO WITH YOU?

After one of his sermons a famous preacher was visited by one of the worthies of the town, a youngish man with advanced ideas, and without beard or earlocks.

"Reb Magid," said the visitor, "I protest against your sermons. Why do you frighten our people with your old wives' tales? Why don't you leave out those lurid pictures of Hell and its demons?"

The *magid* was taken aback but he recovered quickly and spoke to his visitor as follows:

"Let me tell you something that once happened to me. I was on my travels one day when I met an ox. The ox stopped and extended a hoof in greeting.

" '*Sholem aleychem!*' said the ox.

" 'Foolish beast,' said I, 'what have I to do with you?'

" 'You eat my flesh,' the ox replied, and recognizing the justice of his reply, I returned his greeting.

"I proceeded on my way and met a cow. The animal stopped and greeted me.

" '*Sholem aleychem!*' said the cow and held up one of her hoofs.

" 'Silly cow,' said I, 'what have I to do with you?'

" 'You drink my milk,' the cow replied. I had to admit the truth of what she had said and returned her greeting.

"I went on and before long I met a goat. The goat took his stand in front of me, shook his head solemnly, and greeted me.

" '*Sholem aleychem,*' said the goat and lifted one of his forelegs.

" 'Ridiculous beast,' said I, 'what have I to do with you?'

"The goat nodded to me and replied:

" 'Look, I have a beard and so have you!'

" 'You are right,' said I and returned his greeting.

"Finally I met a pig and the pig also lifted a leg and greeted me. I became very angry.

" 'Loathsome beast!' I cried. 'Your flesh I don't eat, your milk I don't drink, of a beard you have no vestige! What on earth have I to do with you?' "

TWO-GUN MOSCOWITZ

The subject of his sermon was "Our Heritage." He had only recently been declared "a preacher and teacher in Israel," and this was practically his maiden effort. He had learned many things; among them the importance of driving home his point by means of a good story.

"My friends," he orated, "let me tell you a little story. It's about a lady whom we will call Mrs. Moscowitz. She visited a department store one day to take advantage of a special sale, and took her youngster along, a boy of about four. In the wild melee around the sales counter, mother and son were separated, and the child—a beautiful child, dressed in cowboy costume, with a pistol hanging at each hip—wandered off alone.

"Presently the child began to cry, and a floorwalker lifted him in his arms.

" 'What's your name?' said the man.

" 'Two-gun Moscowitz, and I want my mommy,' the child bawled.

"In a minute or so the loud-speaker system of the store was heard blaring out and repeating the following message:

" 'Will Mrs. Moscowitz please come to the manager's office on the second floor and pick up her Two-gun!' "

And the youthful preacher continued:

"Now my friends, I ask you: Is that a proper name for a Jewish child? Two-gun Moscowitz? Is that the way to inculcate our sacred heritage into our children? Two-gun Moscowitz! Doesn't the name run counter to all our traditions, to the ideals of our great prophets?

"But you might object and ask me: What then would you call him? Suggest some other name! I am ready, my friends, to meet your challenge. I would call the little fellow (*pause*) Ten-Commandments Moscowitz!"

HAVE MERCY!

We complain against long-winded orators, and who will deny that the complaints are justified, seeing how they make us suffer? But does it ever occur to anyone that the orator himself may also suffer? This is the sad story about one such orator.

He had been holding forth for more than twice the time the

chairman had allotted him, and he was aware that the audience was writhing. "It's high time I wound up," he was now thinking. "I need a good peroration, a whopper." So he began a ringing peroration, but, somehow, before he got very far with it, it lost its ring. "This won't do," said he to himself. "I am heading for an anticlimax." So he abandoned it and launched into another peroration, with the same lamentable result. A third time and a third disaster. The audience now noticed that their tormentor was diligently mopping his forehead. He was like an aviator circling a field, looking for a safe landing. Now the plane comes close to the ground, but there is no safe landing and up it shoots for another round and another.

At length the chairman resolved to let courtesy go by the board. He handed the orator a folded slip of paper on which were written the words "Have mercy!" The speaker stopped long enough to add the words "On me, O Lord!" before handing the paper back to the chairman and soaring up for another round.

And, dear friends, let us pray that for his own sake, if not for the sake of his audience, he has by this time made a happy landing!

STORY WITH A BEARD

The after-dinner speaker droned on and on, indifferent to his listeners; perhaps not even aware of them. He was the only one in the banquet hall who was not bored. He liked to hear his voice and was sure he was propounding important truths and expressing noble sentiments. The people before him yawned and fidgeted, but they were helpless. The chairman slumped in his seat and buried his clean-shaven chin in his shirtfront.

Eventually the chairman was observed to stand up quietly and approach someone seated near him on the dais—observed that is, by everybody except the speaker.

"Mr. Simon," the chairman whispered. "I have to make a number of important calls. I'll be away twenty, thirty minutes. Please take my seat and act as chairman."

Mr. Simon took the chairman's seat and his posture as well. He slumped down and buried his chin in his shirtfront. But Mr. Simon's chin was not clean-shaven. It was adorned with a short black beard.

The speaker droned on and on. The audience began to dwindle. There were others who had important calls to make.

At last the speaker paused. He shook off his self-hypnosis and, becoming aware of his audience, wondered why it was so diminished. Then he glanced towards the chairman and gasped.

"My—my friends," he stammered. "Forgive me, please forgive me. I—I didn't realize I had spoken so long!"

NOTHING LIKE NO SPEECHES

I knew Albert Levy well. Al, everybody called him. Queer chap. When he was elected president of the congregation, some of the members had misgivings. The man had queer ideas. He objected, for example, when rabbis called themselves "spiritual leaders." A diploma from a seminary, he used to say, doesn't make a man a spiritual leader. Such leadership is a gift from a higher source. The name rabbi should be good enough. Silly talk, you'll agree. No?

But the queerest thing about Al was his aversion for orators and speeches, an aversion that amounted to a phobia. "Bores, bores, bores!" was the way he described them all. "I sometimes go and listen to one of them," he once told me, "in order to enjoy the wonderful relief I feel when they finish." When he became president of the congregation they all knew they could expect no more purveyors of "stimulating messages," "fiery appeals," "historic addresses," "illuminating discourses," and so forth. Such purveyors were in plentiful supply at the time, but the doors of this particular house of worship were closed against them.

But it happened that there came to our shores from the Old World a man of towering reputation as an orator and public figure. The admiration he aroused was enthusiastic and universal, and those who were not happy with Al as president saw their chance to take him down a peg or two. They insisted that the illustrious orator be invited to address the congregation and nearly all the others supported them. The pressure became more than Al could resist and he had to give in.

The orator came and he was really good. But good is no word for it. He was just grand. There was no dissenting opinion. When the affair was over and the speaker had left, the members, especially Al's opponents, were anxious to hear what he would say about it.

"What do you say, Al?" they taunted him. "A wonderful speech, wasn't it?"

"Wonderful?" said Al. "Maybe. But let me tell you something. It didn't measure up—just didn't measure up."

"Didn't measure up to what?" they asked him.

"It didn't measure up to no speech at all," Al Levy told them.

Buyers, Sellers, Borrowers

A FOX TERRIER

The Polish squire summoned his Jewish superintendent.

"Yankl," said he, "my wife has made me promise I would get her a fox terrier. Will you go out and buy me one? And remember, I want a good one!"

"Of course, Your Excellency! At once!" the man replied.

"And how much is Your Excellency willing to pay for a good fox terrier?"

"Fifty crowns," said the squire.

"Impossible, Your Excellency," said Yankl.

"How much, then?"

"At least a hundred."

"A hundred crowns?"

"At least, Your Excellency."

"Well—all right. A hundred then. But hurry up!"

But Yankl stood still.

"Why don't you go?" the squire demanded.

"Your Excellency. . . ."

"Yes?"

"Tell me, I beg of you, what is a fox terrier?"

NO PROFIT, NO LOSS

"Shimshn," said Motl the clothing dealer, "you are my *lantsman* and I'll sell you a suit that you'll thank me for all your life. And cheap, do you hear? Why should I make money on you? You're my *lantsman!* Here is the suit, the best in the store! And will I ask you sixty dollars for it, which it is worth? Oh, no! Not sixty, and not fifty and not even forty. Thirty dollars is all you will pay me. Take it, it's yours!"

"Motl," said Shimshn, "I can't see you should lose money on me. Why should you lose on me? You are my *lantsman!* So what will I offer you for this suit? Will I offer you six dollars? Oh, no! I will not offer you so little, and not even eight dollars or ten dollars. Motl, I'll give you twelve dollars for that suit, not a cent less!"

"It's yours, Shimshn," said Motl.

WELL STOCKED

The customer bought a cigar, lighted it, took a few puffs and returned it to the tobacconist.

"I asked you for a good cigar," he cried, "and you give me this stinker!"

The man looked sadly at his customer and said nothing.

"Why don't you say something?" the customer demanded.

"What can I say?" replied the tobacconist. "I'm thinking what a lucky man you are. You have only one of those cigars, but my store is just full of them."

THEY AGONIZE

"Dear friend," wrote a merchant to one of his creditors, "I have settled in a new place and opened a business that cannot fail. I carry two lines: bread and shrouds. People, you know, either live or die. If they live, they need bread; if they die, they need shrouds. The money I owe you is virtually in your pocket. In three months you'll hear from me."

Three months passed, and three more.

"*Nu?*" wrote the creditor to the merchant.

"My friend," the merchant replied, "this is a strange place where I have settled. The people here neither live nor die. They just agonize."

"IT'S A LIE"

They were discussing the latest gadgets in the art of bookkeeping.

"It's all nonsense!" said one. "My grandfather, peace unto him, was ignorant of the art, but he never made a mistake in his accounts."

"How did he do it?" he was asked.

"Very simply. He had a little book where he kept a record of all his transactions. Suppose he gave someone a loan of fifty cents. He'd write down: 'Seventh day of Nissan: So-and-so owes me fifty cents.' When so-and-so paid, my grandfather wrote: 'The above statement that so-and-so owes me fifty cents is a lie!' "

A MASTER CRAFTSMAN

The rich man ordered a new suit of clothes for his son's wedding.

"See that you make a good job," said he to the tailor. "You know the people of this town. If anything isn't just so, they will make merry over it."

"Don't worry," replied the tailor. "I've been practicing my trade now for thirty years, and it hasn't happened yet that people should make merry over my work. On the contrary, they always weep over it."

MORE THAN THE ORDER

The traveling salesman came to a customer and inquired if there was a telegram for him.

"Here it is," said the customer.

The salesman opened it and his face fell.

"My wife," he said sadly, "has presented me with twins."

"Good!" cried the customer. "Now you'll know how it feels to receive more goods than you order."

RED WINE AND WHITE

The wine salesman insisted on the superior quality of his red wine.

"But I am stocked up on red wine," the customer pleaded, "I don't want any."

"My red wine," the salesman began and he went off on another eulogy. Finally the customer lost his temper. He took the salesman by the collar and threw him out.

An hour later the salesman returned.

"What happened an hour ago," said he to the customer, "was in connection with red wine. Now what about white wine?"

LOANS AND HOT DOGS

The hot dog merchant stood with his little stand on the sidewalk near the bank. Along came a *lantsman.*

"How is business?" asked the *lantsman.*

"Not bad," replied the merchant. "I have already put away some savings in the bank, thank God."

"In that case," said the *lantsman,* "can you lend me five dollars?"

"God forbid!" replied the merchant. "I have no right to do it!"

"What do you mean you have no right?" the other inquired.

"You see," the merchant replied, "I have an agreement with the bank that we are not to interfere with each other. I am forbidden to make loans and the bank is forbidden to sell hot dogs."

DESPERATE SITUATION

Dear Max: Surprised, aren't you? Well, the way I figured it, you don't want to talk to me, so maybe you'll read a letter. I don't blame you, mind you, for not talking to me. I didn't act right toward you. I should have paid you. If not all, then something. I won't go into that. I admit I am to blame and I'll not say any more about it. So why do I write to you? Because, Max, I am in a desperate situation. The flood is up to my chin. I'm drowning, Max, so don't be surprised what you hear about me or what you read in the papers.

It happened like this. Yesterday I met Nathan. You remember Nathan? He is in the jewelry business. So we shake hands like the best of friends. So I say, "How is business, Nathan?" So he says, "Not bad, Meyer, not bad. In fact," he says, "I could say it's pretty good." So I say, "I'm so happy to hear it." And I take him aside and ask him to let me have a tenner just for a week, a couple of days. So you know what he says, the low-life? "You?" he says. "Oh no," he says, "not you. I know you too well. I know you from way back." And he walks off. What do you say to a cheap nobody like that?

Well, Max, you can imagine how I felt. It was not the money, mind you, but the principle of the thing, the insult. But I had to have a tenner. So on the way home I step in my drugstore, and I buy a tube of toothpaste. The druggist is a nice chap, a perfect gentleman, refined, educated. So we talk about the heat wave, the latest holdup, and so on. And he is very nice, polite, and smiles all the time. So I say good-by and walk to the door, but I stop and go back and say to him confidential like, "Oh Mr. Resnik, I just remembered, could you let me have a little tenner for a few days, till tomorrow?" Well, the smile on his face goes up the flue, and he says to me, "Sorry, sir," he says, "you come in here once in a great while for toothpaste. I really don't know you. I don't even know your name."

And that, dear Max, is the terrible situation I am in. The people who don't know me turn me down because they don't know me, and the people who know me turn me down because they know me. And those are the only two kinds of people I know. I don't know any other kind.

I am still living at the same address, Max, but who knows how long I'll be there? Who knows? So all I can say to you Max, is good-by. Good-by, Max, dear friend. Don't forget me, no matter what you hear or read. Your true friend, Meyer.

THE HALF OF IT

"I must have your help, my friend. You know, of course, that I am marrying off my daughter tomorrow and I promised to pay down the dowry of five hundred rubles on the wedding day. Well, I'm short exactly half the sum."

"Why worry? Don't you know that nobody pays more than half the dowry he promises?"

"But you don't understand, my friend. That's the half that I am short."

Marriage Brokers and Other Liars

HE HAS THEM ALL

"YOUNG MAN," said a *shadchn*, "I have an excellent match for you; the girl is a beauty."

To which the young man replied: "Please, don't bother me."

"Very well," the *shadchn* continued, "if beauty is not the main thing with you, I have another one, not so beautiful, but not homely either, and she has five thousand rubles."

And again the young man replied: "Please, don't bother me."

"So!" continued the *shadchn*. "I see your standards are very high. Well, I have one for you with twenty thousand."

"Don't bother me," said the young man. "Money is not my object."

"No?" said the *shadchn*. "Is it *yiches*? Well, I have someone for you of the finest family. Ten generations of rabbis!"

"I want you to know," said the young man with finality, "that I am not interested in any of your proposals. I will marry for love only."

"Oh, I see!" said the *shadchn*. "Well, I have one like that also!"

THE RIGHT DAY

There was a young man who was neither handsome, nor rich, nor learned—a very ordinary young man. One day, a *shadchn* called on him and proposed an extraordinary match.

"The father is one of the richest men in town," he said. "The young lady is highly educated and beautiful."

"Then why—," began the young man who was not altogether a fool.

But a *shadchn* knows in advance what a client intends to say.

"Why they would favor you?" said the *shadchn*. "Let me tell you the whole truth. Every half year the young lady goes insane. Her insanity lasts only a day, and she is well again for another half year."

The young man thought it over. Only two days a year—it's not so terrible! One can put up with it.

"Very well," said he to the *shadchn*, "we'll go and see the bride."

"Not today," the *shadchn* replied. "We must wait a few months for the day when she is out of her mind."

NOODLES WITH MILK

He was a simple village lad, and the marriage broker, after arranging the preliminaries, took him to the neighboring town to be introduced to the prospective bride.

On the way the *shadchn* instructed him on proper manners and conversation.

"Remember," he told him, "there are three things that interest women: family affairs, good things to eat, and clever sayings."

The young man promised to remember.

"Have you any brothers or sisters?" he asked the maiden, beginning with subject number one.

"No," she replied, "I am an only child."

There was a pause and the village lad decided to proceed to the next subject.

"Do you like noodles with milk?" said he.

"No," replied the maiden, "I don't like noodles with milk."

There was another pause and the young man felt it was time for the third subject. He thought hard and finally said:

"If you had brothers and sisters, would you like noodles with milk?"

ONE-EYED, BUT—

There was a wealthy man in town who was anxious to marry off his daughter and to him came Shaye Shadchn and proposed a certain young man whom the marriage broker declared eligible on every count. Shaye praised the young man to the skies and the father wanted to meet him.

"There is one thing I must tell you beforehand," said Shaye who knew when to reveal a thing and when to conceal it. "The young man possesses sight in only one eye."

"You mean he is blind in one eye?" asked the astonished father.

"Yes, I must admit it," said Shaye, "but—"

But the father cut him short.

"I'm surprised at you," said he, "that you know no better than to propose a one-eyed husband for my daughter!"

"What's wrong with that?" Shaye demanded. "Do you know that the author of the great book 'Menoras Hamoar'* was blind in one eye?"

"And not only that," continued the aggrieved father, "but the young man, you admit, is very poor."

Shaye became indignant in his turn.

"Who is more illustrious than the poet and philosopher, Abraham Ibn Ezra?"* he demanded. "And yet Abraham Ibn Ezra was a pauper!"

The father jumped to his feet.

"But this young man is an ignoramus!" he cried.

Shaye Shadchn smiled at the man benevolently. He took a pinch of snuff and held out the box to his client.

"Do you find that Rothschild is such a learned man?" he asked.

* See Glossary.

IRRESISTIBLE!

Shaye Shadchn called on a young man who was somewhat infected with modern ideas. The young man gave him a cold reception.

"I think," said he, "I have told you already that I shall marry a girl with whom I fall in love and none other."

"That's exactly why I have come!" said Shaye. "Listen! Five thousand rubles down! The father is seventy years old, as rich as Korach, and she is his only child. And that's not all! She has an old uncle who is also very rich and childless! I ask you now, is it possible not to fall in love with a girl like that?"

IT'S OVER AND DONE!

With another young man Shaye Shadchn struggled valiantly for a long time until every difficulty seemed to have been removed. In the end the prospective groom discovered that the bride limped, and he called the whole thing off.

"I'll not have a lame wife, if she had the wealth of Korach!" he declared.

Whereupon Shaye Shadchn spoke to the young man as follows:

"Let us assume, my young friend, that you take a woman after your own heart and that both her legs are strong and sound. Are you sure that some day or other she won't slip and break one of them? She'll be laid up for weeks and months, you'll ruin your health with watching and worrying, and become impoverished in the bargain! Now take this girl! She has already broken her leg, she has been cured by others, and with other people's money. It has all been done for you; you have nothing more to worry about!"

NO ONE IS PERFECT

There was another young man in town to whom Shaye spoke at length on the bride's dowry.

"Remember," said he, "five thousand down, besides jewels and precious stones, and a trousseau—such a trousseau on every Jewish daughter!"

"But," said the young man, "she limps a little, doesn't she?"

"And what if she does?" said Shaye. "Do you suppose she can't afford a carriage?"

"And her eyes, I understand, are rather weak," the young man added.

"The better for you," said Shaye. "She won't see your faults."

"And besides that, she stammers," the young man continued.

"Lucky man!" said Shaye. "Would you have a wife that would talk your head off?"

"But—but," said the young man, "what about that—that hump on her back?"

"God in heaven!" cried Shaye, jumping to his feet, "Do you want her to be perfect?"

FOUR MORE DAUGHTERS

Shaye Shadchn likes to tell the following story as illustrating the difficulties to be encountered in his profession:

"The bride's father accepted the terms and everything was ready for the betrothal. The last minute he takes me aside and says:

" 'The groom insists on two thousand, and more than a thousand I cannot—'

"I knew my man and interrupted him.

" 'And even a thousand,' I said, 'are you in a position to—'

" 'No, of course not,' he replies, 'but a thousand I could promise.'

" 'And not pay,' I added.

" 'No, of course not,' he admitted.

" 'In that case,' said I, 'why can't you promise two thousand and not pay?'

" 'What are you thinking of?' says my man. 'Don't you know I have four more daughters?' "

HE ASKS TO BE REMEMBERED

When it was all over and the couple was happily married, Shaye Shadchn approached the bride and whispered in her ear: "*Mazl tov!* I have a little favor to ask you."

"What is it?" asked the beaming bride.

"My name is Shaye. I want you to remember my name. Shaye."

"I shall remember your name all my life, Reb Shaye," replied the bride and smiled happily. "But why do you make this request of me?"

"Because," said Shaye, "in later years I don't want you to say it was the devil who brought you to this pass."

SHAYE DEMANDS A FEE

There was a wealthy man in town who found a satisfactory match for his daughter, but not with the help of Shaye Shadchn. The day after the wedding, Shaye appeared and claimed a fee.

"Have you gone out of your mind?" asked the man.

"No, my friend," said Shaye, "but I'm a *shadchn*."

"But I got my son-in-law through another *shadchn*!" the man protested.

"That's exactly why you should pay me a fee," said Shaye. "You should do it out of simple gratitude. You see," he whispered in the man's ear, "not one of the marriages I ever arranged has endured."

ONLY WHEN SHE WALKED

No one could compare to Shaye in the art of persuasion. His manner was soft, artless and disarming.

"Shaye," a young man complained. "What are you trying to do to me? What do you have against me?"

"I want to see you married and happy," Shaye smiled at the angry young man. "You have just seen her. Have you found any fault in her?"

"Have I found—! Why, she has a clubfoot! She limps!"

"You saw her limp? Wait. What was she doing at the time? Was she sitting?"

"No."

"Lying down?"

"No."

"Was she eating, reading, singing? She sings like an angel, the little kitten."

"No."

"Was she sewing, embroidering? What blessed fingers she has!"

"No."

"So! You probably just saw her walk."

"Yes! She was walking!"

"Only that, mind you. Only when she walked did she limp. And for a little thing like that are you going to sacrifice everything else?"

The young man promised to think it over.

KING SOLOMON COULD BE WRONG

"Listen carefully," said Shaye to one of his prospective bridegrooms. "I am taking you now to the bride's home and you'll be very carefully inspected and appraised. So let's face it. You are not very clever. In fact, you are very far from being clever. Your only chance, my boy, is to be silent. Don't say a word. Look as if you are deep in thought. King Solomon himself is my authority. He said: 'Even a fool who is silent is considered wise.' "

The young man promised. In the bride's home he was seated at one end of a table, and at the other sat three of the bride's uncles who were charged with the task of judging the candidate. Shaye hovered anxiously over his "merchandise."

Said one of the uncles, a mild, soft-spoken man, to the others: "Looks like an earnest young man, engrossed in serious thoughts. He should make a good husband for Malkele."

Said the second uncle, who had a dreamy faraway look in his eyes: "A poetic soul, a superior young man."

Up spoke the third uncle. He was a sharp-eyed man, with a pointed beard, pointed nose, and pursed lips. "This young snipe," he said, "is just an ordinary empty-headed fool."

At once Shaye bent down and whispered in the candidate's ear. "Come on," he said. "Let's not waste any more time here. They have found you out." And on the way to the door he added: "Does King Solomon have to be right all the time?"

CAN'T WAIT

There was a *shadchn* whose wife gave him no peace.

"You are providing husbands for all the girls in town," she nagged him, "and our own Rochele is becoming an old maid!"

But what could the poor *shadchn* do? The young men were insisting on a handsome dowry, and where was he to find it? Nevertheless his wife's nagging had its effect and one day he went to the rich man of the town to propose a match for his daughter.

"Reb *Shadchn*," said the rich man, "what's the hurry? My daughter is only fifteen years old. She can wait!"

"Yes," replied the *shadchn*, "but my daughter can't! She is over thirty."

WOLVES!

Zavl Liar's specialty was wolves. His experiences with wolves were hair-raising.

"Once when I was in the forest alone," he narrated, "I was attacked by ninety-nine wolves."

"Exactly ninety-nine?" objected one of his listeners. "Why not a hundred?"

"Well," said Zavl, "perhaps there were a hundred, but I don't like to exaggerate."

On another occasion, however, Zavl made it a hundred.

"Exactly a hundred?" he was asked. "Were you able to count them?"

"Well," said Zavl, "if there weren't a hundred, there were certainly fifty."

"Perhaps there were twenty," someone suggested.

Zavl was a little offended.

"Why must you quibble about it?" he said. "A single wolf is also dangerous!"

"But did you see the wolf with your own eyes?" another insisted.

Now Zavl was really hurt.

"What do you think it was," he demanded, "that made that noise in the bushes?"

FISH FOR THE WEDDING

"So you don't believe in miracles!" said an old-timer. "Well, listen to what I'll tell you, and see what you can make of it. I was on my travels one cold winter day, and I was crossing a frozen river to get to a village on the other side. Suddenly the ice broke under me and I fell into the water. I shouted for help and some peasants came running and pulled me out. When I stood up I was a pillar of ice and my beard was frozen solid. The peasants took me to a Jewish home and I found the place full of people: they were celebrating a wedding. But the host was sad and forlorn: he had been unable to obtain fish for the feast.

"In the meantime, I was beginning to thaw out. They put me into a barrel, and the water ran in torrents from my body and my beard. And what do you think happened? Two good-sized fishes, a carp and a yellow pike, leaped out of my beard and flapped right into the barrel. I leave you to imagine the joy of my host and all his guests!"

AND A WALL-CLOCK!

"Or consider this incident," the old-timer continued. "It was the day before Passover and in my house poverty reigned like a king. There was no vestige of anything: no *matse*, no wine, no eggs—nothing! The wife is in tears, the children are scared, and as for me, what could I do? I went to the market place. I took my stand near a large store and stood wondering whence my salvation would come. A cab pulls up near the store, and my heart goes pitapat! A lady steps out of the cab, arranges her satin dress, takes out her silk handkerchief and a bundle falls out of it right at my feet! 'Oh Lord!' I prayed, 'send me salvation!' And God heard my prayers. I picked up the bundle and opened it. It contained thirty rubles in copper and in addition, guess what! A wall-clock, as I live!"

LUXURY—AND CHEAP

The man from Vilna and the man from Odessa were praising their own cities, and each of them was running down the city of the other.

"Vilna," said the man from Odessa, "is no place to live in. All you have to eat there is black bread and cucumbers, and even that comes high. And what do you drink? Nothing but water. But in Odessa, we live in luxury. We eat and drink of the best, and everything is dirt cheap. You can get a five-pound fish for a kopek and a gallon of wine for five kopeks."

The man from Vilna was roused.

"It's a lie!" he declared.

"A lie, did you say?" replied the man from Odessa. "Very well then, it's a lie. But a kopek for a five-pound fish and five kopeks for a gallon of wine is cheap enough, isn't it?"

SOME SLIGHT CORRECTIONS

"In Odessa," the man continued, "nothing is too good for us. Take the cantor of our great synagogue, for example. The man's throat is like a musical instrument, David's harp! He costs us enough, you may be sure—twenty thousand rubles a year! His name, by the way, is Marcus."

"Twenty thousand a year!" someone objected. "Impossible!"

"Don't say that," interrupted the man from Vilna. "I can vouch for that, except for a few minor details. First, the city is not Odessa, but Kiev, and the man's name is not Marcus but Brodsky. Further, he is not a cantor but a lumber merchant, and instead of making twenty thousand a year, he loses thirty. Everything else is correct."

A TALL ONE

"People talk about high mountains. But if you want to hear about a really high mountain, listen to me. I happen to be a merchant, you must know, and my line of business is geese. Yes, I buy and sell geese, flocks of them! And it happened once that I had to take a flock of geese from one place to another and between the two stood a mountain, the very mountain I want to tell you about. Well, we started, my geese and I, up the mountain, the geese in front and I behind, urging them on. We climbed and climbed and, how long, do you think, did it take us to reach the summit? You'll never guess! Two and a half years, as true as you are looking at me! Well, we got to the top and, naturally, by that time the geese were hungry. But I had nothing to give them. The geese, like all birds of their species, began to peck. Now what, I ask you, did they peck at? Corn? Oats? Berries? No, my friend, the stars, that's what they pecked at, the stars, as true as I am talking to you! So there you are, if you want to know something about high mountains!"

SNOW

"Since you talk about snow, I am reminded of a sleigh-ride a number of us took many years ago. Listen and you'll hear something. The sleigh was not large, we had but one horse, and we started out in high spirits. We were young, you understand! We came to an elevation and by the time we got to the top, it was midday and we were hungry. So we ate, and after eating we felt drowsy. We unharnessed the horse and tied him to a pole that stuck up out of the snow. Then we turned the sleigh upside down, stretched out, and fell asleep. The day was not cold; the sun, in fact, was warm, and we were quite comfortable. When we woke up, we looked around and what do you think! The snow was gone. The sleigh was resting on green grass. So we knew that the sun had melted the snow while we slept. We looked for the horse and the horse too was gone! Where could the horse be? How were we going to get back without the horse? We look here, we look there, no horse! Finally I happen to look up, and there was our horse dangling from the steeple of a church! Now figure out how high that snowdrift was where we had stopped to rest."

THE LION

"Men talk about strength and they talk about wisdom. Which of the two, you ask, is more to be desired? Wisdom, of course! Everybody knows that our people have chosen wisdom, that we are the wisest people on earth! Nevertheless, there are times when strength is also important. What, for example, would

I have done on certain occasions if it were not for my unusual strength? Listen and judge for yourself. I was on my way through a forest when I met a lion. Have you ever met a lion in a forest? No? Don't laugh—it's no laughing matter. The lion roared and rushed right at me, his jaws wide open! Was I frightened? I don't deny that I was—a little. But the next moment I laughed at him. I remembered how strong I was! So what did I do? I plunged my arm right between his jaws! I plunged it deeper and deeper until I came to his tail. I seized his tail and with one powerful wrench I pulled the lion inside out! Then I swung him by the tail over my shoulder and brought him home. Thus I was delivered from great danger and in addition, my wife, God bless her, and I had fur coats for the winter, which was very severe that year. Shall I tell you about the frosts we had that winter? No? Very well, some other time!"

WEDDING GUESTS

A great event was in the offing for the little town: the rich man of the place was marrying off his youngest daughter! It was to be a wedding such as the town had never had before. Everybody was to be there, young and old, rich and poor, men, women, and children.

But as the day approached, the bride's father became worried. The whole town, he learned, was preparing to come! That, he thought, would be too much. Such a throng he was unwilling to receive, or perhaps he was unable to do it! You can't be too sure about your rich men these days! So he instructed the butler to admit only those who had something to do with the preparations for the wedding or could show a relationship to the families, either his or the groom's.

The butler hired two yokels, put them into unforms, and stationed them near the entrance, having first told them what they must do. The people began to arrive, streams of them, and the yokels asked them who they were. Said one:

"I am a brother-in-law of the bride's uncle's grandmother."

"Enter!" said the yokels.

"I am a cousin of the man you have just admitted," said the next.

"Certainly! Step inside," said the yokels.

"I am the man who grated the horseradish for the wedding," said another.

"The horseradish? Inside!"

"My grandfather's father-in-law officiated at the circumcision of the bridegroom's great aunt's son."

"Indeed! Step inside, please!"

"I am the man who pounded the pepper."

"Enter!"

And hard upon the last, came someone whom no one had ever seen before.

"Who are you?" asked the yokels.

"I am the pepper-pounder's son-in-law."

"Enter!" said the yokels in uniform.

And when the rich man looked out upon his guests, it seemed to him the whole town was there after all.

WHAT A STALLION!

When passengers were scarce and business was slack, the wagoners got together at a table in the tavern and talked about ——what? Horses, of course! At one time or another each of them, it seems, had owned at least one horse that was not to be matched for beauty, strength, speed, endurance, sagacity, loyalty, etc. They outdid themselves in telling breath-taking stories which no one challeneged on the principle that you don't challenge me and I don't challenge you. It was a sound principle: it permitted the widest freedom of expression, as the following tale will prove.

"You, good friends," said the teller, "know how smart a horse can be. But did I ever tell you about the one I had ten years ago, a frisky stallion, with legs like steel and a mane that he kept flinging from side to side whenever a young mare appeared on the road? When that stallion neighed—do you hear me?—I felt he was talking to me, and after a while I really understood what he was saying.

"But let me tell you about the time I drove him through a thick forest at night. My wagon was piled with a load of hemp that I was taking to a neighboring village. The moon was full and I had no trouble finding my way. My young eagle skimmed along as if he was soaring through air. But suddenly it became pitch dark and a fierce storm broke over the forest. My stallion got frightened—I could feel it in the way he tossed his head. The lightning flashed, the thunder crashed and off he dashed! Right off the road and in among the trees! I pulled at the reins, I cursed him, I cooed to him, I couldn't stop him. Suddenly one of the wheels hit the trunk of a tree and I was jolted out of the box. As I fell, I struck my head on a stone and lost consciousness.

"How long I lay there on my back unconscious I can't say, but suddenly I felt someone or something nudging me. I opened my eyes and there was my stallion standing over me. He was feeling for something to take between his teeth and lift me up. But in the position in which I lay, unable to move, he found nothing to seize on. So what do you think he did? He turned me over, took the seat of my trousers between his teeth and flung me into the wagon."

"How did he do that?" one of the listeners ventured to ask.

"Very simply. Haven't you ever jerked a pancake up into the air, and it fell back into the pan on the other side? Fortunately, as I have already told you, the pan—I mean my wagon—was full of hemp, so I landed very comfortably on my back. But was that all the stallion did? Far from it. He found the road again and took me straight to the village, coming to a halt before the tavern. The landlord came out and they put me to bed. And what made the stallion act as he did? His sense of loyalty, of course, and his devotion to me personally."

"A wonderful stallion! A true friend and comrade," the listeners all agreed.

"Nevertheless, I must tell you the whole truth," the narrator continued. "He made a mistake and it was a long time before I forgave him. You see, he went and brought me a doctor."

"The tavernkeeper?"

"No, the stallion!"

"Of course! The stallion, of course!" the others chimed in.

"But would you believe it? Instead of bringing me a real doctor, he brought me a veterinarian. Imagine being treated by a horse doctor!"

"A bad mistake," the others agreed.

"But isn't it possible there wasn't a real doctor in the village?" a keen listener spoke up.

"You have found the answer!" the narrator cried. "That was exactly the situation. And when I realized it, then, of course, I forgave him. There are circumstances when it's proper for a horse doctor to treat a man."

"Especially when the man has lived with horses so long, that he has become a good deal of a horse himself," the same keen listener observed.

LIARS AND GANOVIM

In an inn the guests talked about the places they came from.

"In my *shtetl*," said one, "they are all liars. What shall I tell you? You never saw such liars! But the biggest liar of all is the *shames*. Is that man a liar! I have seen liars, I have heard liars, I am myself a bit of a liar! But a liar like that *shames*—the Lord shield and deliver us!"

"In my *shtetl*," said another, "they are all *ganovim*. What shall I tell you? The merchants, the matchmakers, the beggars—them we don't have to talk about. But the tailor is a *ganev*, the shoemaker is a *ganev*, the *shames* is a *ganev*, even the *dayen* is a *ganev*. We do have one honest man in our *shtetl*, the *rov*, so he is also a *ganev*!" *

* See Glossary.

Gluttons, Guzzlers, and Other Sinners

THAT GLASS OF TEA, DOCTOR!

"Am I glad to see you, doctor! I am waiting for you like we wait for Messiah. Help me, doctor. It's my stomach. I have a terrible cutting pain there. It feels like I swallowed a razor. And sometimes the stomach acts like it wants to jump out through my mouth. You think it's something I ate? But what did I eat? I ate the same as I always eat when I come home from *shul* on Saturday. Nothing different. I should tell you in detail everything I ate? The whole menu? Why not? I didn't eat much. The same as every Saturday.

"So, after making *kidesh*—you know, a glass of brandy and a couple of egg cakes—I had a piece of last night's gefilte fish. On the morning after, the fish has a new taste. The spices sort of blossom out, and the frozen soup also tastes wonderful. After that I had some of last night's *tsimes*. Carrots with dumplings. I always have some of Friday night's gefilte fish and *tsimes* on Saturday after *shul*. For years and years—all my life. After that I had my portion of *petcha*. You don't know what that is? It's a jelly made of calf's feet with plenty of onions and garlic. Very delicious, doctor. So you see I had the same things this morning as I always have.

"After that? Well, after that came the regular meal. I should tell you about that also? Why not? There was the soup. You are right. I did have something before the soup. A little appetizer. Chopped liver with onions and radishes, hardly worth mentioning. Yes, I had two portions. I nearly always have two portions. The soup? Plain consomme. *Kreplach* in it, of course; meat *kreplach*. But the consomme I left over. I don't fancy that thin stuff. If I want water I know where to get it. So where are we? Yes, then came the entree. Duck, doctor. I like duck. But wait a minute. I left out the *tcholent*. Potatoes with plenty of meat. Then came the *kugl*. Did I have the *kugl* before or after the duck? I don't remember any more. The way I feel, doctor, I'm surprised I remember anything. The *kugl*? It was the "leafy" kind. Leaves of rolled dough with plenty of fat and spices between them. It's the kind I like and I always have it on Saturdays, always. So there you have it, doctor. I don't have to mention the strudel, it's hardly worth it. Yes, two portions—I always have two portions. So I told you everything, doctor. So what do you think is the matter—?

"Wait, doctor! Wait a minute! I did have something today which I never had before! What got into me, I wonder! I had a glass of tea! I didn't enjoy it, but I drank it anyhow. So that's it!

"That glass of tea, doctor. It laid me out! It just laid me out!"

WHAT A GLUTTON!

"So, Reb Innkeeper, you'll wait on me yourself? I am honored. And hungry! Terribly hungry."

"So what will you have, sir?"

"I'll begin with soup. You have good kasha soup, or bean, or cabbage? Potato will be all right. Anything!"

"Golde Neshe! Any soup left? You threw it away? Sorry, sir. On Wednesday the soup is not good. It's four days after the Sabbath, and the seasoning is all flat."

"No matter, I can do without soup. Bring me a nice piece of beef, not fat, not too lean."

"Meat? Where will I get meat on Wednesday? We have meat only on the Sabbath."

"I see, I see. Then bring me a nice piece of chicken. I prefer the white, but I'll have anything. Drumsticks, wings, the giblets, anything!"

"My dear sir, we can only obtain chickens on Thursday, the market day, when the peasants bring poultry into town."

"Too bad. Unlucky day, Wednesday. Well, I'll have to be satisfied with a nice piece of fish."

"I advise against it. First, I don't have any. Second, it comes in fresh only on Thursday, the market day."

"Two excellent reasons, Mr. Innkeeper, especially the first. It looks as if I'll have to have to get down to an omelet."

"With eggs?"

"You make your omelets without eggs?"

"But where will I get eggs? I told you already—"

"Yes, yes, I know! On Thursday the peasants bring eggs into town."

"How did you know that, sir?"

"Look, Reb Innkeeper, talking makes me even hungrier. Bring me a herring and let's have done with it!"

"Ah, my dear sir, now I must apologize. I served my last herring to a customer only an hour ago. Believe me, this morning I had six herrings. I counted them. But you see, in this town people are—"

"I know! I know! They are just crazy about herring! But I too am going crazy! Do you have any rolls? Any bread?"

"Yes, sir. Right away, sir. Golde Neshe! What are you doing there? Bring the gentleman a slice of bread!"

"What do you mean, a slice of bread? Bring me ten slices, fifty slices! I am starved, I tell you!"

"Golde Neshe, did you hear that character sitting there at the table, Golde Neshe? He must come from the big city. Are they gluttons over there, Golde Neshe! The Lord shield and deliver us!"

FILIAL PIETY

A young modern was observing the anniversary of his father's death, and in keeping with the occasion, he went to a kosher restaurant. It was a Saturday and the menu included a delicious Sabbath pudding. The young man finished his portion and a wave of filial emotion swept over him.

"Waiter!" he called, "bring me another portion of pudding! My father—he should rest in peace—deserves it!"

NO NEWS

A stranger sat down at a table in the tavern, and ordered fish. When the waiter brought it, the stranger examined it closely, then bent down over the plate and began to whisper. The other customers looked on with amazement. The stranger continued to whisper to the fish, and, between whispers, he seemed to listen. Finally the proprietor approached the man.

"What are you doing?" he demanded.

"I'm having a little chat with the fish," said the stranger. "I said: 'How do you do?' and he answered: 'Thank you. How are you?' I said: 'How is it down in your world?' 'Pretty good,' said he, 'sorry I had to leave it.' 'Where do you come from?' I asked him. 'From a river not far from here,' he told me. 'And what's the latest news down in your river?' I asked him. 'News?' he answered. 'Don't ask me, It's more than a month now since I left the place!' "

CAUSE FOR REJOICING

On the festival of "Joy in Torah," the tippler, even while he danced and drank, was heard to chant the well-known words: "Man's origin is dust and his end is dust."

"What sort of words are those for a joyous day like this?" someone protested.

"They are the right words," the tippler replied. "If man's origin were gold and his end dust, he would have reason for regret. But if his origin is dust and his end is dust, and he manages in between to empty a bottle or two, why shouldn't he rejoice?

NO MATTER WHEN

Before lying down for his afternoon nap, a certain tippler refreshed his spirits and said to his wife:

"Woman, wake me up as soon as I get thirsty."

"What kind of nonsense is that?" said the woman. "How will I know when you are thirsty?"

"It doesn't matter," the man replied. "Whenever you wake me up, I'll be thirsty."

A QUESTION OF DATE

After consulting his doctor, an old guzzler met a friend.

"What did he tell you?" asked the friend.

"He told me I must stop drinking. It's a question of life and death."

The two walked on in silence. As they passed the tavern, the sick man turned and went inside. He ordered a tall glass of liquor and brought it down at a gulp.

"Are you tired of living?" asked his friend.

"Not exactly," replied the other. "I'm only assuming that I saw the doctor tomorrow instead of today."

NOT CRAZY FOR THE STUFF

"Rifkele," said a husband to his wife, "I am not feeling so well. It must be the cucumbers I ate. Is there a drop of brandy in the house?"

It was in the dead of night and the woman was fast asleep,

but the matter was important and the man didn't hesitate to wake her.

"Brandy?" she repeated in a loud angry whisper. "In the middle of the night he has to have brandy! Go to sleep! There's no brandy in the house!"

"If you think I'm crazy for the stuff, you're mistaken," said the man resignedly and turned his face to the wall.

It was not long, however, before he called her again.

"Rifkele," said he, "our neighbor always has some in his house. Couldn't you get me a drop from him? I don't feel so well."

"Have you gone crazy?" said the woman. "What kind of idea is it to go knocking on people's doors at this time of the night for liquor? Go to sleep! You'll feel better in the morning."

"All right!" said the man. "Only I don't want you to think I'm crazy for the stuff."

But soon enough he called her again.

"Rifkele," said he, "I have just remembered. Tomorrow there is a fair in town and the peasants arrive during the night. The tavern must be open already. Couldn't you run down and get me a little glass of brandy?"

But now the woman was in a rage.

"May all the evil dreams I dreamt this night and every other night descend on your head!" she cried. "Guzzler! Drunkard! In the middle of the night, in a bitter frost, I should go and get him brandy!"

"Hush!" the man whispered, "you'll wake up the children! Do you think I'm crazy for the stuff? Only if you don't care to go, I'll get up and go myself."

THE RIDDLE

"Yoshek," said one peasant to another, "we've sat together for three hours, drinking all the time. But I don't feel so happy. How about you?"

Yoshek laid his head on his arm and groaned.

"No, Stepan," he replied, "I don't feel happy either."

"Listen, Yoshek!" Stepan continued, "I hear the Jews tell each other a lot of funny stories. They tell riddles and things that make you laugh. Go to their synagogue, Yoshek, little brother. Stand near the windows and listen, and bring back a good story or a riddle. I want to laugh, Yoshek, do you hear? I must laugh!"

Yoshek staggered out and made his way to the synagogue and stood near an open window. Inside a group of men sat together and gossiped. Said one of them, who had a long red beard:

"Guess this one: my parents have a son, but I have no brother. Who is it?"

"It's yourself!" a number of voices replied.

Yoshek laughed and staggered back to his friend.

"Stepan, dear little brother," he said, "guess this one: my parents have a son, but I have no brother. Who is it?"

Stepan looked at Yoshek long and mournfully. But he found nothing to say.

"Stepan, little brother," said Yoshek at last. "You're stupid. It's the Jew with the long red beard in the synagogue!"

And Yoshek and Stepan laughed uproariously together, embracing each other and slapping each other on the back, until they rolled together under the table.

PENANCE

"Have a good year, Velvl? And how did the fasting go?"

"The fasting, Berl? *Nu*!"

"What do you mean, *nu*?"

"I mean—*nu!*"

"Tell the truth, Velvl. Did you fast or not?"

"Did you, Berl?"

"I asked first, Velvl."

"I can see, Berl, that you didn't fast. On Yom Kippur you didn't fast!"

"And I can tell that you, Velvl, didn't fast either."

"Berl, my friend, we committed a big sin, both of us."

"I had terrible dreams all night."

"I was awake all night."

"We have to do something, Velvl!"

"What shall we do, Berl?"

"Let me think, Velvl. Ah! I know what! Let's go to the *rov* and confess. If a sinner confesses and repents, he is forgiven."

"So, my children, you confess that you committed this grave sin. And because you confess you think God will forgive you. No, Velvl! No, Berl! Confession alone is not enough. You must do penance before you are forgiven. I will impose a penance on you, and see that you carry it out. This, my children, is the penance. Put peas inside your shoes, and for the next three days go about your usual business, but wear no other shoes except those with the peas inside."

"Velvl, my friend, you look terrible!

"How should I look after going about three days with peas in my shoes?"

"But you are so pale and haggard, Velvl. Did the peas torture you so much?"

"You need to ask? But you, Berl, don't look bad at all. You look fine. Ah, Berl! I know you, you rascal! You didn't do the penance!"

"I didn't do—? How can you say such a thing, Velvl?"

"You put peas inside your shoes?"

"Of course, I did. Only——"

"Only what?"

"Only first I boiled them."

CARDSHARPS

In a tavern sat two worthies, eying sharply all who came and went. They were of dubious appearance and restless demeanor. They were, in fact, looking for someone whom they might persuade to join them in a game of cards. But there finally remained only one other person in the room, an elderly man of dignified appearance who did not look like very promising quarry. Having no choice, however, they approached the man and asked him if he would join them in a game.

"Eh, what?" said the elderly man. "A little louder, please!"

The invitation was repeated.

"What? What's that you say?" the man shouted.

"Will you play cards with us?" the two shouted in return.

"Cards?" the man repeated. "Wait a while. First I must say my afternoon prayers."

The old man went through his prayers slowly and with great devotion. When he sat down the two said to him:

"Will you play now?"

"Eh? What?" the man shouted.

"Will you play cards with us now?" they shouted.

"Oh, cards!" said the man. "Just a little while—I must eat something first."

The man ordered food, ate very slowly and said grace.

"Well now," said the two, "how about a little game?"

"Eh, what?" said the man.

"A game of cards!" the two shouted.

"Oh, that!" said the man. "Yes, let's play now."

So they sat down and played; and since they were playing with a deaf opponent, the two communicated freely with each other, telling each other about their hands and advising each other on their plays. And they won without difficulty—that is to say, they won the first few games. Then their opponent began to win, and he won without interruption. Never had they witnessed such a streak of luck. At the end of two hours they were without means to continue.

"Stranger!" shouted one of the two to the elderly man. "You play cards like a shark!"

"Perhaps so," the man replied. "But why do you shout like that? Do you think I am deaf?"

FORGOT HIS MAKER

The ignorant village innkeeper lived all year round among the peasants, far removed from the people of his faith, and once when he came to town for the High Holy Days, the rabbi spoke harsh words to him. The man stood before the rabbi, ashamed and confused.

"It wouldn't surprise me," said the rabbi, "if you didn't even know who made you!"

"It's true, rabbi," the man confessed, "I don't know."

The rabbi turned to a small boy who stood near.

"Tell me, son," he asked him, "who made you?"

"God!" the youngster replied promptly.

The rabbi turned again to the villager.

"The child," he declared, "knows more than you!"

"I know why," the innkeeper ventured. "He was born not so long ago and still remembers. But how can I remember so many years back?"

Renegades and Anti-Semites

A MATTER OF PRINCIPLE

In Czarist Russia there was a well-known convert to Christianity, Necander Zussman by name, who was a confirmed drunkard. In the company of a Jewish writer he once entered a tavern, and after pouring himself a large glass of liquor, he crossed himself, and drained the glass at a gulp.

His companion looked at him ruefully.

"Why," he asked, "do you have to cross yourself into the bargain?"

"That, my friend," replied the convert, "is a matter of principle with me. I do it for the sake of my former coreligionists. Why should I give some anti-Semite a chance to say that he saw a Jew drink like a fish?"

EAGER FOR A FRIEND

"Barney," said Herman to his friend, "believe it or not, I have just been baptized. I'm a Christian now."

"Well, of all——" Barney began.

"Never mind all that," Herman interrupted. "I've come to ask you to do something for me."

"Oh, really?"

"Yes, Barney, I want you to get baptized also."

Barney stared at Herman.

"I was a little in doubt before," he said at last, "but now I am sure you're crazy!"

"I'm not crazy, Barney, and I want you to do it. Do it for me!"

"But why?" Barney demanded.

"I'll tell you, Barney. It's because I want to have at least one Christian friend."

HE HELD FAST!

They told Levi Yitzchok, the famous rabbi of Berditchev, that a certain old man of seventy had become baptized.

"Lord of the Universe!" exclaimed the rabbi. "See how steadfast your people are to serve You! For seventy years that man held fast, and was faithful to you!"

NOTHING FOR PASSOVER

He stood before the missionary, ragged and resigned, and told him he came to be baptized.

"Splendid!" cried the missionary. "Tomorrow I'll take you to the minister and he'll teach you the fundamentals of our faith!"

"Could—could you take me today?" asked the would-be convert.

The missionary was puzzled.

"Why?" he asked. "What's your hurry?"

"You see," was the answer, "tomorrow is Passover."

"What if it is?" asked the missionary.

"There isn't a thing in the house for Passover," the man confided, "no *matse,* no wine—nothing! I'm penniless!"

BORN AGAIN

Feitl and Feivl went together to the baptismal font, and the first to be called in was Feitl. When he came out, his friend met him eagerly.

"Nu, Feitl?" he asked.

"In the first place," replied the other with asperity, "my name is not Feitl but Philip. In the second place, I don't talk to an accursed Jew like you. You crucified our Lord!"

TIME FOR MINCHE

There were two in the anteroom waiting for the missionary. It was late afternoon and they had been waiting several hours.

"He takes his time, doesn't he?" remarked one of the would-be converts.

"He certainly does," the other agreed.

"Shall I tell you what I'm thinking?" said the first after a pause.

"Nu, what?"

"I'm thinking it's time for *Minche.*"

"And I too," agreed the other.

And both men stood up and recited the Afternoon Prayer.

CARLSBAD SALTS

Two Jews were strolling through a park in the Petrograd of the Czars. One of them had a residence permit in his pocket, the other didn't. Suddenly they looked up and saw a policeman ambling towards them.

The man with the permit turned to his friend:

"As soon as he is near us I'll run. He'll go after me and you will have a chance to escape."

The policeman approached, the man with the permit ran, and the policeman ran after him. Before long the runner looked around, and making sure that his friend was out of sight, he stopped, and was seized.

"Name!" the officer demanded.

"Zelig Brodsky."

"Your permit!"

Zelig Brodsky produced his permit. The policeman examined it and became enraged: the document was in perfect order.

"What's the meaning of this?" he shouted. "Why did you try to escape?"

"I try to escape?" Zelig repeated.

"But you ran!" the officer shouted.

"Oh!" said Zelig. "I take Carlsbad salts and after taking them I have to exercise. My doctor insists."

"Why didn't you stop when you saw me chase you?"

"You chase me?" said Zelig. "It never occurred to me!"

"But you saw me run, didn't you? Why did you think I ran?"

"I thought you, too, were taking Carlsbad salts!"

HOW HE KNEW

"My *porets,*" confided one Jew to another, "was in a terrible rage yesterday. Five times he wanted to slap me."

"How do you know he wanted to do it exactly five times?"

"Because I had the presence of mind to count."

"So he did slap you! Then why do you say he *wanted* to slap you?"

"Foolish question!" replied the first. "If he hadn't wanted to, would he have slapped me?"

DELICIOUS!

The chief rabbi and the cardinal sat side by side at the table. The occasion was a state banquet and the food which the management had the good taste to provide for the rabbi was kosher. But the cardinal was inclined to amuse himself and handed some of his own food to the rabbi.

"Your Eminence," said the rabbi, "don't you know we are forbidden to have non-kosher food?"

"What a pity!" replied the prelate. "It's delicious!"

As they rose from the table, the rabbi turned to the cardinal.

"Your Eminence," said he, "will you be good enough to convey my greetings to your wife?"

The cardinal drew himself up.

"Don't you know," said he, "that a priest is forbidden to have a wife?"

"What a pity!" replied the rabbi. "It's delicious!"

THE LEOPARD

Shmerl and Zelig were strolling through the streets and stopped to read a police notice in bold letters:

"A leopard escaped last night from its cage in the menagerie," ran the notice. "Whoever comes upon the animal is obligated to kill it and notify the Police Department."

Said Shmerl to Zelig:

"I'm leaving town at once!"

"What an idea!" said Zelig. "Are you afraid you'll be killed? You are not a leopard."

"You don't understand, my friend," Shmerl explained. "They'll kill you first and then how are you going to prove you are not a leopard?"

"OPERATE OPERATE"

From his wife who was taking the cure in a place across the border, a husband received a telegram reading as follows: "Says to operate operate." To which the husband sent a telegram in reply reading: "Says to operate operate."

Several days later the man was summoned to police headquarters. The police chief confronted him with copies of both telegrams and demanded to know what sort of correspondence he was conducting with persons across the border.

"It's plain," said the official, "that you are using a secret code."

"Your Excellency," pleaded the man, "this is no code! This—"

"Your denial won't help you!" the police chief declared. "We know a code when we see one. The best thing for you to do is to confess!"

"Let me read the telegrams to you, Your Excellency!"

"Are you implying that we can't read?"

"No, but these telegrams, Your Excellency—"

"Then go ahead and read them!"

"You see, Your Excellency, my wife is ill, and before she left we arranged that she would go to a surgeon. She did so and sent me this telegram: 'Says to operate. Operate?' And I replied: 'Says to operate? Operate!' "

NOT WITHOUT FRIENDS

"So you too have a Jewish orderly," said the Russian captain to the major, during a lull between drinks. "What's his name?"

"Avremko", said the major. "What's yours?"

"Berko. Tell you something, major. I don't like your Avremko. Don't like the way he pours the vodka."

"Y'don't like my Avremko? Well, I don't like your Berko. Don't like that—that glint in his eye."

"If you don't like my Berko, major, you're no friend of mine. Lemme tell you—"

"Lemme tell you, captain, whoever don't like my Avremko, I don't like him! No, not I."

For a while they drank in gloomy silence.

"Captain!" the major suddenly jumped up, "I just wanna crack your Berko in the jaw! Yes, in the jaw!"

"No, y'don't! If you crack my Berko in the jaw, I'll break your Avremko's nose. His nose, I tell you! Yes, I will."

"Y'call yourself a friend?" said the major. "You no friend! I'll show you!" The major lunged at Berko, his fist landing on Berko's chin.

"You dare? You—" the captain shouted. "I'll show you! There!" And his fist landed on Avremko's nose.

Now they were really furious with each other, and they continued pummeling each other's orderlies. Then they fell, weeping and slobbering, into each other's arms.

"Avreml," said Berl between groans, "do you realize what this means? Did you take it in, Avreml?"

"I took it in," said Avreml. "I surely did."

"It means," Berl went on, "that we are not without friends. Yes, we Jews are not without friends."

"Not without friends and protectors."

"Praised be the One Above!" they said together.

PHARISEES AND SADDUCEES

The Sunday Afternoon Circle of the Ladies' Church Auxiliary was having tea, and as usual the chief topic of conversation was the sermon which the minister delivered that morning. He was a small town clergyman, but his learning was impressive.

"Who were those people he spoke about?" asked one lady. "I've already forgotten their names."

"The Sadducees and Pharisees," came from another.

"Yes, I remember now," said the first. "They didn't get along well together, did they? Always bickering and wrangling."

"They were Jews," said a third matron, "so what can you expect? They don't get along with others, they don't get along with each other. Here in Hicksville there are just two of them, and do you know they don't talk to each other? It's true they are both in the clothing business, but being the only two of their kind in town, you'd imagine they'd stick together, wouldn't you?" They all imagined so and one of them wondered what the reason could be.

"It must be," ventured a fourth, "that one of them is a Sadducee and the other a Pharisee."

And they all agreed it could be nothing else.

SIMPLE SOLUTION

The admission of Dr. Berkowitz, a distinguished globetrotter, into the exclusive Traveler's Club left Dr. Von Pupke, an eminent Prussian explorer, unreconciled. He felt rabid about it. It was an outrage, a challenge to every drop of the pure Teutonic blood that flowed in his veins. Perhaps a systematic campaign of insult would force the intruder to resign.

He made his first move at a gathering where he found the intruder chatting with a group of members about his recent experiences in Central Africa.

"I, too, was in Central Africa," the Prussian intervened, "and I came upon one area that I found unique. There wasn't a single pig or Jew in the entire region."

In the hush that followed Dr. Berkowitz's voice sounded serene and suave.

"What a pity!" he said. "And just think, Dr. Pupke, how easily you and I could correct the situation."

"You and I?" the Prussian bridled. "What do you mean by that?"

"I mean that we could both go there."

En Route

MAZL TOV!

A NEW PASSENGER entered the third-class coach and found every seat occupied. There was an old woman, however, who was in possession of two seats and preparing to take a nap.

"*Mazl tov,* grandmother!" said the new passenger to the lady.

She thanked him and moved over to make room for the courteous stranger, who sat down beside her.

"A *mazl tov* is always welcome," said she, "but what's the occasion?"

The man made himself altogether comfortable.

"You see," he explained, "this is the first time I've seen you since your wedding."

A CONVERSATION

The two travelers found themselves in the same compartment and recognizing a coreligionist in each other, they wanted very much to engage in conversation, but hesitated. Each perceived in the other a certain aloofness and feared that the attempt might meet with rebuff.

At last one of the travelers expressed himself.

"Oy!" he groaned.

"Right!" the other responded. "That's exactly what I've been thinking!"

ANOTHER CONVERSATION

In the case of another pair of travelers, conversation moved much more smoothly.

"Where, may I ask, do you come from?" asked one.

"Of course you may ask," replied the other. "I come from Warsaw and I'm going to Vilna. My business is dry goods—retail. My first name is Gimpl, my family name is Abramowitz. I'm neither rich nor poor, just average. I have two sons, both married. Yes, I have daughters also—three of them, one is married, one is engaged, and the third is not yet of age. I've no hobbies, I'm not looking for any new line of business, I don't take snuff, I don't smoke, I know nothing about politics. If I've forgotten anything, be kind enough to ask me now. I really would like to take a nap."

CONFIDENCE FOR CONFIDENCE

They were fellow passengers on board an ocean liner, both Jews, one a hunchback, the other endowed with the telltale nose. For a few days the second avoided his fellow Jew. In the end, however, he made up to the hunchback.

"My friend," said he with the nose one day, "I'm going to impart a little confidence to you. I'm a Jew."

"Confidence for confidence," said the other. "I'm a hunchback."

PHILOSOPHY

"May I ask," said a passenger with a philosophic turn of mind to his neighbor, "where you are going?"

"I'm going far," replied the other.

"That's how it is," mused the first, "the only place where we are happy is the place where we are not."

"Yes," said the other, "that's where I am going."

HE LIED

In the railway coach Shmerl met his friend Berl.

"Where are you going?" asked Shmerl.

"To Grodno," said Berl.

Shmerl became indignant.

"You're telling me you are going to Grodno so as to have me think you are going to Vilna. But I know you are really going to Grodno, so what's the idea of lying about it?"

THEY LOOKED AT EACH OTHER

"You know," said a returned traveler to his friend, "on the trip from Warsaw to Lodz the conductor looked at me very queerly."

"Just how did he look at you?" asked the friend.

"He looked at me as if I had no ticket."

"So what did you do?"

"What could I do? I looked at him as if I had one!"

SAME COLOR

They were two strangers in a first class compartment of a railroad car and one of them lighted a cigar.

"Smoking is not allowed here!" said the other testily.

"I know it," replied the smoker calmly and continued to puff away.

The second traveler called the conductor.

"He is violating the rules," he complained. "This compartment is reserved for nonsmokers."

"And I say," replied the smoker, "that it's he who is violating the rules. He is travelling in a first-class compartment on a second-class ticket."

The accusing passenger turned pale and went out hastily.

On the platform of the station the two met again. The curiosity of the nonsmoker overcame his resentment.

"Are you a clairvoyant?" he asked his fellow passenger. "How did you know I had a second-class ticket?"

"I'm no clairvoyant," replied the other. "I saw a corner of your ticket stick out of your pocket and it was the same color as mine."

THE ART OF PANTOMIME

The two from the *shtetl* were visiting the big city and stopped before a garish display in front of a theatre.

"Look," said one, "they are giving a pantomime in this theatre. What is a pantomime?"

"You don't know what is pantomime? So I'll explain it to you. Pantomime has to do with the way you talk, but in pantomime you don't talk with your mouth. Otherwise it's the same thing. You talk as you always talk."

GINSBERG!

My friend Ginsberg is quite a traveler. He is a good, simple soul, not exactly a paragon of culture, but poised and self-assured. A little pompous, in fact. Years ago he happened to be in Mount Clemens, the famous health resort in Michigan. At that time the word *blech*, meaning *tin*, had acquired a certain vogue. It had come to mean the equivalent of *inferior*—a contrast to gold. Someone tried to sell you, say, a job lot of shirts and praised the merchandise to the skies, laying the ground, of course, for a high price. "It's *blech*," you told him, and the price took a dip. In time, the word, as words have a way of doing, extended its range, and was applied to the condition of one's health. "I am *blech*" meant "I don't feel too well."

To come back to Ginsberg. In the morning he entered the dining room of his hotel in Mount Clemens and the headwaiter seated him at a table where another guest was having breakfast. This worthy was small and sallow with a woebegone look in his eyes and a sour expression about the corners of his mouth. For a while nothing passed between them. Then their eyes happened to meet.

"I am *blech* from colitis," said Ginsberg's neighbor.

Instantly Ginsberg stood up.

"Ginsberg from Philadelphia," he responded solemnly and bowed.

That story came to me from someone other than Ginsberg. What follows is something he told me himself.

It happened on a French luxury liner on which Ginsberg was returning from an extended tour abroad. Again it took place in the dining room. Ginsberg was having his first breakfast alone at a large table, when a family—a French family consisting of husband, wife, and an assortment of offspring—entered and approached the table. The Frenchman held the back of his chair, smiled and said:

"*Bon appétit!*"

Immediately Ginsberg stood up, bowed and said:

"Ginsberg!"

At luncheon, at dinner the same ritual was enacted:

"*Bon appétit!*"

"Ginsberg!"

Both men were puzzled. Ginsberg wondered why the Frenchman, having once introduced himself, did so again and again, forcing him to do the same. The Frenchman wondered what language it was in which *ginsberg* meant *thank you.* Or did it mean *likewise*? So they made inquiries and each of them was duly enlightened.

The following morning, the Frenchman, smiling broadly, stood at the table.

"Ginsberg!" said he.

"*Bon appétit!*" Ginsberg replied.

HE DIDN'T LOOK IT

In a place called Kai-fong-fu, some five hundred miles south of Peiping, there existed, and perhaps still exists, a Jewish community that goes back to very ancient times, its members being undistinguishable in appearance from their Chinese neighbors. This community was once visited by a European Jewish Orientalist who, on a Sabbath morning, sought out its place of worship and attended the service. He knew enough Chinese to follow it.

The westerner created a little stir, and the sexton approached him to bid him welcome.

"Are you Jewish?" he asked the visitor.

"I am," was the answer.

The sexton smiled affably, but his expression was quizzical. "You don't look it," he told the traveler.

BEST OF FRIENDS

"So you are from Suwalk, hey? I know someone in Suwalk, Shmuel Feigfinger. Do you know Shmuel Feigfinger?

"Shmuel Feigfinger? You know Shmulikl Feigfinger?"

"Not too well. But you seem to know him, too. Can you tell me something about him?"

"Of course! Where shall I begin? Let me see, we are alone here, so I can tell you the whole truth. First of all, there is the story about him and the servant girl. Not a pretty story. It cost his father a fortune. His father took him into his business, but had to watch the till all the time. And watching didn't always help. Shmulikl has nimble fingers. With cards also. Would you believe it, they found a deck of cards on him with five aces. There are other stories. That servant girl, it seems, was not the only one. Once he was caught with—"

"But wait a minute! How is it you know so much about him?"

"About Shmuel Feigfinger? Why Shmulikl and I have been the best of friends from boyhood!"

DIFFICULT CONVERSATION

They were sitting in the same compartment, an alert man of the world from the distant city of Tomsk in Siberia, and a self-absorbed scholar from the pious city of Berditchev in Ukrainia. The man of affairs took the initiative.

"We are both of the seed of Abraham," he said, "so why shouldn't we talk?"

"Oh!" the other responded, "it will be a pleasure."

"So tell me, I pray you, where are you from?"

"From Berditchev."

"Berditchev. I heard of Berditchev. Are there many Jews in Berditchev?"

"In Berditchev? In Berditchev we are all Jews."

"You don't say! You mean there are no *goyim* in Berditchev?"

"Oh, yes. We have some *goyim* in Berditchev."

"How many about would you say you have?"

"As many as we need."

The traveler from Tomsk was rather taken aback. He dropped the initiative. But the man from Berditchev felt that good manners required that the conversation should go on.

"And where, if I may be so bold, are you from?" he ventured.

"From Tomsk."

"Tomsk? I never heard of Tomsk. Is it far?"

"It's in Siberia."

"Ah, Siberia. I hear it's very cold in Siberia."

"Yes, it's cold." And again the conversation fell off. But the man from Berditchev made another attempt.

"Tell me," he said. "Do you have many Jews in Tomsk?"

"We have some. Not many."

"And *goyim?* Do you have many *goyim?*"

"*Goyim?* Thousands and thousands of them!"

"Really? Why do you need so many *goyim?*"

Gallant and Gay

Humor of Reborn Israel

Foreword

MODERN ISRAEL was born in toil, battle, and anguish. Its birth was preceded by a long and bitter tug of war with a powerful empire; it was attended by an unequal contest against implacable neighbors; it was followed by an era of privation and peril which is not yet over. And as a somber backdrop to the epic struggle, the annihilation of east European Jewry loomed over it.

Nevertheless, in the humor of reborn Israel there is little of the grimness that might have been expected. It is the humor of a people schooled in suffering, but without bitterness or self-pity. Its laughter, in fact, is wholesome and spontaneous.

Consider some of its choice targets: the American Jewish tourist; the *pakid,* or bureaucrat; the *yeke,* or immigrant from Germany. The American tourist is the purse-proud benefactor, and of course receives his meed of ridicule, apart from the unpopularity which is the usual lot of a benefactor. But his critics, one feels, are at the same time grateful for the hearty laughter which his ignorance and presumption afford them. The sarcasm, at any rate, has no venom in it.

As for the *yeke,* he is found to have too much of the Teuton in him. He is charged with being rigid, arrogant and absurdly in awe of authority. Perhaps he affords a weclome opportunity to avenge the traditional superior attitude of the *Westjude* to the *Ostjude.* But the somber and common tragedy he recalls takes the sting out of the ridicule.

The *pakid*, or minor bureaucrat, is found vulnerable on two counts: first, he is inexperienced and inept—a babe in the woods; second, he owes his position to a species of nepotism in that he belongs to the right political party. But the community as a whole is the real target of the satire directed at him. Everybody, as member or voter, is identified with a political party and hopes, in one way or another, to benefit from it; and the *pakid*'s dilemmas are only a minor sector of the problems faced by the entire community, endowed suddenly with the formidable gift of statehood.

That, indeed, is the hallmark of the humor of Israel: it scintillates with irony that is aimed at itself, and it is this quality that makes it so hearty and salutary.

Through the Mocking-Glass

MIRACLES

THE ILL-TRAINED and ill-armed soldiers of newborn Israel had repelled the simultaneous onslaught of all her Arab neighbors.

"To what do you ascribe your victory?" an army officer was asked.

"As I see it," he replied, "there were two causes: one natural, the other miraculous. The natural cause was the will of God. The miracle was the courage of our fighting men and women."

When things were not too rosy this bit of advice was offered by a pious Jew: "Don't rely on miracles. Pray devoutly and chant the Book of Psalms every day."

And the whole course of events was summed up by the man who said: "After all we have been through you still don't believe in miracles? Then you have lost all sense of reality."

HAPPY LANDING

The press bureau of the Egyptian government issued the following statement: "We are happy to report that a substantial portion of our air force has already landed in Israel."

The report was true. The "substantial portion" had been shot down.

ONCE IS ENOUGH

Egyptian headquarters called the commander of one of its units.

"Why," he was asked, "didn't you attack and capture the Jewish settlement?"

The officer replied: "My men insisted they heard the radio report that our forces had already taken this settlement. They saw no point in taking it twice."

POOR OLD LADY

After a severe shelling of Egyptian positions in the Gaza Strip, Cairo reported "no damage or casualties except one old woman who was wounded." To this report one correspondent added: "The old woman burned for four days. There was not enough water to put her out."

DRASTIC MEASURES

"Have you read what the Egyptian representative said in the UN yesterday? He said if we don't agree at once to an armistice in the Negev his government will be forced to take drastic measures."

"I remember a similar case. Where I come from two chaps once got into a fight. One was knocked down on his face and the other seated himself on his back and wouldn't get off. 'People!' cried the man on the ground, 'Get him off my back or I'll kill him!' "

PECULIAR BUS DRIVER

She was a little old lady who had lived all her life in a small town in Poland where the only language she spoke was Yiddish. When she got to Palestine she heard them speak in the holy tongue, but she didn't take it seriously. It was a fad, an affectation. When it came to something serious, she was sure they spoke Yiddish. How else?

Then came the days of turmoil and trouble. The Jews were preparing to set up a state and the Arabs were determined to prevent it. Roads were blocked and buses were shot at from ambush. And this old lady, as it happened, was travelling by bus one day from Jerusalem to Tel Aviv when the vehicle became the target of gunfire.

"All passengers get down on the floor of the bus!" the driver shouted—in Hebrew, of course.

Said the little old lady to the passenger who lay next to her on the floor of the bus, and in Yiddish, of course.

"What do you say to this driver of ours? Out there they are shooting and he has to talk Hebrew!"

HE TRIED USING FORCE

When the state was established and functioning this old lady—or was it another one?—felt she ought to do something towards earning her livelihood. So she called on her ancient skill in baking and went out peddling with a basket of *beygl* and *pletsl.*

A policeman approached her, an affable young man with a perfect command of Yiddish, and asked her if she had a permit.

"What do you mean a permit?" she inquired.

The policeman explained. She must go to the police station and obtain a permit or license to peddle.

The old lady smiled at him. "You have nothing else on your mind?" she asked him.

The next day the same policeman asked her the same question.

"Listen, young man," she replied. "Does it hurt you that an old lady is trying to make a living?"

He asked her the same question on the third day and this time she was just a little angry.

"Young man," she told him. "Don't you think you should find something to do with your time?"

But now the affable policeman was also a little ruffled.

"Grandmother," he warned her, "you must get a permit, and better do it without delay."

On the fourth day she was really angry.

"You look like a nice young man," she said, "but you are really a *gazlon*. You can't bear to see someone make a living."

But now he too was angry.

"This is the last time I'll warn you," he told her. "The next time I find you peddling without a permit I'll arrest you."

And the next time he really did take her by the arm, saying: "Come with me!"

She turned on him with amazement. "What are you doing, young man?" she cried. "I see that you don't know me. So let me tell you this: with force you won't get anywhere with me!"

THE LAW TRIUMPHS

How this unfortunate difference between the old lady and the law was resolved is not on record, but in another and similar case the law was triumphantly vindicated. This time the offender was a testy old man whom the uniform of the police officer failed to impress, and the policeman was a man of compassionate nature who abhorred violence.

After numerous warnings, to which the lawbreaker responded with scornful indifference, the policeman decided he must arrest him and so informed him.

"I'm sorry," he apologized, "I have to take you to the station, so please come with me."

The old man couldn't believe his ears.

"Have you gone out of your mind?" he demanded. "Where do you think we are, in Russia?"

The man in uniform realized the force of the argument and turned away, embarrassed.

But before long he sensed that his superiors were beginning

to look at him dubiously: he hadn't made an arrest since he joined the force.

So he went to the old curmudgeon and said: "You are not being fair to me. I am in danger of losing my job and I have a wife and five children."

The lawbreaker eyed the policeman gloomily.

"It's you who are unfair," he told him. "What you are using against me is worse than force. What can I do? I'll have to go with you."

TALE OF TWO LIONS

They were old friends, the two lions, and having decided to savor the taste of freedom, they broke out and escaped from the Tel Aviv Zoo. They took separate roads, but at the end of a fortnight they were recaptured and found themselves together again in the same cage. One of them looked sleek and smug with that cat-full-of-canary expression. The other was drawn and haggard, the ribs on his flanks bursting out of his hide.

"My poor friend," said the first, "you seem to have had a hard time of it."

"Hard is a mild word for it," the second replied. "I nearly starved to death. It happened like this. I made my way into one of the government offices. It was tea time, and a porter was bringing in tea and cookies. He didn't look bad, so I pounced on him, thinking that I too was entitled to refreshments. Well, you should have seen what a rumpus the bureaucrats raised over a mere porter! They ganged up on me with everything they could lay hands on and chased me all the way to the Negev. I barely escaped with my life, but in the wastes of the desert what could I live on? I just managed to subsist on a couple of scraggy old Bedouins that I picked up, and I am glad to be back."

"Too bad, old friend," said the other lion. "You made an unfortunate start. You should have let the man with the tea things alone. He is too important."

The lean lion looked gloomily at his sleek friend. "You don't seem to have fared badly at all," he remarked.

"I did all right," the other said. "I had myself a fat little bureaucrat every day. Mmm, delicious!"

"And the others did nothing about it?"

"Nothing," said the fat lion. "It seems that nobody missed them."

ODYSSEY OF AN APPLICANT

There are those who report that when an applicant for a government post enters the application room he finds himself faced by two doors: one marked "Experienced;" the other "Inexperienced." Let us follow such an applicant. He takes the door marked "Experienced" and finds himself facing two new doors marked "Under Forty" and "Over Forty." He goes through the first and behold, two more doors: "Single" and "Married." He opens the door marked "Single" and, sure enough, there are two new doors, one marked "Member of Party A" the other "Nonmember of Party A." And since he is not a member of any political party, he passes through the second door and steps right out upon the sidewalk.

QUESTION AND ANSWER

Q: Why is a bureaucrat like a headless nail?
A: Because once he is in you can't yank him out.

MILK AND HONEY

It happened when they were rationing water in Jerusalem, and one housewife asked another how she liked her new apartment.

"I like it well enough," she replied, "but it's a nuisance to have a faucet that gives you water only twice a week."

"Why complain?" said the other. "You know what the faucet is for on the other days of the week, don't you?"

"I can't say I do."

"Ah, you've forgotten your Bible. Milk and honey, of course!"

SENSIBLE ADVICE

It was in the gaunt days of austerity, when food and other necessities were strictly rationed, and one citizen hit upon an ingenious device for not going hungry. He took his stand at the door of one of the cabinet ministers with a bundle of straw, which he chewed until the minister came out.

"Why are you eating straw?" the minister inquired.

"I'm hungry," the man replied.

The minister took out a five pound note and handed it to him.

The following morning he repeated the performance at the door of another minister with the same happy result.

The third morning he made the mistake of trying it at the door of the Minister of Supply and Rationing.

"My good man," said this minister. "You should save the straw for the winter. It's summer now, so why don't you go out and eat grass right off the field?"

TOO RISKY

They got to talking about the economic problems that beset the newborn state: the unfavorable balance of trade, the lack of hard currency, the shortages of food and other necessities.

"It's a gloomy prospect," one of them summed it up.

"But I have a solution!" another one declared, and they all turned toward him.

"I derive it," he went on, "from what has happened during these postwar years. Take West Germany, Japan, Italy, all of whom fought the United States in the war, and see how their victorious enemy has enabled them to get on their feet again.

My proposal, therefore, is that we have a war with America and when it's over our problems will also be solved."

All agreed it was an excellent idea, except one.

"What's wrong with it?" they asked the dissenter.

"It's too risky," he said.

"Too risky? What do you mean?"

"I mean: suppose we win the war?"

THE POOR WIVES!

In the days of austerity three citizens of Tel Aviv talked about the dire effect which the reduced diet was having on their wives.

"The other day," one reported, "my wife insisted she had to have a new dress. So I said, see what you can do about it. She took an old shirt of mine, cut away the sleeves and collar and made herself a dress. I thought it fitted her perfectly, but she said it was too long and too wide. She is going to shorten it and take it in at the waist. What? You don't believe me?"

"I believe you," said the second, "in view of what happened to my own wife. Last week she swallowed an olive pit. When she went out to stand in line at the food store, her neighbors came over and told her she mustn't be on her feet too long. They held her hand, caressed her shoulders and wanted to know when she expected the blessed event. But you don't believe me, I can see it."

"When I think of what happened to my wife, how can I help believing you?" said the third. "Last night she took a bath, and when she was through she pulled out the stopper. The water began flowing down the drain and took her along. She disappeared and I haven't heard from her since. I don't expect I'll ever see her again. You know a good *shadchn*, either of you?"

TRANSIT PROBLEMS

"We in America," said a tourist to a friend in Israel, "also do a lot of traveling by bus. In fact, more and more people now go by bus to the most distant places."

"We are accustomed to being imitated," the Israeli modestly observed.

"But we have some wonderful buses," the American held up his end. "You start out in one of them and three days later you are still traveling in the same one."

"We have such buses also," the Israeli assured him.

One bearded man stood patiently in line, waiting for a bus. The vehicles stopped at long intervals, took on passengers and sped away. At last he was able to squeeze into one of them. He took out of his pocket a reduced-fare ticket to which school children are entitled, and handed it to the driver.

"How do you come by this ticket?" asked the driver sarcastically.

"I received it before I joined the line," the passenger informed him.

She looked up from the paper she was reading and informed her husband that the population of the country had risen above the two million mark.

"I'm not surprised," he observed. "You should have seen how crowded the buses were today!"

COVERAGE

"Why do you put on a *yarmelke* when you sign a check?"

The question was addressed to Eliezer Kaplan, the first Finance Minister of newborn Israel.

"It's the only coverage I have," he explained.

CHANGE OF NAME

After the establishment of the State there was a rush of name-changing in Israel. Names of Slavic and Germanic origin were Hebraized.

There was an immigrant from Morocco whose schooling fell

short of the ability to sign his name. When he received his salary he stamped his fingerprint in the space reserved for the signature. One day he did something which made the clerk curious.

"You always use your thumb," he said. "Why do you now stamp with your middle finger?"

"I've changed my name," the man answered proudly.

MEN OF LITTLE FAITH

The government decreed a bonus for families with six or more children.

A young woman from Morocco appeared at the proper bureau and applied for the bonus. She held a baby in her arms and led a little two-year-old by the hand.

"How many children have you?" she was asked.

"These two," she answered.

"But you have to have at least six!"

The young mother burst into tears.

"You don't trust me," she wailed. "My mother had seventeen, and me you don't trust to have four more."

HERE AND THERE

The immigrant from behind the Iron Curtain was not too communicative. Finally someone asked him the overall question:

"How did you find living conditions over there?"

"Thank God, I couldn't complain," he answered.

"And how do you find living conditions in Israel?"

"Thank God, I *can* complain."

SIMPLE SOLUTION

"So Israel intends to keep her doors wide open for all Jews who wish to enter?" a foreign journalist asked a group of Israeli colleagues.

"We do," was the answer.

"But your country is so small! Sooner or later you will have to impose restrictions."

"Why?"

"Well, suppose the Soviet Union permits its Jews to emigrate and they come flocking to Israel. What will you do then?

"It's simple. The rest of us will get out."

POOR CZAR!

The Russian ambassador to Israel was entertaining a prominent figure on the Israeli political scene.

"So you were born in my country," said the ambassador, "and you left as early as 1905. But tell me, I pray you, why did you leave?"

"Well, Nicholas II was Czar at the time, and there was no room for both of us."

"I see," the ambassador smiled. "You got into each other's way."

"That's right, and when it became clear that one of us must go, I felt that I should be the one. You see," he concluded, "I had somewhere to go, but the Czar didn't."

SPECIAL WORRIES

They were nicknamed *yekes,* the immigrants from Germany, and they were believed to have peculiar worries. Shortly before the British surrendered the mandate and departed, a *yeke* was said to have come up with the following question: "What are we going to do if the British leave and forget to lift the curfew? How are we going to go out at night?"

Another immigrant from Germany found himself in an even worse predicament. When he debarked he was unable to obtain a lodging for the night, so he crept into a covered truck and decided to sleep there. It was a cold night and well before dawn he was found standing outside the truck in his nightshirt, smoking a cigarette and shivering.

"What's wrong?" someone asked him.

"I couldn't sleep," he explained, "so I decided to have a smoke."

"So?"

"So I came outside."

"And why?"

"There's a sign inside that says 'No Smoking.' "

OPTIMISM UNLIMITED

"What happened to your left shoulder? What makes it sag down like that?"

The question was addressed by one who had not seen the man with the sagging shoulder for several years.

"I've been having a hard time with this shoulder," the man replied. "It's suffering from optimism."

"You see," he went on, "in my business I meet a great many people. After we compare notes and shake our heads over the way things are going, they brace up and smile and say: 'Don't worry, old chap, things will be all right!' And as they say it, they invariably bring their right hand down on my left shoulder."

RECOGNITION DENIED

The emergence of the Republic of Israel brought the question of recognizing the new state before every other republic and kingdom, including, of course, the Animal Kingdom. The lion met with his Supreme Council and it was decided to send an investigation commission to Israel before granting recognition. As members of the commission the lion appointed a cow, a rooster, and an ass.

"Your Majesty," said the fox, "let it be a white ass."

"Why white?" His Majesty demanded.

"In Israel," the fox explained, "there are people who believe that the Messiah has come or is on the way, and since the Messiah must ride on a white ass they will appreciate it if you send them one. It will be a nice gesture on your part."

His Majesty graciously consented and the commission departed. In surprisingly short time, however, they were back again. The first to speak was the cow.

"This new state," she reported, "has adopted a policy of unlimited milking. Whatever the people do, a tax is levied upon them and they get milked. If that's what they do to their own people, I said to myself, what will they do to poor me? So I got out as fast as I could."

The cow was followed by the rooster.

"I left in a hurry," he reported, "or I would have died from frustration. In this new state you have to get a permit for everything you do. I would have had to get a permit every time I wanted to crow. Now, when the inner urge comes over me, can I stop to get a permit? So I got out as fast as I could."

Now came the turn of the ass.

"I barely escaped with my life," he reported. "My intentions were of the best. I aimed to show those people that I was familiar with their traditions and respected them. So I stood in the principal square of their capital and issued a call: 'Let the Messiah come forward and ride on me!' Then it happened. They rushed upon me from every direction. They jostled and trampled each other, trying to get on my back. Finally they knocked me off my feet, and how I managed to scramble out and escape I don't rightly know."

N.B. The Animal Kingdom has not yet recognized the State of Israel.

Enter the Tourist

THE GUIDEBOOK

"BEFORE WE start," said the tourist to his driver, "I'd like you to step in somewhere and buy me a guidebook."

"Very well, sir," said the driver. He stopped at a book shop and when he came out he handed the tourist a book.

"But this—this is a Bible!" the tourist exclaimed.

"That's right, sir. That's our guidebook," the driver informed him.

WAILING WALLS FOR ALL

"Today," said an American tourist to his guide in Tel Aviv, "I want to visit the Wailing Wall."

"In that case we'll have to go to Jerusalem, sir."

"What?" the tourist demanded. "We have sent you so much money and you haven't gotten around to putting up a wailing wall in Tel Aviv?"

"But there is only one Wailing Wall in the entire country, sir," the guide tried to explain.

"Well," the tourist declared, "get this straight. Before we Americans are through every town and village in this country will have its own wailing wall."

But the tourist did make the trip to Jerusalem to see the Wall. What could he do? It was the only one in the country. When he got back, a friend asked him did he see it and what did he have to say about it.

"What's to say?" he replied. "A wailing wall like all wailing walls!"

THEY HUNG FROM HER EARS

The American lady tourist seemed to have taken all her jewels to wear on the trip, and conspicuous among them was a pair of large diamond earrings. She "did" every place there was to be "done," including the farm settlements. At one settlement she was conducted by the manager, who was intrigued by those earrings. In the end his curiosity overcame his tact.

"Madam," he said, "would you forgive me if I asked how much your earrings are worth?"

"I don't mind telling you," she answered. And she named the figure, in dollars, of course.

The farmer did some rapid mental arithmetic.

"Madam," he told her, "you may not believe it, but you have a bull and six cows hanging from your ears."

DR. HERZL'S OFFICE HOURS

There is a room in the Jewish Agency building in Jerusalem which has been fitted up as an exact replica of the room in which Dr. Theodor Herzl did his work in Vienna. Herzl's desk is there, his chair, his books—everything.

The party of tourists followed the guide into the room and examined everything with interest.

An eager lady from America approached the guide.

"Can you tell me," she cooed, "what Dr. Herzl's office hours are? I'd love to see him."

A DISTINGUISHED WAITER

An American tourist was visiting a *kibbutz* in the Emek and stayed on over the Sabbath. One of the members of this *kibbutz* was a prominent deputy of the Knesset who made it a practice to spend his Sabbaths with his comrades in the settlement and, like them, perform whatever chores were assigned to him. During the Sabbath meal this deputy waited at the table and served the tourist his soup and *Kugl* and other Sabbath dishes.

Not long afterwards the tourist sat with a friend in the visitor's gallery of the Knesset and saw among the deputies someone who looked remarkably like the man who waited on him in the *kibbutz*. The American was dazed. He never saw such a perfect resemblance.

"You see that man over there?" he said to his friend. "If I didn't know he is a member of the Knesset, I would swear he is a waiter."

REAL ESTATE

Perhaps the cruelest jibe at the American tourist is contained in the story of one who was out walking in the Orthodox quarter of Jerusalem one summer morning and heard sounds of distress issuing from a humble structure, apparently a synagogue. It was the Ninth of Ab, the day when Jews mourn the destruction of the Temple, but the American was blissfully ignorant of it all: he was in the real estate business.

The groaning and wailing which he heard alarmed him. He rushed inside and hurried up to someone who appeared to be in charge.

"What is it?" he asked anxiously. "What's going on here?"

The man he questioned took him in at a glance.

"Don't you know?" he replied. "Our Temple was destroyed."

"You don't say!" the American was shocked. "How did it happen? An explosion? I didn't hear it."

"No," he was told. "It was burnt down."

"Burnt down, hey? When was the fire?"

"About two thousand years ago."

The American opened his eyes wide and gasped.

"Two thousand years ago!" he finally managed to say. "So

why do you carry on like this? The lot alone is now worth the money!"

KEEN OBSERVER

This dignified lady tourist was doing not just Israel but the whole Near East, and wherever she went she made copious notes. Her society in Chillicothe, Ohio, expected a full report.

Her observations in Jerusalem, the Holy City, she set down in special detail, and Mea Shearim, the Orthodox section of the city, intrigued her in particular.

"What was the most interesting place you saw in Jerusalem?" she was asked on her return.

"The Jewish Quarter," she replied.

A VISA AND A HUSBAND

"How do I go about getting a visa to America for a husband?" asked the lady tourist. Her manner was brisk and businesslike.

"You must apply to the American consul," she was told.

"The address?"

She was given the address and wrote it down.

"Now," she continued, keeping her pencil poised, "how do I go about getting a husband?"

TRUE BLUFFS

This tourist had been a Zionist propagandist in America, where numerous audiences had gone away inspired by his eloquent portrayals of the wonders the Jews had wrought in the land of their fathers. After many years of speechmaking these wonders came off his tongue glibly, without effort, and, let it be said, without inner conviction.

The officers thought well of his work, and rewarded him with a trip to the Land, all expenses paid. He came and he saw. He saw the busy port of Haifa, the ships, the docks, the factories. He saw the suburbs rising up the slope of Carmel. In the valley of Jezreel he saw the settlements, the grainfields, the new forests. Along the coast he saw the vineyards, the citrus groves, the truck farms, the dairy farms. He saw Tel Aviv and was caught up in the swirl of its vibrant life. He saw and saw and saw.

He was happy and dazed. He cabled to his President: "Feeling grand. Must tell you those bluffs I handed out in my speeches are all true, every one of them."

DUCKS AND GEESE

The tourist from Manhattan was exuberant. He found everything in the settlement just wonderful. He stopped with his companion before the poultry shed.

"Look," he said. "They are raising geese here."

"Those are ducks, not geese," the guide explained.

"What did I tell you?" he said to his friend. "Our farmers, God bless them! Their cherries are like plums, their ducks are like geese!"

ISAIAH AND DISARMAMENT

The Dead Sea scrolls were on display and attracted numerous visitors. Among them was a tourist from Arizona whose habit it was to follow the crowd. He stopped before one exhibit and wondered why people looked at it so intently.

"What is this?" he inquired.

"The Scroll of Isaiah," he was told.

"Isaiah, hey? Big shot, I suppose."

The other looked him up and down, and then explained as follows:

"This scroll contains the disarmament program of one of our most famous experts. The program got around and a lot of people quoted from it, especially the part about beating swords into ploughshares. Unfortunately, however, Isaiah's proposals were never adopted. The Americans said he favored the Soviets because he said the heavens belong to God, not to men: in other words, he was against the "open skies" plan. The Russians denounced him as an imperialist; they suspected him of being a Zionist. So all he could do was to put his ideas down on a scroll which he hid in a cave near the Dead Sea. Well, this is the scroll. Somebody found it and brought it here. Now do you see?"

"Plain enough," said the man from Arizona.

Bivouac Banter

MIRACLE BROOM

It was in the days when the British still governed the country. News reached them that the Arabs had launched an attack on a certain settlement and were driven back. A British officer was dispatched to look the situation over. Among the settlement guards he saw a gray-bearded man with an old musket.

"What?" said the Briton. "Don't you have any age limit here?"

"No," the old man replied. "But we have an old Yiddish proverb."

"What is that?"

"*Az Got vil, shist a bezem.*" (God willing, even a broom will shoot.)

NARROW ESCAPE

During the War of Independence there were rumors in heaven that the army of Israel was being recruited from older and older age-groups. Finally there were unconfirmed reports that old men were actually being put into uniform. It was decided in the heavenly council to send someone down to investigate, and Methuselah was summoned and ordered to go.

"You Methuselah," he was told, "are the oldest of us. You will be safe."

Methuselah went and came back in a hurry.

"I escaped just in time," he reported. "They were already calling up my age-group."

A MONTH AT THE MOST

There was a resident of Tel Aviv during the War of Independence who appeared among his friends one day and predicted with confidence that the war would last a month at the most.

"What makes you so sure?" they asked him.

"My son was drafted into the army today."

"So?"

"Well, that young snipe has never yet held a job longer than a month."

DUTIES OF A SERGEANT

"What," said the sergeant to the new recruit, "was your civilian occupation?" His tone was not exactly cordial.

"I worked in a bank," the novice answered.

"I can imagine what your work was," the sergeant continued. "You dusted the tables, filled the inkwells, cleaned the pens, and laid out the forms."

"Oh no!" said the recruit. "For those chores we employ an elderly sergeant."

NEW APPROACH

Everything the new recruit received he found tolerable except the pants. They were too long and too tight. They made him look ridiculous. But what could he do? They kept telling him there were no others. Finally he appeared before the quartermaster with a book which he held out toward the officer. It was a Bible.

"Lay your right hand on this book," said he, "and swear you don't have another pair of pants."

It appears there was another pair after all.

WHY EAT IT?

The soldier came to the commissary and complained about the soup. There was too much sand in it.

"You must learn to take it," he was told. "A good soldier must be willing to suffer for his country."

"Yes," the soldier replied. "But must he also eat it?"

HARMONY RESTORED

They tell this about a captain in the army of Israel who saw a private of his company walking towards him in a street in Tel Aviv. The private passed his captain without saluting.

The captain was nonplussed. Then he turned, strode quickly towards the private and overtook him.

"Isaac," he said, "you didn't salute me."

Isaac was surprised and embarrassed.

"Moshe," he said, "I didn't see you. I swear I didn't see you."

"All right, Isaac," the captain replied. "I thought you were angry with me for some reason or other."

A SLIGHT ERROR

You think I stand in awe of officers? Not I. The other day the captain asked me to make a copy of a report he got from Headquarters. He found out I had a good handwriting. After reading it through I said to him: "Captain, the clerk over at Headquarters made a mistake. Instead of writing *Intelligence Officer,* he wrote *Intelligent Officer*. Do we have any like that?"

RIFLE VERSUS TANK

When rifles were in short supply and positions had to be held, an officer gave one of his men a broomstick and instructed him as follows:

"You are on guard tonight and this is your rifle. If you hear footsteps approaching you cry out: Who goes there? If you get no answer and the footsteps come closer you cry: Halt, or I shoot! If you get no answer, you rush upon the intruder and lay him out with your broomstick."

The man took his post, and sure enough he heard footsteps approaching. He followed instructions but there was no answer. He was about to rush upon the enemy with his broomstick when he recognized one of his comrades.

"Velvl," he cried, "I could have killed you! Why didn't you answer?"

"How could I?" Velvl replied. "The captain told me I was a tank."

ALL FIGURED OUT

"Men!" said the officer before giving the signal to attack. "We have complete information on the strength of the enemy. They and we are exactly equal in number. All that is necessary is that each one of you take care of one of them."

"I'll take care of two!" an eager recruit responded.

At once another recruit stepped forward.

"In that case," he asked the officer, "can I go home?"

THE PASSWORD

An American Jewish pilot who flew for Israel in the War of Independence was brought down near the coast and parachuted into the sea. He managed to reach shore, and there before him was a Jewish settlement. But he was afraid he might be mistaken for an Egyptian and shot down before he could explain, so he ran towards the settlement, shouting and repeating with all his strength: "Gefilte Fish! Gefilte Fish!" They were the only Jewish words, Yiddish or Hebrew, that he knew.

GREAT EXPECTATIONS

"My wife is expecting," the soldier explained, and he got his furlough.

His buddy accompanied him to the jeep that stood ready for him.

"Good-by!" his buddy said. "And tell me, how soon do you expect the blessed event?"

"I don't know exactly," the happy man leaned over and whispered, "but I would say in about nine months after I return."

TWO TALL ONES

When he brought in the Egyptian prisoner, they wanted to know how he captured him.

"I shot him through the heart and took him in," he reported.

"Very good," they complimented him. "But first you raised him from the dead, didn't you?"

"I didn't have to," he explained. "The moment I pulled the trigger his heart fell into his pants, and I was able to take him alive."

It was the turn of the paratrooper.

"I know you won't believe my story, but I'll tell it just as it happened. It was my turn to jump. I had jumped only once before, and I was nervous. Why should I understate it? I was more than nervous. I was in a blue funk. The officer was barking out commands and instructions, but his voice was drowned by the roar of the engines. I was in no condition to listen, even if I could have heard him. But then I saw him point at me and at the open door, and his face was purple with fury. I was half-dazed. I stepped out into the void, and I remembered that I had not finished adjusting my chute. 'It's all over,' I said to myself, 'it won't open.' And I was right. The confounded thing never opened, and before I knew it I was on the ground. 'What is this?' I wondered. 'I'm conscious, I'm breathing, I'm alive!' I felt my ribs, my legs, my arms. I was sound and whole. I had hardly a scratch."

"Congratulations!" they cried, and one of them added: "The moment you jumped you became an angel and a pair of wings sprouted out of your shoulders."

"Wings nothing," the paratrooper replied. "I didn't need any. The plane was still on the ground. It hadn't taken off yet."

HE KNEW WHERE TO GO

The occasion was in honor of the first president of Israel, and those in attendance included members of the diplomatic corps and many distinguished citizens. There was a large sprinkling of army officers in carefully furbished uniforms, but one of them stood out by the magnificent sword that clanked at his side.

"Where on earth did you get that blade?" a fellow officer asked him.

"Don't you know that before the war I had charge of the property room of the Habima Theatre?" the man with the sword replied. "Well, I still have access to the place."

SUDDEN EPIDEMIC

As soon as the pretty nurse appeared in camp a long line formed outside her door.

"What is this?" the sergeant demanded. "An epidemic?"

"Yes," he was told, "and it's serious."

"How did it start?"

"Well, sergeant, have you seen the new nurse?"

"No."

"You're lucky. If you had, you too would be standing in line."

WHICH WAS IT?

When he came home for his furlough, he took her in his arms, looked deep into her eyes, and whispered in her ear as he kissed it:

"You are beautiful."

She thought it best to moderate his ardor.

"It's because I spent four hours in the beauty salon today," she bantered.

"I wonder——" he began.

"Wonder?"

"Yes. I wonder if it's because you spent four hours in the beauty salon or because I spent four months in the Negev Desert."

L'ENVOI

Don't write to your girl too often. She might fall in love with the postman.

Ben-Gurionana

HIS WORKING CLOTHES

The Prime Minister was booked to address a workers' convention, but prior to it, he attended a diplomatic reception where, of course, he appeared in the formal attire prescribed for such occasions. With no time to change, he came in the same attire to the convention. "Fellow delegates," he said, "before beginning my address, I want to apologize to you for coming here in my working clothes."

TO MAKE THEM HAPPY

It was in the days of austerity, but to celebrate Purim a huge throng had gathered in Tel Aviv. The Minister of Finance, the Minister of Supply and Rationing and the Prime Minister went up in an airplane to have a better view of the festivities.

Said the Prime Minister: "What with high taxes and strict rationing, I don't think the people are really happy."

Said the Minister of Finance: "I suppoese I could make them happy if I threw them down a few bags of gold coins."

Said the Minister of Supply and Rationing: "They would be even happier if I threw them down a few bags of sugar."

Said Ben-Gurion: "They would be most happy if I threw both of you down."

TWICE THIRTY-FIVE

"Yes," said an Israeli to his American friend, "Israel does have a pretty good army. The military experts seem to agree on it."

"And to what do you ascribe it?" the American asked.

"There is more than one reason," the other replied. "But an important one is the fact that our officers are young men. The average age of our top commanders, for example, is, I am sure, not more than thirty-five."

"But you forget that your commander-in-chief is over seventy!"

"Ben-Gurion? You are mistaken. He just happens to be two young men of thirty-five."

NOT FAIR

"I am for changing our political system," a certain critic opined. "In ancient time we reached our pinnacle of power under a monarchy. Why not restore the monarchy?"

"And whom would you have as king?"

"Ben-Gurion, of course. Whom else?"

"But do you think it fair that he should go down in history as David the Second?"

THE STRAIN

Some friends asked Ben-Gurion how he was bearing up under the burden of his office.

"It's not easy," he answered. "I often feel like the man who was employed as a sorter in an orange grove. 'I don't know what will happen to me,' he complained to his wife. 'There are big oranges, small oranges and middle-sized oranges, and I have to put each one in a different box. The strain is beginning to wear me down. All day long it's nothing but decisions and decisions.' "

QUOTED ON THE EXCHANGE

The youngsters in Jerusalem established an "Autograph Exchange."

For weeks after the removal of the Knesset from Tel Aviv to Jerusalem they hounded the members for autographs. When the manhunt was over many a youngster discovered he had a number of autographs of some members and none of others. Hence the "Exchange." In principal demand were the autographs of Ben-Gurion and Menachem Beigin, the leader of *Herut* (Freedom Party), the second largest political party in the country. As on every exchange quotations fluctuated. But in general three Beigins were offered for one Ben-Gurion.

THEN AND NOW

It got around that while the Sinai campaign was in progress Ben-Gurion summoned two distinguished rabbis to his residence. Curiosity ran high and soon a large group stood outside to learn the cause of the summons. When the visitors came out they were surrounded.

"He wanted us to explain a simple matter," they informed the questioners. "How did the children of Israel under Moses manage to survive the climate of the Sinai Peninsula for forty years?"

WHO INDEED?

At dinner the head of the family reported there were rumors that Ben-Gurion was going to resign.

Up spoke five-year-old Miriam.

"Daddy," she asked, "if Ben-Gurion resigns, who is going to be Ben-Gurion?"

Sparks from the Small Fry

CAUSE AND EFFECT

He was only five, but he knew how to make a real nuisance of himself. He kept rampaging all over the barn and getting in the way of the men who were working there. They ordered him and warned him but made no impression on him. Finally one of them caught him and held him.

"What would you say," the man threatened, "if I took off my strap to you."

"I would say," he answered, "that your pants would come down."

HE FELT LIKE A BUS

She was feeding her four-year-old, and with motherly insistence, cramming things into his mouth.

The little one gulped down a big mouthful and protested.

"Why do you keep cramming me like that?" he cried. "Am I a bus?"

ALMOST

The two youngsters were friends. They attended the same school in Tel Aviv and their fathers were both policemen.

"This morning," said one, "I almost saw your father."

"Almost? What do you mean almost?"

"Your father's number is 1521, isn't it?"

"That's right."

"Well, I saw a policeman this morning and his number was 1522."

HE'LL RETALIATE

The four-year-old was bad that morning, wilder than usual.

"If you don't stop stamping and yelling, I'll lock you up in the chicken coop," his mother threatened.

"Lock me up there, if you want to," he warned her. "But I'm not going to lay any eggs."

POOR MORDECAI!

He was only seven, but the pictures he drew were so good, people said he would be a fine artist.

For Purim he made up an album of the leading figures in the Megillah. Esther was beautiful, Haman was huge and menacing, and Ahasuerus had a tipsy smile on his fat face. But Mordecai was lean and shrunken.

"Why is Mordecai so skinny?" they asked him.

"What do you expect?" he replied. "With the Jews having so much trouble, you want him to be nice and fat?"

HOW TO ABUSE A DONKEY

The two tots were taking a ride on the donkey. But the beast balked. He just wouldn't stir.

The front rider became angry.

"Donkey!" he cried, "why don't you move?"

The other intervened.

"A donkey," he said, "doesn't mind if you call him Donkey. Try calling him Man."

IT'S A WISE CHILD

On Independence Day the Jerusalem stadium was the scene of an impressive military display. Admission was by ticket only.

Close to the field sat a tot of five or six watching the exercises. He was approached by a guard.

"You are all alone?" the guard asked him.

"Yes."

"You sneaked in, didn't you?"

"No!"

"You have a ticket?"

The little one took out a ticket and handed it to the guard.

"This is made out to your father, isn't it?"

"Yes!"

"Where is your father, then?"

"He is home now, turning everything upside down, trying to find the ticket."

THE CYCLE OF LIFE

The two little ones were engaged in a serious conversation.

"Do you know what it means to die?" asked one.

"Of course," said the other. "First people are born. Then they go to school and then to work. Then they get married. They become father and mother, then grandfather and grandmother. Then they begin to speak Yiddish and die."

WHO WANTS TO BE A COPYCAT?

"*Mazl tov!*" he said to his four-year-old son, "You have a little sister now."

But the tot looked none too happy.

"Aren't you glad?" his father asked him. "Would you have liked it better if you got a little brother?"

"Yes," he answered with assurance.

"But why?"

"My friend Dani got a little sister last week, and he always says I'm a copycat."

A TIME TO LAUGH

It was her bedtime, but this six-year-old refused to retire. Her father wheedled and threatened and finally she went. But she did it under protest and her face showed it.

After a while the man had a twinge of remorse. He felt he ought to placate her. He found her in bed where she sat reading. He sat down near her and stroked her hair.

"You know," he said, "I heard a good one today. I meant to tell you but I forgot. Here it is. Why does a rooster close his eyes when he crows? Do you know the answer? No? Well, it's because he knows it by heart! Ha, ha, ha! It's real funny. Why don't you laugh?"

"I am not on good terms with you," she replied. "When you go out I'll laugh."

Glossary

Pronunciation Key

a	= a in *far*	o	= o in *for*
ay	= y in *sky*	u	= u in *put*
e	= e in *pen*	ch	= ch in Scottish *loch*
ey	= ai in *rain*	tch	= ch in *chair*
i	= i in *wit*	ts	= ts in *wits*

agode (Heb. *Haggadah*), the story of the Egyptian bondage and liberation read at the *seyder*
akshn, stubborn man
balagole, wagoner
beygl, ring-shaped roll
bime, synagogue platform
chale, white bread
cholile, God forbid!
chossid (lit. *pious man*), adherent of the religious movement founded by Israel Baal-Shem-Tov (1700-1760).
chutspe, insolence
dayen, Rabbinic judge
Dubno Magid, Jacob Krantz (1741-1804)
eyneni yodea (Heb.), "I don't know."
gabay, trustee
ganev (pl. *ganovim*), thief; shrewd person
gazlon (pl. *gazlonim*), brigand
giml, third letter of Hebrew alphabet (= g in *get*)

goy, non-Jew (pl. *goyim*)
Ibn Ezra, Abraham (1092-1167), poet and philosopher
kabtsn, pauper
kaftn, long coat
kayssn, irascible man
kibbutz, collective settlement
kidesh, benediction chanted on eve of Sabbaths and holidays
kreplach, little bags of rolled dough stuffed with chopped meat
kugl, Sabbath pudding
lamdn, learned man
lantsman, countryman
litvak, Lithuanian Jew; crafty fellow
magid, preacher
matse, unleavened Passover bread
mazl, luck
mazl tov, congratulations!
Megillah (lit. *scroll*), the Book of Esther in the Bible.
melamed, teacher
Menoras Hamoar, "Candlestick of Light," religious work by Isaac Aboab (ca. 1300)
minche, Afternoon Prayer
mitsve, religious ordinance; good deed
naches, happiness; pleasure
nebach, the pity of it! alas!
parnosse, livelihood
pletsl, flat roll
porets, squire
Reb, Mister
rebe, teacher; Chassidic rabbi
rov, rabbi
seyder, Passover home service
shadchn, marriage-broker
shames, sexton; servitor
shlemiel, ne'er-do-well
shma Yisroel, "Hear O Israel!", first two words of the profession of faith: "Hear O Israel, the Lord is our God, the Lord is One!"
sholem aleychem, peace unto you! (greeting)
shtetl, small town
shul, synagogue